Reasoning and Thinking

Ken Manktelow

University of Wolverhampton, UK

Psychology Press
a member of the Taylor & Francis group

Copyright © 1999 by Psychology Press Ltd. a member of the Taylor & Francis group.
All rights reserved. No part of this book may be reproduced in any form by photostat, microform, retrieval system, or any other means without the prior written permission of the publisher.

Psychology Press Ltd
27 Church Road
Hove
East Sussex, BN3 2FA
UK

British Library Cataloguing-in-Publication Data

A catalogue record for this book is available from the British Library

Library of Congress Cataloging-in-Publication Data are available

ISBN 0-86377-708-2 (hbk)
ISBN 0-86377-709-0 (pbk)
ISSN 1368-4558

Front cover illustration:
Indecision, oil painting by Andrea Landini (1847–c.1911).
Reproduced by permission of Plymouth City Museums and Art Gallery.

Cover design by Joyce Chester
Typeset in Palatino, by Facing Pages, Southwick, West Sussex
Printed and bound in the UK by TJ International Ltd, Padstow, Cornwall

REASONING AND THINKING

5

In memory of John Bennett,
who first taught me psychology

Contents

Series Preface

Cognitive Psychology: A Modular Course, edited by Gerry Altmann and Susan E. Gathercole, aims to provide undergraduates with stimulating, readable, affordable brief texts by leading experts. Together with three other modular series, these texts will cover all the major topics studied at undergraduate level in psychology. The companion series are: *Clinical Psychology*, edited by Chris Brewin; *Developmental Psychology*, edited by Peter Bryant and George Butterworth; and *Social Psychology*, edited by Miles Hewstone. The series will appeal to those who want to go deeper into the subject than the traditional textbook will allow, and base their examination answers, research, projects, assignments, or practical decisions on a clearer and more rounded appreciation of the research evidence.

Other titles in this series:

Essentials of Human Memory
Alan D. Baddeley

Laboratory Psychology
Julia Nunn (Ed.)

Imagery
John T.E. Richardson

Acknowledgements

Anyone who does research builds up a huge store of debts and thanks. It is difficult to do justice to my own list, so rather than try to include everyone, and risk missing somebody out, I shall just pick out the three people who have been my main inspiration in the work I have done over more years than I will admit to in public: Jonathan Evans, David Over, and Peter Wason. I have been pretty lucky with research students too, especially Neil Fairley, Steve Kilpatrick, Tom Ormerod, and Ed Sutherland. Thanks also to all the other psychologists from round the world with whom I have exchanged ideas, papers, and drinks bills.

I would also like to express my gratitude to the people I work with at Wolves, particularly Ann Henshaw and Kevin Hogan, for their constant support through both good and less good times.

The manuscript of this book was read and commented on by Roger Dominowski, Neil Fairley, David Hardman, Linda Miller, Mike Oaksford, David Over, and Fred Vallée-Tourangeau, and I am grateful for the trouble they took over this. You should be too: they are responsible for the improvements on the raw material. Rachel Windwood and, latterly, Linda Jarrett, at the publishers, were also very helpful in dealing with my queries and excuses. Finally, my special thanks go to Linda Miller.

K.I. MANKTELOW

Reasoning and thinking: A four-way introduction

1

The psychological study of thinking has both a very long and a very short history. Its long aspect comes from its antecedents in philosophy, where ideas can be traced back to classical antiquity: Aristotle, in particular, casts a shadow stretching over more than 2000 years. On the other hand, the psychology of human thinking, as a branch of cognitive psychology, can hardly be older than cognitive psychology itself, and the birthday of the latter is often located in the late 1950s (see e.g. Baars, 1996). In fact, we can look to even more recent times for the beginnings of a true cognitive psychology of thinking, to Wason and Johnson-Laird's *Psychology of Reasoning: Structure and Content*, published in 1972.

Thought and reason are, of course, foremost among the list of properties that we often invoke when we try to mark out what makes us different from other animals. Making inferences is also a fundamental requirement of intelligence, so you might expect the subject to be right in the mainstream of psychological research. In fact, this has not been the case until very recent times. The reason for this probably lies in the ways in which the field relates to, and feeds from, not only other areas of psychology but other disciplines too. The clearest instance of this relation is in the way the study of reasoning has often seemed to assess people against idealised criteria derived from formal systems such as logic, probability theory, and decision theory. The place of normative standards in the psychological account of thinking and reasoning is one of the core issues we shall be concerned with in this book.

Of course, it would be a strange kind of psychology that did not concern itself with thought, and there is now a huge and proliferating literature on reasoning and thinking, informed by the theoretical and empirical methods of both cognitive psychology and cognitive science. So huge, in fact, that I shall have to start by drawing some lines, before outlining what will be covered in this text.

Some boundaries

First let me reassure those readers who dread having to get to grips with technical systems. Although in studying reasoning you cannot totally avoid contact with logic, and in studying decision making you must at some point look at decision theory and probability, systems such as these will be set out only in as much detail as is necessary for the psychology, and with a minimum of maths.

Second, as this field has taken its place in the mainstream of cognitive enquiry, so the borderlines between it and other fields have become blurred. As a consequence, we shall need to refer to ideas from (among others) the psychology of problem solving, language, intelligence, memory theory, social cognition, and cognitive development from time to time; and, outside psychology, from philosophy, economics, and artificial intelligence. As with the technical material, these references will be made in the context of the psychological topic in hand, and won't be treated as separate issues.

Fields, issues, theories, and tasks: A four-way perspective

Having noted where the borders are, it is time to set out what will be found within them. To help organise your reading, you can think about the material from four angles.

Fields

First there are the fields of research that we shall consider. A traditional division is that between inductive and deductive thinking, with the latter most often equated with reasoning. This division is helpful, but should not be regarded as rigid: as we shall see in later chapters, there are increasing trends towards integration across subfields. Put simply, inductive thinking is what you do when you arrive at a conclusion on the basis of some evidence. Detective work is a good example: a series of crimes may contain common elements such as locality, frequency, or a characteristic method. When put together, they suggest a pattern, which in turn suggests a "model" for the suspect. "Suggest" is an informal label for an inductive process. Thus, induction increases information, in the sense that an induction rules out possible models. However, there is a price: an inductive conclusion cannot be guaranteed to be true. This is because a conclusion may be based on irrelevant evidence, relevant evidence may be ignored, new evidence may force one to change it, or there may be bias in the way evidence is treated; and the wrong suspect may be arrested, or the real one missed. If induction guaranteed truth, we could replace the courts by logicians.

Deduction, on the other hand, involves arriving at conclusions on the basis of statements, called premises, whose truth value can be assumed. The nature of the conclusion is given by the structure of the argument, not its content, and these structural principles are the province of logic. A true set of premises can never lead to a false conclusion. Thus, while deduction is truth-preserving, it does not increase information: no more models are ruled out by the conclusion than were ruled out by the premises. A deduction at best makes explicit what was already there. Deduction is one way of testing inductive hypotheses.

Both these areas cover distinct but related sub-areas. For instance, there is a major area of research involved in exploring how it is that we form judgements about the likelihood of things, which is a very common type of induction. Are the summers getting warmer, do we live in especially violent times, is it safe to eat seafood? As with deduction and logic, there is an obvious relation between human judgements of probability and a formal system of principles, in this case statistical.

Even from these examples, it is clear that assessing likelihoods is only one aspect of the kinds of everyday decisions that we make. Most of the time, we also place a value on the object of the judgement: it may be something we would like to happen, or prefer not to happen. Is it worth buying tubes of factor 20 sunscreen this summer? You need to think about the benefits and costs involved, as well as the likelihood of relevant events happening: are you worried about skin damage, do you think it is likely your skin will be damaged if you do not protect it? Is an uncertain long-term risk enough to put you off the immediate pleasure of being out in the sun? As Baron (1994a) puts it, such decisions depend on both your beliefs and your goals. Once again, there are formal systems that have been developed to set out in principle how these judgements of probability and utility can be expressed: this is the field of decision making.

This last example shows how, in many aspects of our thinking, we are not just considering what is or is not the case, but what we should or should not do. This kind of thinking has attracted a lot of research interest recently, and is known as deontic thinking. Contemplating the blazing sun, and bearing in mind your assessments of the risks of skin damage, you might say to your friend (or yourself), "you must (or should, or ought to) put on some sunscreen" (a statement of obligation), or "if you put on some sunscreen, then you can go out" (a permission). Deontic thinking is an area in which the distinction between reasoning and decision making has become fuzzier.

These then are the major fields of thinking and reasoning we shall cover in this book: deduction, hypothesis testing, induction, judgement, and decision making.

Issues

There are several central questions addressed by researchers in thinking and reasoning that cut across the areas they explore. The one that has led to more experiments and theory than probably any other has already been mentioned several times: the relation between formal systems and human behaviour. Some authors call this the relation between *normative* and *descriptive* accounts of thought. Formal systems are called normative because they appear to set out norms, or ideals, of thought. Psychological theories aim to describe, and explain, what people actually do when tested or observed.

The simplest hypothesis about this relation is to propose that we have some kind of formal system in our minds. There have been many exponents of this view. Piaget, for instance, was the most famous of those theorists who argue for a "mental logic" (e.g. Inhelder & Piaget, 1958), and similar proposals have been made about decision theory, especially by economists. A subtler form of this argument which is still actively debated today, is that the mind contains systems of "natural" inference rules. Both the original mental logic idea and its present-day form have been hotly contested.

One of the central problems that inference rule theorists have to confront is that of content. If our minds contain logic-like inference rules, which are by definition abstract, then all problems of a given structure should produce the same solutions. But they do not. People reason better about concrete rather than abstract problems, and about problems with which they are familiar (Garnham & Oakhill, 1994). The role of content in reasoning is a second central issue, one that also cuts across fields of research.

However, this is not to say that people are helpless in the face of more or less unfamiliar problems. They generally perform above chance level, although they may be prone to systematic biases as well as being influenced by content (Evans, Newstead, & Byrne, 1993a). A complete theory of thinking would have to explain all three of these observed properties of human performance.

One general question that arises from these observations and arguments concerns the question of *rationality*. What does it mean to say that people, singly or in general, are rational or irrational? For years, it has been assumed that rational meant close adherence to a formal system. Psychological demonstrations of bias or content-dependency sometimes seemed to terrify theorists who held this view, as they seemed to put human rationality in serious question. Some theorists (e.g. Cohen, 1981) responded by denying that experiments could ever tell us anything about rationality. Others (e.g. Stich, 1985) took the opposite stance and seemed to accept general irrationality as a demonstrated fact. In recent years these views have been challenged by an "ecological" argument. This reflects a second usage of words such as "rational" or "irrational" in ordinary language, where we often mean that someone did or did not do the right thing in the circumstances: rational thought in this second sense is that which helps us achieve our goals. Questions of rationality and irrationality also cut across research fields.

Lastly, an issue related to the rationality question has also begun to be addressed by theorists, and that is the matter of the relation between psychological research, based on controlled experiments, and wider views of human thought. Do laboratory tasks tell us anything useful about thought in the real world? The discovery of the central role of content in thought makes this question an important one for theorists. On the other hand, environmental considerations have opened up a new way of characterising laboratory performance using Anderson's (1990) method of "rational analysis." The relation between the laboratory and the real world is addressed, in the field of decision making, by Fischhoff (1996) in a paper with the arresting title "The real world: what good is it?".

Major issues that will recur throughout the book are therefore those of the relation between formal systems and psychological observations, the questions of competence, content, and bias, the question of rationality, and the relation between laboratory performance and everyday thinking.

Theories

It would have been neat, if boring, were theories of thinking linked tightly to fields of research, but, like the basic issues just outlined, they are not. I have already mentioned how formal systems have been recruited as theories of thought, and this has happened across fields. Not so long ago, these were the nearest thing we had to general theories of thinking and reasoning, but in the early 1980s there was what at least one writer has described as a theoretical revolution (Byrne, 1996).

A measure of this progress in theory can be seen by looking at a classification made by Evans in 1991. He set out four types of theory: inference rules, content-dependent rules (or schemas), mental models, and heuristic approaches. The second and third of these have been developed since 1980, the fourth since 1970, while the first is still delivering new theories in the 1990s. We shall look in detail at all of them.

The most ambitious of the newer approaches, in terms of its scope and the degree to which it has been tested empirically, is the theory of mental models expounded by Johnson-Laird and his colleagues (Johnson-Laird, 1983, 1995; Johnson-Laird & Byrne, 1991). This has been applied across the board, originally to deduction but latterly also to induction, and also outside the field, e.g. to linguistic inference. The trial between mental models and mental logic theories is an especially lively current debating point.

As if that were not evidence enough of the rate of theoretical progress, note that Evans's classification is already out of date. In the mid-1990s we have seen the arrival not only of elaborations of existing approaches, but distinct, new approaches that have taken their cue from theories outside the field of thinking, and have been successfully and influentially applied within it. An example is information gain theory, developed by Oaksford and Chater (e.g. 1994a) from Anderson's (1990) rational analysis approach.

In the areas of judgement and decision making, a parallel story can be told. For many years, it was believed that people were, in the main, good "intuitive statisticians" (e.g. Peterson & Beach, 1967), and would make decisions along the lines assumed by economic theories of utility maximisation. From the 1970s, however, it began to appear that both these assumptions could be questioned. People's tested probability judgements seemed, e.g. in the work of Kahneman and Tversky and their followers, to be prone to systematic biases, and their decisions did not always follow the canons of economic theory. Lately, however, alternative approaches have emerged, such as the "ecological" approach of theorists such as Gigerenzer, in which judgemental accuracy and the rationality of decisions can been seen in a rather more favourable light. And, as already mentioned, such developments have led to the beginnings of an integration of ideas from the areas of reasoning and thinking, which for so long have been kept separate.

We shall therefore survey a range of general theoretical accounts: inference rules both abstract and domain-specific heuristic approaches, mental models, relevance, and information gain. We shall also look at Bayesian probability theory, frequentist or "ecological" approaches, formal utility theory, and descriptive accounts such as prospect theory.

Tasks

In 1973, the late Allen Newell famously criticised cognitive psychology for its reliance on small-scale laboratory tasks of dubious merit, in terms of actually telling us anything about the nature of human mentality. That argument was alluded to earlier. It has less force these days, but is still worth bearing in mind, because psychological research in the field of reasoning and thinking has been dominated by a relatively small number of well-known tasks. As we shall see, there are two main reasons for this: one is to do with the ancestry of the area, particularly its logical strand, and the other is that experimental methods create a kind of self-perpetuating dynamic whereby interesting findings with one kind of experiment lead to further studies using adaptations of the same experiment, and so on, if you are not careful, indefinitely. This is not necessarily a bad thing, and all areas of experimental psychology have this property, but there is a risk that whole architectures of theory can be balanced, rather precariously, on a narrow empirical base. As Fischhoff (1996) puts it, "Live with a task long enough and it may become more real than the situation from which it was abstracted." We shall consider the relation between laboratory performance and real-world thinking at various points, especially in Chapter 10.

The reasoning task with the longest history is the syllogism: such problems date back to Aristotle's time. There are many kinds of syllogisms now, used to address many kinds of problem. They are all based on a common form: at least two premises and a conclusion that you either produce, select from a range of options, or evaluate when given it. Here is one of Aristotle's "perfect" syllogisms, so called because it seems immediate and obvious:

All A are B	Premise 1
All B are C	Premise 2
All A are C	Conclusion

This is clearly a paradigm for investigating deduction. Alternatives include the inference task, the truth-table task, and the Wason selection task. Inference tasks are often used in the study of conditional (if–then) reasoning, one of the largest areas of deductive reasoning research. As with syllogisms, you have two premises and a conclusion which you produce, select, or evaluate, e.g.:

If p then q	Major premise
p	Minor premise
q	Conclusion

By convention, Aristotelian syllogisms tend to be explained using A and B, whereas conditionals use p and q. Remember that, logically, these symbols can be replaced by anything at all: an argument's validity depends solely on its structure. A valid argument is one where the conclusion must follow given the premises, so if the premises are true, the conclusion must also be true. The abstract symbols may be confusing at first, so it is as well to get used to them as early as you can. In the rest of the book, I shall use concrete examples as often as possible.

Truth-table tasks ask you to judge whether, given a sentence and a logical instance of it, the sentence is true or false, e.g.:

Sentence:	If p then q
Instance:	p q

They have not been widely used in experiments, in stark contrast to the next case.

The Wason selection task has often been claimed to be the single most investigated experimental paradigm in the psychology of reasoning. Not surprisingly, therefore, it will loom large at several points in the book. Here is the most common version of the basic form introduced by Peter Wason in 1966. If you have not seen it before, have a go at it now: it will be a useful experience.

You have seen a pack of cards, all of which have a single letter on one side and a single number on the other. Four cards are taken from the pack and placed on the table in front of you, thus (these always seem to be the ones used in examples):

$$\boxed{E} \quad \boxed{K} \quad \boxed{4} \quad \boxed{7}$$

I make the following claim about these cards:

If a card has a vowel on one side, then there is an even number on the other side.

Which of the cards would you need to turn over to tell whether my claim is true or false?

The effect this apparently simple problem has had on reasoning research has been almost incredible. It has been used in investigations of several different fields, and responsible for the raising of several important issues. You will have to read Chapter 3 to see if you have got it right. A warning: you almost certainly have not.

In the fields of judgement and decision making, the grip of specific paradigms has been looser, but is still there. The more venerable tradition in research on statistical intuitions has been to give people a sampling problem, such as the urns-and-balls task. Here, you are presented with, or asked to imagine, two urns containing coloured balls in varying proportions, and are asked to estimate these proportions, or guess which urn is which, after seeing samples from them. Alternatively, more realistic scenarios are described and your judgements sought; or estimates of the probabilities of real-world events can be taken. A stable finding from the latter is that people tend to overestimate the likelihood of rare events (compared to their objective frequency), such as dying in an air crash, and underestimate common events, such as dying from heart disease.

A methodological revolution in the field occurred with the work of Kahneman and Tversky and their colleagues, beginning in the 1970s (see Kahneman, Slovic, & Tversky, 1982), on heuristics and biases in thinking. As with Wason's selection task, the impact of this work has been enormous; unlike the selection task, it has spread beyond the psychology of thinking—beyond psychology, even. However, their theoretical ideas, once accepted by many psychologists, economists, and biologists almost without demur, have recently come under intense critical scrutiny, as we shall see in Chapter 8.

Their methods have also been widely adopted. Here is a famous and well-used example of the kind of problem that has become central to the heuristics and biases research programme:

> Linda is 31 years old, single, outspoken, and very bright. She majored in philosophy. As a student, she was deeply concerned with issues of discrimination and social justice, and also participated in anti-nuclear demonstrations.

Which descriptions are most likely to be true of Linda? Rank them in order of probability (go on—it will be useful later):

1. Linda is a primary school teacher.
2. Linda works in a bookshop and takes Yoga classes.
3. Linda is active in the feminist movement.
4. Linda is a psychiatric social worker.
5. Linda is a member of the League of Women Voters.

6. Linda is a bank clerk.
7. Linda sells insurance.
8. Linda is a bank clerk and is active in the feminist movement.

(Adapted from Tversky & Kahneman, 1983.)

In Chapter 8 you will see how results from tasks such as this have been interpreted. You should be particularly interested in such results if you have ranked the last "Linda" sentence more highly than the third or the sixth. If you did, you have committed an apparent fallacy of thinking by judging that Linda is more likely to have two properties than one of the properties alone. That is logically impossible.

Judging likelihoods and frequencies is only part of the process of making decisions: the other part is assessing the values which we put on the options we are deciding between. Here is a famous problem (adapted from Tversky, & Kahneman, 1981) that makes the relation between the two quite clear.

Imagine you are a government official deciding on how to cope with a new disease that is about to break out. The best medical opinion available is that it will kill 600 people. Two treatment programmes are available. Programme A will definitely save 200 lives, and Programme B will have a one-third (0.33) chance of saving 600 lives. Which programme do you opt for? Your colleague in the health service has a similar problem with another disease, which is also expected to kill 600 people. She has to choose between Programme C, which will certainly result in 400 deaths, and Programme D, which has a two-thirds chance (0.67) that 600 people will die. Which programme will she support?

Once again, the answers you come up with are unlikely to match those you should come up with, according to formal decision theory: for instance, you probably thought that you would go for programme A, whereas your colleague would go for programme D. Formally, this is inconsistent; in Chapter 9 you will see why, and also why, on psychological rather than formal grounds, it might not be.

Organisation of the book

The next four chapters are devoted to deductive reasoning. Chapter 2 surveys syllogisms, and also begins to introduce some of the major theories that have come to dominate the whole field of deduction.

Chapter 3 mainly looks at conditional ("if") reasoning, and introduces the main experimental tasks that have been used in this research. Chapter 4 extends this topic by addressing the questions of the biases that appear in the research data, and the effects of problem content, the main research question for many years in the psychology of deduction. In Chapter 5, we look in detail at the theories that have been proposed to account for these findings.

Reasoning with conditionals is closely related to the kinds of thinking involved in science, and in Chapter 6 we address this topic explicitly by considering hypothesis testing, both in experiments and in the real scientific world. We then go on to consider inductive thinking, one of the other cornerstones of scientific thinking, in Chapter 7. Most of the conclusions you come up with when thinking inductively concern probabilities, so we look in detail at judgements of probability in Chapter 8. This form of thought is central to one of the most familiar and important tasks we face in everyday life: that of making decisions. When we make decisions, we consider the values of the options before us and their potential outcomes, as well as the chances of their happening. This then is the subject of Chapter 9. Finally, in Chapter 10, we confront a topic which is relevant to all the others in the book, and which is currently the centre of much debate: that of human rationality.

Typically, textbooks are not books in the sense that novels are, they are more like stores of information. Although the same goes for this one, it has also been designed to be read from beginning to end, so that successive ideas build on one another and an integrated picture of this fascinating area of research can emerge.

Deduction: Experiments with syllogisms 2

As we saw in Chapter 1, there are several ways of approaching the topic of reasoning. In this chapter we focus on syllogisms, and in Chapter 3 we look at experiments on deductions using what are called propositional connectives, especially "if". This will allow you to see how the empirical base of the subject has developed. Alongside the empirical foundations I shall also set out in simple terms the formal, logical norms by which performance on the tasks has traditionally been assessed. The status of these norms is controversial; the relation between norms and performance will occupy us not only here but also in Chapter 4 (on content and context), in Chapter 5 (on theories of reasoning), and in Chapter 10 (on rationality).

In this chapter, most of the experimental results will be from syllogistic tasks in their basic "abstract" form. Findings from versions of the problems designed to be more realistic will be dealt with later. It might seem strange at first that anyone should be interested in performance on tasks deliberately designed to be detached from everyday life. There are two related reasons why psychologists have done this.

First, remember that historically the study of reasoning is anchored in logic, and to the question of the degree to which people adhere to or deviate from logical rules. Using abstract problems might allow for a comparatively "pure" means to do this, avoiding the contamination of inferences by prior knowledge or motives. There is a similarity here to early work on memory begun by Ebbinghaus in the 19th century: he used nonsense syllables with the aim of excluding existing associations. A subtler and more modern form of this argument was put forward by Evans (1982): realistic problems run the risk of evoking memories of similar tasks rather than actual reasoning, so the only way one can be sure that this is not happening is to use problems that defeat this kind of analogical thinking. Of course, we then run the risk of compiling findings that miss something essential about thinking in its natural context. All psychological research has to confront this trade-off, and some recent theorists have begun to follow its implications seriously (see Chapter 10).

Syllogisms formed the core of reasoning research for years. There are still many new studies published every year. In this section, we shall look at the fundamental Aristotelian or *quantified* form.

Aristotelian syllogisms

Although these problems have existed for longer than any other in the study of thinking, they represent a rather restricted form of reasoning. All the same, they have, along with other tasks, formed a vehicle for exploring wider issues. For now, let us look at their basic forms and the findings associated with them.

Aristotelian syllogisms contain single instances of four fundamental *quantifier expressions*: All A are B, Some A are B, No A are B, and Some A are not B. These can make up the two *premises* and the *conclusion* that form the classic patterns of a syllogistic argument, known as *moods*. The quantified statements are labelled A, I, E, and O respectively. In addition, they can be classed as affirmative (A and I) or negative (E and O), and as universal (A and E) or particular (I and O). This terminology can be hard to remember, so Table 2.1 sets out these properties.

Thus, the "perfect" syllogism referred to in Chapter 1 is in AAA mood because the two premises (above the line) and the conclusion (below the line) are all universal affirmative (A) sentences:

All A are B	e.g.	All archbishops are believers
All B are C		All believers are Christians
All A are C		All archbishops are Christians

Note that the conclusion always states a relation between the two *end terms* A and C, with the *middle term* B being eliminated: deriving the relation between A and C, which has not been explicitly stated, is the essential syllogistic inference.

In addition, syllogisms can be characterised by their structure, or *figure* as it is known. We shall keep to the A, B, C notation and follow

TABLE 2.1

The quantified statements used in syllogisms

A	All A are B	Universal	Affirmative
I	Some A are B	Particular	Affirmative
E	No A are B	Universal	Negative
O	Some A are not B	Particular	Negative

the analysis suggested by Johnson-Laird (1983; Johnson-Laird & Byrne, 1991). He uses "figure" to refer only to the arrangement of premises, ignoring the conclusion. On this basis, it is easy to see that there are four possible figures, depending on whether the first premise relates A to B in the order A–B or B–A, and whether the second premise relates B to C in the order B–C or C–B, as Table 2.2 shows.

Validity

A valid conclusion is one that must be true if the premises are true, or in other words, where there is no possibility of reaching a false conclusion given true premises. How can we decide which syllogisms have valid conclusions? This is not an easy question to answer, as shown by the fact that different counts have been arrived at by different writers. Aristotle himself is often said to have recognised only 14 valid syllogisms (of the 512 that can be constructed), largely because initially he did not include the first figure in Table 2.2 in his system. Others have gone as high as 48; Johnson-Laird admits 27 (Johnson-Laird & Byrne, 1991). Adams (1984) goes into extensive detail on this subject. Reasons for the different counts include whether or not "weak" conclusions are regarded as acceptable, and whether a statement such as "all A are B" implies the existence of As and Bs, the so-called existential presupposition. For instance, from some AA premise pairs one can validly draw not only an A conclusion but also an I conclusion (Some A are C), in the sense that this conclusion cannot be false given these premises. Johnson-Laird's scheme omits the weak conclusions, and accepts the existential presupposition.

Deciding formally on which syllogisms can be proved to be valid has been addressed by a number of writers. Two methods are described clearly by Garnham and Oakhill (1994, Ch. 6), and a third based on Euler diagrams (see later) is given by Wetherick (1993).

Empirical studies and psychological models

Syllogisms produce a wide range of performance: some valid ones are correctly accepted by almost everyone, including children (e.g. the "perfect" example given earlier), whereas others produce no better than

TABLE 2.2

Four syllogistic figures suggested by Johnson-Laird (1983)

A–B	B–A	A–B	B–A
B–C	C–B	C–B	B–C

chance responses. Similarly, invalid syllogisms are sometimes erroneously accepted as valid. Here is one that in a recent study produced no correct answers at all from one group of subjects (see Ford, 1995):

No A are B
All B are C
?

This syllogism has a valid conclusion: Some Cs are not As (it is therefore a syllogism in EAO mood). Using realistic content may help to show this:

No Americans are Belgians
All Belgians are Christians
Some Christians are not Americans

There have been many cunning attempts to devise realistic syllogisms using words beginning with A, B, and C. The effects of content are actually a serious psychological matter, as we shall see in Chapter 4. For now, we shall stay with the main empirical findings from the basic tasks and how they have been explained. We shall then consider the theories of mental models, mental logic, and information gain; these reappear at several points in the book, so this is a good place to start to get acquainted with them.

As the two examples already given will have shown, syllogisms range in difficulty from those that are so easy as to be obvious, to those that are so difficult that they are very hard to understand, even once the answer has been given. These observations contain three empirical findings that must be explained: (i) people generally perform at above chance level overall, while (ii) they also make make errors, and (iii) syllogisms differ in their difficulty. Since the 1930s, several attempts have been made to account for these results. Some have been restricted to the domain of syllogisms, whereas others have consisted of the adaptation of larger-scale theories to the area. We shall deal with the two classes of theory in that order.

Theories of syllogistic reasoning

Atmosphere, matching, and conversion

The earliest attempt to account for the observed effects was by Woodworth and Sells (1935), who proposed the atmosphere theory; it was refined by Begg and Denny (1969). The idea is simply that the mood of the pair of premises conveys an overall mood, or atmosphere, which suggests conclusions of certain types. Thus, two universal premises will suggest a universal conclusion; two affirmative premises will suggest an affirmative conclusion; at least one particular premise will suggest a particular conclusion; and at least one negative premise will suggest a negative conclusion.

Approaching syllogisms in this way will lead to quite a good level of logical performance, as many of the valid arguments are consistent with atmosphere, and the theory also accounts for a high proportion of observed errors. On the other hand, this implies that not much actual reasoning is used in solving these problems. Furthermore, as Evans et al. (1993a) point out, the atmosphere theory serves only to describe patterns of performance, it does not explain *why* people might behave in this way; neither does it explain the differences in difficulty between syllogisms.

A related idea has recently been put forward by Wetherick and Gilhooly (1990), and is known as the *matching* hypothesis. "Matching" because the hypothesis is that reasoners prefer a quantifier (Some, All, etc.) in the conclusion that is the same as one in the premises (you can see how this explanation fits the relative difficulty of the two examples given earlier). With two different quantifiers in the premises, reasoners prefer the one that is most *conservative*, i.e. that commits the speaker to the lowest number of possible cases. Thus, No is preferred to Some or Some ... not, and Some is preferred to All, when these are alternatives.

Atmosphere and matching both refer to the processes used to make a response, so essentially they are response bias theories (see Chapter 4 for more on biases). Other writers have suggested other sources of error. One that has attracted attention both recently and longer ago concerns the ways in which people interpret the premises. Two kinds of interpretational effect have been proposed: conversion and Gricean implicature. The conversion hypothesis was suggested by Chapman and Chapman (1959) and elaborated by Revlis (1975). It states that errors arise because people may interpret premises as implying their converse, e.g. taking All A are B as implying that All B are A. It is easy to see that this can be an error if you substitute category names for A and B, e.g. archbishops and believers.

In fact, only A (All A are B) and O (Some A are not B) statements can be subject to this "error", because I (Some A are B) and E (No A are B) can be validly converted. This can be appreciated by using everyday content or, more reliably, by using a graphic device such as Euler circles. These diagrams are named after a Swiss mathematician who used them to explain logic to a countess. The idea is simple: the terms in the premises are represented by circles, and the moods can be matched to particular arrangements of the circles. When one circle is inside another, or overlaps it, the area under both belongs to both. The circles reveal how some moods are consistent with more than one possible arrangement, a fact we shall return to when considering the theory of mental models. The system is set out in Fig. 2.1.

The conversion theory is also a descriptive rather than explanatory theory. Ceraso and Provitera (1971), for instance, showed that blocking conversion with additional information (e.g. giving "All A are B, but some B are not A" as the first premise) led to fewer errors, and other studies have shown that people do sometimes misinterpret

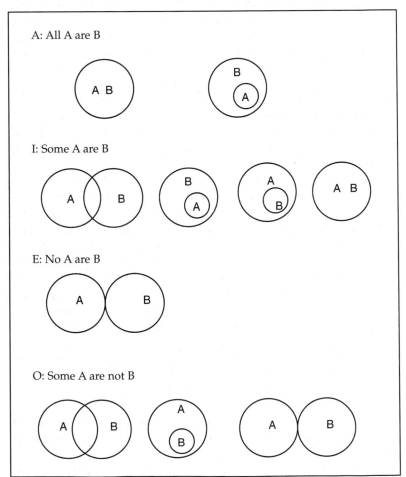

FIG. 2.1.
Euler circle representations for syllogistic premises.

premises in the ways predicted. However, conversion can only ever be a partial account, because there are two premises for which conversion is valid (I and E), and there is no clear theoretical reason as to why people might tend to convert premises. One possibility is that converted premises are cognitively simpler because they impose lower demands on memory.

Gricean implicatures are named after the linguistic philosopher Paul Grice. He is famous for his *principle of cooperation*, from which he derived a list of conversational maxims (see Grice, 1975): quantity (do not give too much or too little information), quality (say what is true or justified), relation (be relevant), and manner (be clear). Newstead (1989, 1995) has studied the possible role of two of these, relevance and quantity, in syllogistic reasoning. These maxims are potentially important because there is an imperfect fit between the logical reading of the quantifiers, particularly Some, and their informal use in everyday language. Logically, Some means "at least one and possibly all". Remember, in logic a statement is true if it is not false: finding that all A are in fact B would not refute the statement that some A are B, because there would be no cases of A that are not B. Conversationally, "some" is usually taken to mean at least one but not all; hence "some A are B" suggests that some A are not B (if your bank told you that some of your money was missing, you would be even more upset to discover that all of it was gone).

Newstead found that (mis)interpretations of premises along Gricean lines were quite common. He used two methods to determine this: Euler circles (see Fig. 2.1) and immediate inference. With Euler circles, subjects were given a premise and asked to indicate which of the diagrams fitted it. Immediate inference involved linguistic presentation, with people either assessing presented conclusions or producing their own. However, the proportion of non-logical *interpretations* did not directly correspond to the proportion of errors on syllogistic *inference*. According to Newstead, the "logical demands" of a task largely determined the effects of the Gricean implicatures: syllogistic problems produced the least effects, because their logical demands were greatest, whereas simple interpretation produced the most. Conclusion production, where you have to think of your own answer, was less prone than conclusion evaluation, where you choose one from a given set; the former is more demanding.

There is a third class of explanation, those invoking some aspect of the way the information in the premises is *combined*. Erickson (1974) used Euler circles and proposed that experimental subjects' errors could be attributed to their considering only one of the possible relations between terms in a premise, when more than one interpretation was possible. His account of which of the alternatives is chosen is essentially *post hoc* (see Adams, 1984, p. 297) and rests on an assumption that people represent classes (e.g. "archbishops'), these classes being combined in reasoning. This idea is explicitly denied by Johnson-Laird in his theory of mental models. In the next section, we shall introduce this theory, and then compare it with two other recent general approaches: mental logic theory and information-gain theory.

Theories of reasoning applied to syllogisms

Mental models

The theory of mental models began in a study of syllogistic reasoning by Johnson-Laird and Steedman (1978) and was fully articulated by Johnson-Laird (1983). It was subject to a major revision by Johnson-Laird and Byrne (1991) and has received further fine-tuning since (e.g. Bara, Bucciarelli, & Johnson-Laird, 1995; Johnson-Laird, 1995; Johnson-Laird, & Byrne, 1996). We'll consider the mental model theory of syllogistic reasoning from the standpoint of the 1991 version because this is the one you are most likely to encounter in wider reading. The theory will reappear several times later in this book.

Mental models theory proposes that there are three stages of thinking people go through when reasoning; these are shown in Fig. 2.2. The first stage is to *understand the premises*, using your knowledge of language and any relevant general knowledge (the Comprehension stage). Thus, reasoners *construct models* of the states of affairs conveyed by the premises; in the case of syllogisms, this is done by representing an arbitrary number of instances of each premise, not by representing classes (cf. the Erickson theory).

The second stage is to *combine the premise models* to derive a description of the state of affairs they jointly define: the Description stage. (It is this stage that has been the subject of theoretical revision, or "tinkering" as the theorists phrase it. See Bara et al., 1995; Johnson-Laird & Byrne, 1996.) The composite mental model that results must include new information, i.e. it must state something that was not already explicit in the premises: a conclusion, in other words. If reasoners cannot find such a model, they will respond that no conclusion follows. If they can, then they will pass to the third stage: that of Validation. This involves *searching for any alternative models* that are consistent with the premises but in which the putative (i.e. candidate) conclusion is false. If there is one, then the conclusion is false; you should then search for another conclusion and validate it, until there are no more. A valid conclusion is one where there are no alternative models that falsify it.

Johnson-Laird and Byrne also include an important psychological constraint to explain the difference in difficulty between syllogisms. This is a principle of economy, and it basically means that, because of the restricted capacity of working memory, reasoners will try to do as little cognitive work as possible. They will try to construct a minimum of models, with a minimum of information explicitly represented in each.

These elements of the mental models theory, the stages and the economy principle, lead to clear and testable empirical predictions. Let us see how they can be applied to syllogisms, using some general hypotheses and a couple of examples.

Modelling the premises will depend on the comprehension stage and the economy principle. From these two factors comes a distinction between an initial model and a fully explicit model. The initial model will contain only as much explicit information as is necessary for the meaning of the premise, but people will be able to extend this knowledge if need be: they will be aware of what may be implied but not stated by a premise. Thus, an initial model will contain both *explicit* and *implicit* information. The model theory portrays this using the following notation, with the A premise All A are B (e.g. All archbishops are believers) as an example:

> [archbishop]   believer
> [archbishop]   believer
>   ...

in abstract terms:

Premises and general knowledge
|
COMPREHENSION
|
Models
|
DESCRIPTION
|
Putative conclusion
|
VALIDATION: search for alternative models falsifying conclusion
|
Valid conclusion

FIG. 2.2. Three stages of reasoning in mental models theory. From Johnson-Laird and Byrne (1991). Reprinted with permission.

```
[a]      b
[a]      b
   ...
```

There are two bits of notation here which are important for the theory and its predictions. The first is the set of three dots: this denotes the implicit information. The next is the square brackets, as in [a]. These signify that this item is *exhaustively represented*, so in this case it embodies the knowledge that an a cannot appear in any other case (which is of course what we convey by using the word "all").

There is a third bit of notation which we need before we can work through how the theory explains syllogistic performance: a symbol for negation. Because mental models are held to contain tokens for single instances, and not classes, negation can be represented directly, using the symbol ¬ . We can see this in operation when we consider the fully explicit representation of the model for the A premise:

```
[a]      [b]
[a]      [b]
[¬a]     [b]
[¬a]     [¬b]
```

This conveys the logical possibilities that whereas there can only be As that are Bs, there can be Bs that are not As. There may also be things which are not B and also not A; this would follow when all As were Bs and all Bs were As. Table 2.3 gives all the initial and fully explicit models for the four syllogistic statements.

Now we can see how these models can be combined in solving syllogisms, and how the theory predicts patterns of performance. First, the "perfect" AAA syllogism. The initial model for the first premise has just been given; the second premise will look similar:

```
[b]      c
[b]      c
   ...
```

These can be combined following the constraint that reasoners will not represent explicitly more information than they have to; in this case, they will not represent b twice over, so the combined model will look like this:

```
[[a]     b]  c
[[a]     b]  c

   ...
```

TABLE 2.3

Mental model representations of syllogistic premises.
(After Johnson-Laird & Byrne, 1991)

		Initial Models		Explicit Models	
A:	All A are B	[a]	b	[a]	[b]
		[a]	b	[a]	[b]
		...		[¬a]	[b]
				[¬a]	[¬b]
I:	Some A are B	a	b	a	b
		a	b	a	b
		...		¬a	b
				a	¬b
				¬a	¬b
E:	No A are B	[a]		[a]	¬b
		[a]		[a]	¬b
			[b]	¬a	[b]
			[b]	¬a	[b]
		...		¬a	¬b
I:	Some A are not B	a		a	¬b
		a		a	¬b
		a	[b]	a	[b]
			[b]	¬a	[b]
		...		¬a	¬b

¬   tag for negation.
[ ]   indicates exhaustive representation.
...   alternative model(s) with no explicit content.

This is the only way in which the information about a, b, and c could be combined—there is no need to consider the content of the implicit models. These models are consistent with the conclusion that "all A are C", and as there is no alternative model which is not consistent with this conclusion, it is valid. This should therefore be an easy syllogism to solve, because it only needs one combined model and does not require consideration of the implicit information, and it is: Johnson-Laird and Byrne found that 89% of people get it right.

Other syllogisms are not so straightforward, and the theory explains why. Consider this one, which has been found to be one of the hardest:

All B are A	e.g.	all burglars are agnostics
No B are C		no burglars are churchgoers
?		?

From Table 2.3 you can retrieve the initial models; when combined, Johnson-Laird and Byrne suggest they will produce the following composite:

```
[a      [b]]
[a      [b]]
                [c]
                [c]
    ...
```

which supports the conclusion "No C are A" (and this is the most common conclusion that people draw). However, the premise models can also be combined in this way:

```
[a      [b]]
[a      [b]]
    a           [c]
                [c]
    ...
```

which is not consistent with this putative conclusion, because the third line introduces the possibility of Cs that are As. There is a third possible combination as well, which expresses the situation when there are no Cs that are not A:

```
[a      [b]]
[a      [b]]
    a           [c]
    a           [c]
    ...
```

The three possible composite models are consistent with only one conclusion: Some A are not C (which you can see in the first two lines in each possible combination). Very few people produce this answer, and the model theory attributes the difficulty primarily to the need to consider more than one combined model. Johnson-Laird and Byrne (1991, Ch. 6) give a full description of all the 27 valid syllogisms in initial and combined model terms, together with their observed difficulty in experiments. The 10 one-model problems produced 76% correct conclusions, whereas the 17 multiple-model problems averaged 25% correct, thus confirming the hypothesis that a source of difficulty arises when more than one model has to be considered.

You should note, in passing, that there is another potential source of difficulty: the need to go beyond the initial models and retrieve implicit information. This process is known as *fleshing out*, and would have been necessary to arrive at the Some A are not C conclusion, as ¬c is not explicitly represented in the models. Fleshing out will be considered in more detail in the next chapter when we look at propositional inferences involving *if* and *or*.

Mental logic

Writing in 1991, Johnson-Laird and Byrne were able to state that "No-one has proposed a full theory of syllogistic inference based on formal rules." In fact, they outlined themselves what such a theory might look like, so as to be able to knock it down. Now, however, there is a contender: the PSYCOP theory of Rips (1994). PSYCOP comes from the phrase PSYChology Of Proof. Ford (1995) also proposes a rule-based theory, but we shall only have space for Rips' here; Rips' theory is, in any case, based on a more general account of thinking.

PSYCOP is an extension of an earlier theory known as ANDS (A Natural Deduction System), and shares with this earlier theory the aim, as its name implies, of making a psychological theory out of the philosophical system of "natural deduction". Natural deduction is a term for logical proof systems that allow suppositions to be made in the course of assessing arguments, in contrast to axiomatic systems, where proofs rest entirely on rules.

Natural deduction systems rest on inference rules containing the basic logical operators for conjunction (and), negation (not), and the conditional (if … then). PSYCOP makes use of the fact that syllogistic sentences can all be expressed using these terms along with variables to avoid having to construct a separate rule system for quantifier expressions (All and Some). PSYCOP also includes the Gricean implicatures, e.g. that Some A are B implies that some A are not B, and the existential presupposition, that there are As and Bs to begin with. The translations of the four quantified statements and their implicatures given by Rips are shown in Table 2.4.

Once the four sentences have been expressed in this way, they can be included in the proof procedures of PSYCOP. For Rips, deductive reasoning consists in finding mental proofs using inference rules and suppositions. The number of different steps needed to find a proof, and the nature of the rules involved, should predict the difficulty of a deductive problem. There are several layers to this argument, and we will keep to one or two examples at this stage.

TABLE 2.4

The four syllogistic sentences expressed in words (first lines), their translations into the notation for PSYCOP's inference rules (second lines), and their implicatures (third lines). English equivalents are given in brackets on the right. (Adapted from Rips, 1994, ch. 7)

Mood

A	All A are B	
	IF A(x) THEN B(x)	[if x is A then x is B]
	A(a) AND B(a)	[there are things, a, which are A and B]
I	Some A are B	
	A(b) AND B(b)	[there are things, b, which are A and B]
	A(a) AND NOT B(a)	[there are things, a, which are A and not B]
E	No A are B	
	NOT (A(x) AND B(x))	[it is not the case that x is A and x is B]
	A(a) AND NOT B(a)	[there are things, a, which are A and not B]
O	Some A are not B	
	A(b) AND NOT B(b)	[there are things, b, which are A and not B]
	A(a) AND B(a)	[there are things, a, which are A and B]

x is a variable (i.e. a label for a class); a and b are "temporary names", (i.e. labels for possible instances).

The basic idea behind a mental proof is that reasoners address a deductive problem by generating sentences that link the premises to the conclusion; these links are provided by inference rules corresponding to those in a natural deduction system. A simple inference rule is that of *modus ponens:*

If A then B; A; therefore B.

We have seen in Table 2.4 how this rule can be related to the A statement. Applying these rules generates suppositions that can be used along with further rules to prove subgoals: these subgoals are necessary steps along the way to deriving a proof. You may not always succeed in finding a proof: you may lack a necessary inference rule, or be prevented by working memory restrictions from completing all the steps, or the problem may not be "deducible", i.e. no possible proof exists. Nevertheless, an attempt at a proof will always be made.

Inference rules can be applied in a forwards or backwards direction, a notion that is important in accounting for how some deductions can be made. The difference lies in whether you proceed from the premises to the conclusion (forward), or from the conclusion to the premises (backward). To take the example of *modus ponens* earlier, consider an argument of the following kind (adapted from Rips, 1994, Ch. 3):

If John is an archbishop then he is a believer	[premise 1]
If John is a believer then he is a churchgoer	[premise 2]
John is an archbishop	[premise 3]
John is a churchgoer	

Does this conclusion follow? Applying forward modus ponens, we combine the first premise with the third and derive the assertion "John is a believer" (a subgoal in the proof); combining this with the second premise, we derive the assertion "John is a churchgoer", and hence prove the conclusion (the main goal). Using backward modus ponens, we start with the conclusion. This matches the second part of the second premise, and backward modus ponens states that this goal is satisfied if we can prove the first part of the premise, so this forms the subgoal. To do this, we apply the same backward rule again: now, the first part of premise 2 matches the second part of premise 1; if the first part of premise 1 is true then the subgoal is proved. Premise 3 asserts just this, so the subgoal is proved and hence so is the conclusion.

There are 10 forward rules and 14 backward rules. Also, for syllogisms and other forms of argument using quantifiers, Rips supplements them with three additional forward rules: transitivity, exclusivity, and conversion, because syllogistic inference cannot be captured without them. The transitivity rule is one we have met in other guises before (see Table 2.4 for an explanation of the x, y, and z symbols):

If $A(x)$ then $B(x)$
If $B(y)$ then $C(y)$
If $A(z)$ then $C(z)$

and is sufficient to prove the "perfect" AAA syllogism. Because this argument requires only one easily available rule, it should be simple, and as we have seen, it is: around 90% of subjects typically solve it. The exclusivity rule looks like this:

If $A(x)$ then $B(x)$
Not $(B(y)$ and $C(y))$
Not $(A(z)$ and $C(z))$

and suffices to prove the argument:

All A are B	All archbishops are believers
No B are C	No believers are cannibals
No A are C	No archbishops are cannibals

Again, because this is a one-rule argument it should be easy, and it is (85% correct in Rips' own data). The conversion rule simply allows us to reverse the item order in an E sentence, so that No A are B is equivalent to No B are A:

$$\frac{\text{Not A(x) and B(x)}}{\text{Not B(y) and A(y)}}$$

Consider, on the other hand, the AOO syllogism:

All churchgoers are believers
Some agnostics are not believers
Some agnostics are not churchgoers

According to Rips, this argument requires the application of four inference rules, known as forward and-elimination, backward and-introduction, backward not-introduction, and backward if-elimination (for further explanation of these rules, see Chapter 5 and Rips, 1994, Chs. 6–7). Not surprisingly, it turns out to be much harder: in Rips' own data, only 35% of subjects agreed, correctly, that the conclusion followed.

Models and rules compared

We have seen that Johnson-Laird and Byrne's mental model theory and Rips' rule theory can make predictions about human syllogistic reasoning. How well do they measure up to the data from experiments? As you might expect, both claim that the answer is "rather well". Comparing the two claims is not always straightforward. This is largely because of methodological differences: Johnson-Laird and Byrne ask their subjects to produce their own conclusions from pairs of premises, whereas Rips gives complete syllogisms and subjects have to judge whether the conclusion "would have to be true in every situation in which the first two sentences are true" (Rips, 1994, p. 233). Other researchers ask subjects to select from a range of possible conclusions. Each set of authors considers the other's method to be open to unwelcome biases, and each produces impressive statistics showing how well their approach accounts for their data. Since these theories and the related experiments are so exactly specified and conducted, we have to look for other distinguishing criteria.

There are two aspects of the model theory that seem to give it the edge over the rule theory. The first is that the model theory is more parsimonious than the rule theory: Rips has to introduce, as we have seen, special components to extend his system to syllogisms, and to account for conclusion-production methods; Johnson-Laird and Byrne need do neither of these things. The second is that the model theory goes further than predicting which arguments will lead to more or fewer errors: it predicts what kind of errors will be made, something beyond the range of the rule theory. For instance, in the case of syllogisms requiring an initial model to be fleshed out, errors should be consistent with the initial model, and where more than one model is required, errors should be consistent with a model that is produced, if the full set is not. There is evidence for both of these effects (see Johnson-Laird, 1995).

Rational analysis and information gain

Recently, a third kind of theory has appeared, and has already been mentioned briefly: the information-gain theory of Chater and Oaksford (in press). We shall go into more detail about this theory in Chapter 5, as it is a general approach to the explanation of thinking and reasoning. Its overall case that reasoning depends not on models or rules, but, following Anderson (1990), that cognitive behaviour is adapted to the structure of the environment.

Gaining information means reducing uncertainty: reasoners are said to have this as a cognitive goal. A statement is informative to the extent that it is improbable, i.e. surprising. This idea may not be immediately obvious, but it is basic to the formal description of information. Thus, finding out that some archbishops are Catholics is unsurprising and hence uninformative, but finding out that some archbishops were cannibals would be very surprising and hence highly informative. In this example, the probability is varied by using content, but Chater and Oaksford apply this principle to syllogistic premises independent of content.

They do this by conducting formal, algebraic analyses of the probability of each of the four quantified statements (and two others, as we shall see) being true—it is a practical impossibility simply to count real occurrences of them—to derive an index of their informativeness. They then work through the theoretical consequences of this principle to predict syllogistic performance. This is known as the technique of *rational analysis*. Because not every aspect of the structure of syllogisms or human performance with them can be captured purely in terms of mathematical probability, Chater and Oaksford introduce some heuristics to account for these features. A heuristic is a general principle that is usually adhered to, but heuristics are not hard-and-fast rules like those of arithmetic or logic. The resulting theory is called the Probability Heuristics Model.

Now let us see how the informativeness of the premises in a syllogistic argument can be calculated, using graphic illustrations from Chater and Oaksford's paper. The assumptions on which these illustrations rest are justified theoretically, using a mathematical analysis, in the original paper.

Chater and Oaksford's first step is to express the meanings of syllogistic sentences in quantifiable terms, using *conditional probabilities*. A conditional probability is the probability that something is B given that it is A, e.g. the probability of being a believer given that you are an archbishop; it is written as prob. (B│A). These probabilities are represented in Fig. 2.3, where you can see the six statement types used by Chater and Oaksford (they include two which do not appear in any other theory, or in classical syllogistic logic; more on this later), and are set against lines representing ranges of conditional probability, from zero (certain not to be the case) to 1 (certain to be the case).

Taking each one in turn: The A premise states that All A are B. This means that the probability of B given A must be 1—it is certain that you are B given that you are A, if the A statement is true. So in the figure, A appears at the right-hand end of the probability line.

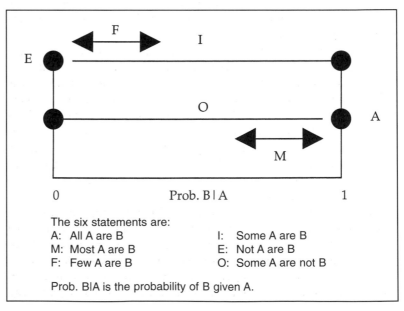

FIG. 2.3. Graphical representation of the information values of six syllogistic moods in Chater and Oaksford's Probability Heuristics model. From Chater and Oaksford (in press). Copyright © Academic Press, Inc. Reprinted with permission.

The six statements are:

A: All A are B   I: Some A are B
M: Most A are B   E: Not A are B
F: Few A are B   O: Some A are not B

Prob. B│A is the probability of B given A.

The M premise states that Most A are B. This means that prob. (B | A) is high but does not reach 1, hence the gap in the line next to the arrow representing this range.

The F sentence states that Few A are B. This means that prob. (B | A) is low but does not reach 0. The M and F premises are the "new" ones that do not appear in standard syllogistic logic or other theories.

The I sentence states that Some A are B. This means that prob. (B | A) can lie anywhere from just above 0 to 1 (in logic, remember, finding out that all A are B does not make Some A are B false, so prob. (B | A) could be 1 here).

The E sentence states that No A are B, so prob. (B | A) is at the 0 end of the probability range.

Finally, the O sentence states that Some A are not B (and again, possibly all A are not B), so prob. (B | A) can be anywhere from 0 to just short of 1.

This analysis, as you can see from Fig. 2.3, brings out some additional properties of the quantified sentences: for instance, O and A, and I and E, together take up the whole range of prob. (B | A): this means that if one of the pair is true, the other must be false. For instance, if All A are B is true, then Some A are not B must be false. It also shows that some statements are "entailed" by others, which Chater and Oaksford call *p-entailment* (p stands for probabilistic). Thus, A is included in I, and so are M and F; similarly, E is included in O and so, again, are M and F; O and I cover almost all of each other's ranges, which means that I and O statements are often compatible with M and F statements, although they are not strictly implied by them.

Expressing the sentences in terms of probability enables Chater and Oaksford to calculate their informativeness, and introduce their main heuristic. This is called the *min-heuristic*, and is based on an analogy with a chain: a chain is only as strong as its weakest link. Hence, the theory states that people will aim to draw the strongest and most reliable conclusion that they can, but that a conclusion cannot be more informative than the argument's least informative premise. To find out how informative, in principle, each premise is, we can relate informativeness to probability using the methods of a mathematical approach known as information theory.

As we saw with the earlier example of archbishops and cannibals, a statement is informative to the extent that it is surprising, and another way of saying "surprising" is to say "low probability". So informativeness is inversely related to probability. In addition, Chater and Oaksford assume a property for natural statements called *rarity*: that natural terms refer to only a small subset of possible objects. Thus the term "archbishop" refers to a rare property in the world: there are vastly more objects in the world that are not archbishops (or priests, men, or human beings, come to that). We can see how the rarity assumption is important by considering the E statement (No A are B). If statements respect rarity, then E will most often be true, because the probability that an object will be both A and B is close to zero (pick two property terms at random and you will see). Thus, E statements will be unsurprising and hence uninformative. Without rarity, properties would overlap and E statements would hardly ever be true, and would thus be surprising and highly informative.

Now, how often are the various syllogistic premise statement types true? We cannot just count them, but, using informativeness and the rarity assumption, we can arrive at an ordering that is justified theoretically and mathematically. Again, I will use the authors' graphic device, and leave the full technical details for you to go through in the original paper if you wish.

In Fig. 2.4 you can see the frequency with which E statements will be true on this analysis represented by the vertical arrow on the left. A-statements will hardly ever be true, and this is shown by the little black box on the right. Two areas under the curve show how often M and F statements will be true—remember that they mark out particular ends of the probability range. From Fig. 2.3 and the discussion of the p-entailments, there will be a region in between that is not specific to any statement: this is marked with the letter Z. The frequency with which I-statements are true is thus the sum of the areas occupied by A, M, Z,

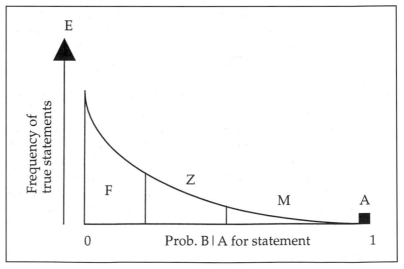

FIG. 2.4. Graphic representation of frequencies of true statements as a function of prob. B|A in Chater and Oaksford's Probability Heuristics model. From Chater and Oaksford (in press). Copyright © Academic Press, Inc. Reprinted with permission.

and F, while the frequency with which O-statements are true is the sum of M, Z, F, and E. Recalling that small areas mean lower probability and hence higher informativeness, the analysis gives the following theoretical informativeness ordering for the six syllogistic premise types considered by Chater and Oaksford:

$$A > M > F > I > E \gg O$$

The double symbol indicates that O is extremely uninformative—it is almost always true. Some cats are not furry, some dogs do not bark.

Expressing quantified statements in terms of probability means that validity can also be given a probabilistic interpretation: on this view, drawing a conclusion is not the all-or-nothing matter it is in logical systems. This notion of validity is called *p-validity*. On the information gain account, a syllogism concerns two probabilistic premises, one relating A and B, and one relating B and C. The goal of syllogistic reasoning is to relate A and C using the information conveyed in these premises. The conclusion can therefore also be a probabilistic statement. If, given the premise information, the probability of A and C is greater than zero, then an I conclusion follows p-validly. If this probability *is* zero, then an E conclusion follows. If the probability of A given C or C given A is 1, then an A conclusion follows. M and F conclusions depend on there being a small probability that prob. $(C \mid A)$ or $(A \mid C)$ does not reach 1 (for M) or zero (for F).

We are still not in a position to state exact predictions about, first, the type of conclusion that will be drawn for each of the 144 A-M-F-I-E-O syllogisms and second, the order of terms in the conclusion, as the previous paragraph implies. Two more heuristics are needed. These are known as the *max-heuristic* and the *attachment-heuristic*. Every syllogism has a max-premise as well as a min-premise: the max-premise is the most informative of the two. The max-heuristic determines the *confidence* that a reasoner will have that a conclusion of a given type will follow (type being determined by the min-heuristic). It states that this confidence is based on the form of the max-premise: the more informative the max-premise, the more confident a reasoner will be in the conclusion, and hence the more likely it is that the conclusion will be drawn; the response that no valid conclusion follows will obviously take the reverse of this pattern. Looking at all the syllogisms with given max-premise types, Chater and Oaksford derive the following order:

$$A > M > I > F > O \geq E$$

Thus, the likelihood of a given type of conclusion being drawn is determined by both the min-heuristic, for the type itself, and the max-heuristic, for confidence that it does in fact follow.

Conclusion order (A–C or C–A) is said to be determined by the attachment-heuristic. The heuristics described earlier (and also the p-entailments, which provide alternative, lower-probability conclusion types) generate a candidate conclusion type. The attachment-heuristic states that if the conclusion mood matches exactly one of the premise moods, and that this matched mood has A or C as its subject, i.e. first term, then this subject term is selected as the subject of the conclusion; if there is no match, then the end term (A or C) of the max-premise is selected. A fifth heuristic is to avoid O-conclusions, as they are so uninformative. An unspecified testing procedure is also mentioned in Chater and Oaksford's paper, to allow for the possibility that people may try to check their conclusion in some way; the authors claim that such testing will play only a small role in performance.

The elements of the theory are summarised in Table 2.5. The theory predicts what people should do when given syllogistic problems, if they are acting to gain information rather than performing some kind of rule-based logical analysis. The theory can be summed up in terms of the major predictions it makes, as follows: (i) the min-conclusion should be preferred for all syllogisms; (ii) the p-entailments will be drawn, but as a less frequent alternative to the min-conclusion; (iii) the frequency with which conclusions will be drawn will follow the order predicted

TABLE 2.5

The processing stages of syllogistic reasoning according to Chater and Oaksford's Probability Heuristics model

GENERATE conclusion

CONCLUSION TYPE
1. Min-heuristic: select a conclusion type that takes the form of the least informative premise.
2. p-entailments: select a conclusion probabilistically entailed by the min-conclusion if the min-conclusion is not drawn.
3. Max-heuristic: confidence in the min-conclusion is determined by the expected information conveyed by the most informative premise.

CONCLUSION ORDER
4. Attachment-heuristic: match the mood of the conclusion with the mood of one of the premises and use its end term as the subject of the conclusion; if no match, use the end term of the max-premise as the subject of the conclusion.

TEST conclusion
5. Avoid O-conclusions; use some assessment of validity.

by the max-premise, and "no valid conclusion" responses will follow the reverse order; (iv) O-conclusions will be avoided; (v) conclusion term orders will follow the attachment-heuristic. Do experimental subjects actually produce the predicted responses? To assess this, Chater and Oaksford conduct a "meta-analysis" of the results of five reported experiments, including those of Rips and Johnson-Laird, in which the full range of syllogisms was given to subjects. They find a very high degree of consistency between their theory and these data, higher even than the fit between the theories (mental logic and mental models) that motivated the experiments in the first place.

For instance, remember the distinction between single-model and multiple-model problems made by Johnson-Laird: syllogisms that require two or more models should be more difficult than those that require only one. It so happens that all the valid two- and three-model problems have O conclusions, which the information gain theory says should be difficult on that basis alone. The one-model problems turn out to be ones with "informative" conclusions (those with A, E, or I conclusions). Furthermore, Chater and Oaksford predict and observe differences within the classes of two- and three-model problems, which mental models theory does not. Note that Hardman and Payne (1995) have also drawn attention to the role of O conclusions in the model theory's account of syllogisms. They argue that Some A are not B "does not seem to say anything much of interest" (p. 946) in everyday language, and go on to explore the difficulty posed by O conclusions in terms of perceived relevance—an idea that seems consistent with Chater and Oaksford's general idea of informativeness.

An additional strength of the Probability Heuristics Model is that it includes in its analysis, and on the same terms as the "classical" quantified statements, the Most and Few expressions, and consequently makes empirical predictions for them. As no other investigations have included them, Chater and Oaksford use their own tests. As with the traditional syllogisms, problems involving the M and F sentences also produced performance closely in line with what this theory—and no other—predicts.

Some of the elements of the information gain theory may remind you of earlier accounts such as atmosphere and matching theory. Chater and Oaksford recognise this, and remark that these theories can be seen as "coarser" versions of theirs, whereas information gain provides a motivation for the principles of atmosphere and matching that otherwise rest only on intuition.

This new approach to reasoning clearly poses a challenge to the existing major accounts of thinking, such as mental logic and mental models: Chater and Oaksford have supplied evidence that human performance mirrors the patterns which rational analysis says are present in the cognitive environment. Information gain thus raises the intriguing possibility that very little of what we recognise as thinking is taking place at all when people respond to reasoning problems, whether they get them right or wrong. We shall return to these issues later in the book, especially in Chapter 5.

Summary

1. In this chapter we have reviewed studies of performance on traditional syllogistic reasoning problems, an area of research that has the longest history in psychological research on thinking and reasoning. Syllogisms traditionally consist of two quantified premises and a conclusion that may be valid or invalid.
2. Several strands running through this and other areas of the psychology of thinking were identified: the comparison between the formal description of the problems' structure and subjects' performance; explanations and theories that are specific to these experiments, such as atmosphere, matching, and conversion; and theories that are based on general accounts of thought applied to this area: mental logic, mental models, and information gain.
3. Mental logic theory proposes that people are equipped with proof procedures in the mind involving suppositions and inference rules. Deductive reasoning involves deriving a mental proof. Problems requiring the use of many rules for a proof will be more difficult than those requiring few rules.
4. Mental models theory proposes that reasoning is based on the derivation of a structured mental representation of the problem elements, the generation of a possible conclusion, and a search for counter-examples to this conclusion. It predicts that problems requiring multiple models will be more difficult than those requiring single models.
5. The information gain approach proposes that reasoning is a matter of searching for the most informative conclusion, based on probabilistic information conveyed by the premises. The outcome of this search is determined by a set of heuristics based on justifiable assumptions about the probabilistic structure of the cognitive environment.

Deduction: Experiments with "if" and other connectives 3

In the last chapter, we saw that work on syllogistic reasoning contains several themes: (i) the formal description of the elements of the problems, (ii) the observation of human performance on those problems, (iii) the question of the extent to which human performance approaches or deviates from the norms established by the formal properties, and (iv) the kinds of explanation, from the particular to the general, that have been produced to account for this performance. These themes are common to all fields of reasoning research, and so will be continued in this chapter.

Here, we shall be concerned with the kinds of inferences associated with words that serve to connect linguistic propositions, and which consequently come under the general heading of *propositional reasoning*. These words are known as connectives, and include *not*, *and*, *or*, and *if*. You may recognise that these are closely related to certain functions in computer programming languages, and they can also be related to logical connectives. As with the syllogistic mood terms, though, the parallel, although close, is not exact.

We shall deal primarily with *if*. Letter for letter, this little monosyllable is probably the most interesting word in the English language, if you measure interest by the amount of study devoted to it. It has captivated a multitude of philosophers, logicians, and linguists as well as psychologists: a flavour of the interdisciplinary range of this work can be sampled from the volume edited by Traugott, ter Meulen, Reilly, and Ferguson (1986). There is still no complete universally accepted account of its use. We shall also look at *or*, which, although not quite having the star quality of *if*, has also come under some close scrutiny, and presents explanatory problems all of its own. A sentence with *if* in it is known as a conditional; a sentence containing *or* is called a disjunctive. First, then, an outline of the formal properties of *if*.

Reasoning with conditionals

Truth-tables

The simplest kinds of propositions are those that are not made up of other propositions, but stand alone. These are technically known as atomic propositions. Truth values can be assigned to an atomic proposition: it is, in logic, either true or false. Sentences that are made up of atomic propositions can therefore also be given truth values; in fact, sentences can be put together in chains and the validity of inferences decided on this basis. This is the method of truth-tables, and it can be used to characterise inferences involving the connectives.

The simplest truth-table is the one for *not*, because *not* operates on single propositions:

p	¬p
true	false
false	true

Thus, when p is true, ¬p is false, and vice versa. You will see that we are now, along with most other authors, using a different section of the alphabet for these variables, and we are also using ¬, the handy symbol for "not" adopted in Johnson-Laird and Byrne's mental model theory.

The simplest truth-table for a connective, where two propositions are related, is the one for *and*:

p	q	p and q
true	true	true
true	false	false
false	true	false
false	false	false

This shows that the sentence "p and q" is only true when both propositions are true, otherwise it is false. Variables can be replaced by any propositions, so here is an example: you are introduced to someone who your friend Clyde tells you is pleasant (p) and quiet (q). You will infer that Clyde was wrong if the person turns out to be pleasant and noisy (p, ¬q), quiet and unpleasant (q, ¬p), or an irritating boor (¬p, ¬q). Even this connective, though, behaves differently in logic and everyday language. Consider these two cases:

Janet screamed and Clyde dropped the tray.
Clyde dropped the tray and Janet screamed.

Of course, both are true when it is true that Janet screamed, and true that Clyde dropped the tray, but the "and" here also implies a temporal and causal relation that is different in each sentence: we could add "so" or "then" or "as a result" to emphasise this (cf. Johnson-Laird & Byrne, 1991, Ch. 3). A similar point will be made about *or* later in this chapter.

Conditionals are more complicated, because there are different logical ways in which conditionals can be characterised. We shall enlarge on this point in later chapters: it is fundamental to the problems of explaining reasoning with conditionals. The first characterisation is often regarded by logicians as basic, i.e. as what they mean when they use the term "conditional"; it is sometimes called *material implication*:

p	q	if p then q
true	true	true
true	false	false
false	true	true
false	false	true

As you can see, with this reading of the conditional the sentence is false when p is true and q is false; otherwise the sentence is true. Imagine that Clyde says to you that if someone is a student, then he or she is poor. To prove him wrong, all you have to do is find a student who is not poor. Impoverished scholars and people who are not students, rich or poor, verify his claim. The idea that a roomful of chiropodists, interior decorators, musicians, and so on—i.e. instances of ¬p—confirms this sentence strikes most people as odd. But remember, in logic a statement is true if it is not false, so the fact that these cases do not falsify the original claim allows it to stand as true. This is one of the complications in relating the formal properties of *if* with its psychological properties: the two do not always match.

Another complication arises from an alternative way of characterising "if p then q". In the case of implication just given, we have a sentence that corresponds to the A mood in syllogistic reasoning, All A are B. If you look back to Fig. 2.1, you will see that there are two Euler representations for this sentence, one where A is a subset of B, and one where A and B are the same. Implication corresponds to the first of these; the second in *if* terms is known as a biconditional, or *material equivalence*. In other words, in some cases All A are B can be also read as All B are A, and equally If p then q can sometimes be read as implying If q then p. Here is the truth-table for the biconditional, or equivalence:

p	q	if p then q
true	true	true
true	false	false
false	true	false
false	false	true

The difference compared to the truth-table for implication is that the third line, ¬p q, now makes the sentence false. Imagine that Clyde tells you he has discovered that animals with a Y chromosome are always male, and that males always have a Y chromosome. He expresses this revelation by saying that "if an animal has a Y chromosome, then it is male". Because the class of things that are male is, as far as he knows, equivalent to the class of things that have a Y chromosome, you can now prove him wrong in two ways: by finding an animal with a Y chromosome that is not male and by finding a male without a Y chromosome.

Logicians use the expression "iff", or the connective "if and only if" to denote a biconditional rather than a conditional, but you only ever come across these in textbooks. In real life, the context of the sentence does the job, which is a simple way of stating a very complex relation. We shall return to questions of context in considering other kinds of reasoning, such as causal and deontic thinking, in later chapters.

Four inferences and two readings

What we have just seen is a set of truth conditions for two kinds of conditional sentence. We can also describe the formal properties of conditional inferences, using a form similar to the Aristotelian syllogism. For instance:

If p then q

p

?

Just as with quantified syllogisms, we have two premises above the line and a conclusion below it. Here, the first premise consists of the conditional sentence, and is called the *major premise*. The second premise consists of an assertion of the p part or the q part of the sentence, or negations of them, and is called the *minor premise*. The conclusion can be selected, evaluated, or, as in the earlier case, generated. We can now start to analyse these arguments in terms of validity, as we did with the syllogisms in Chapter 2. We shall look at the implication conditional first and consider equivalence after that.

The p part of a conditional sentence is called the antecedent and the q part is called the consequent. Reasoning with a conditional syllogism calls for inferences to be made about one from the status of the other, in relation to the sentence. There are four inferences that are commonly drawn. You have already met the first: given "If p then q" and the assertion that p is true, you are likely to conclude that q is also true. Thus given that the claim about students is true, "If someone is a student then he/she is poor", and the information that Alex is a student, it follows that Alex is poor. This inference and all the others have been given names, in this case a Latin one, *modus ponens* (MP). It can be summarised like this:

Modus ponens (MP):

If p then q	If someone is a student then he/she is poor
p	Alex is a student
q	Alex is poor

But what if the antecedent is negated, i.e. it turns out that Alex is not a student? You are likely to draw the following inference:

Denial of the antecedent (DA):

If p then q	If someone is a student then he/she is poor
not p	Alex is not a student
not q	Alex is not poor

We can do the same with inferences from the consequent to the antecedent. First, the likely inference when q is affirmed:

Affirmation of the consequent (AC):

If p then q	If someone is a student then he/she is poor
q	Alex is poor
p	Alex is a student

and lastly when q is denied—this one also has a Latin name:

Modus tollens (MT):

If p then q	If someone is a student then he/she is poor
not q	Alex is not poor
not p	Alex is not a student

These are the likely inferences to draw, but are they valid? A valid inference is one which must be true if the premises are true. We are dealing with implication here, which corresponds to a Euler representation of a small p field inside a larger q field (see Fig. 3.1). Thus, whereas students are always poor (assuming the claim is true), there are other ways of being poor besides being a student. MP is therefore clearly valid: all the possible cases of someone being a student are also cases of someone being poor.

With DA, knowing someone is not a student cannot tell us anything about whether he or she is poor or not: a field representing not-p could be wholly inside the q field (when the rest of the population is also poor) or wholly outside it, or overlapping its borders. DA is therefore an invalid inference. With AC, we know that someone is q, and that the p circle is inside the q circle. There will thus be more q people than people who are both q and p. All we can say then is that Alex may be p; she may not. AC is therefore an invalid inference. On the other hand, the minor premise in MT tells us that she is not q: as all the p people are contained within the q set, it follows that anyone outside the q circle cannot be a p person. MT is valid.

Fig. 3.1. Euler circle representations for implication and equivalence readings of conditional sentences.

Now we can do the same for equivalence, although we can be briefer. Under equivalence, or the biconditional, the p and q Euler circles cover the same field—they are equivalent (see Fig. 3.1). So, using Clyde's biological example, it should be fairly straightforward to see that all four

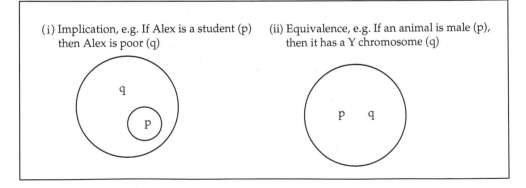

(i) Implication, e.g. If Alex is a student (p) then Alex is poor (q)

q

p

(ii) Equivalence, e.g. If an animal is male (p), then it has a Y chromosome (q)

p   q

inferences are valid. This much would follow anyway from the fact that a biconditional can be validly converted, so an AC inference from the original If p then q statement becomes an MP inference when the statement is converted to If q then p. Thus, if you accept that all animals with a Y chromosome are male, and that all males have a Y chromosome, you can validly change "If an animal has a Y chromosome then it is male" to "If an animal is male then it has a Y chromosome". Now you can conclude that if Ashley has a Y then he must be male (MP); if Ashley does not have a Y then she is not male (DA); if Ashley is male then he has a Y (AC); and if Ashley is not male then she does not have a Y (MT).

The difference between implication and equivalence then is that under equivalence, all four inferences are valid, whereas under implication only MP and MT are valid, and DA and AC are fallacies. The four inferences and their validity status under the two readings of the conditional are summarised in Table 3.1. We shall often refer to them later in this and subsequent chapters. Now, having outlined the formal properties of conditionals, we can look at psychological research on what people actually do when asked to reason with them.

Conditional reasoning research

Psychological work on conditional reasoning, like that on Aristotelian syllogisms, follows to some extent the formal descriptions: people have been given inference tasks and truth-table tasks to perform. However, conditional reasoning has also been extensively explored using Wason's selection task. You were introduced briefly to all these problems in Chapter 1; now we shall go into the research that has employed them. Reviewing this research will spread over the next two chapters as well as this one; here we begin with basic abstract tasks. In Chapter 4 we

TABLE 3.1

Conditional inferences and validity under implication and equivalence

			Inference Type	Implication	Equivalence
Major premise		If p then q			
Minor premise	(i)	p	Modus ponens (MP)	Valid	Valid
	(ii)	not-p	Denial of the antecedent (DA)	Invalid	Valid
	(iii)	q	Affirmation of the consequent (AC)	Invalid	Valid
	(iv)	not-q	Modus tollens (MT)	Valid	Valid

shall cover the issues associated with content, context, and biases, and in Chapter 5 we shall consider the major theories that have been put forward to account for the research findings.

Conditional inference tasks

An obvious kind of experiment is to give people conditional syllogisms or inference tasks and record which inferences they make or accept. There are several examples of such work in the literature, and some stable patterns have emerged in the data. These studies were reviewed by Evans et al. (1993a). They found that MP was almost universally drawn, followed by MT, then AC and DA in equal proportion. Wide variations in acceptance of the last three inferences were apparent across these studies, but weighted average frequencies were as follows:

	MP	DA	AC	MT
%	96.6	39.6	39.5	60.2

These data come from studies that were designed to rule out the influence of prior beliefs or knowledge, so they involved meaningless materials such as letters or numbers, or names of imaginary characters. We can see straight away that there is evidence that people are not simply going along with either an implication or equivalence reading of the conditional. If they were, we would expect first that DA and AC would be relatively infrequent: they are fallacies under implication, but valid under equivalence, so might be accepted only by some people some of the times. We can see that there is just such a pattern here. Second, however, MT should always be accepted, along with MP, because both inferences are valid under both readings—but it is accepted much less frequently than MP.

This lack of endorsement of the logically valid MT inference is the focus of theories of conditional reasoning; all explain it by appealing to extra cognitive processing that it may require compared to MP. Here is an outline of this explanation from two standpoints, those of mental logic/inference rules, and mental models. These theories will be reviewed in much more detail in Chapter 5; a third explanation will be described in the next chapter, when we look at the role of negation.

Mental logic theories assume that MP is held as a rule in the mind (e.g. Rips, 1994)—it is part of the "lexical entry" for *if* (Braine & O'Brien, 1991). Thus the MP inference is immediate and automatic, and should therefore be made almost every time; we have seen that it is. MT on the other hand is not held as a rule, but must be derived by the application of more basic rules in a line of reasoning. Here is an informal inference-rule account of MT adapted from Rips (1994), using the conditional syllogism:

> If Calvin deposits 50 cents then Calvin gets a Coke
> Calvin does not get a Coke
> ————————————————————————————
> Calvin did not deposit 50 cents

The line of reasoning goes like this:

1. IF Calvin deposits 50 cents then Calvin gets a Coke
   [Premise 1]
2. NOT Calvin gets a Coke
   [Premise 2]
3. Calvin deposits 50 cents
   [Supposition]
4. Calvin gets a Coke
   [MP from 1 and 3]
5. Calvin gets a Coke AND NOT Calvin gets a Coke
   [conjunction of 4 and 2]
6. NOT Calvin deposits 50 cents
   [reductio ad absurdum from 3 and 5]

There are two additional rules needed here: for conjunction (given x and given y, conclude x and y) and *reductio ad absurdum*. The latter states that if a supposition leads to a contradiction, then the supposition is false, and we can see that happening above: the supposition that Calvin deposits 50 cents leads to the conclusion that he gets his Coke, but Premise 2 has denied that. It cannot be true that Calvin gets a Coke and does not get a Coke, so the supposition must be wrong. Clearly there is much more to this argument than there is to MP: for instance, a reasoner might not know about, or neglect to apply, the *reductio* rule, and that would prevent MT being drawn. Hence there should be less likelihood overall of drawing MT, and as we have seen, there is.

Mental models theory also includes the principle that MT is a more complex inference than MP, but does so without inference rules (although note that the theory does have rules for how information may be combined in models; see Chapters 2 and 5). Johnson-Laird and Byrne (1991) specify that a conditional sentence will initially be represented thus:

[p]   q
...

You will recall from Chapter 2 that each line represents a different model, that the three dots indicate an implicit model (i.e. that there are unspecified alternative models), and that the square brackets mean that an item is exhaustively represented—it cannot occur in any other model. For MP, then, we are given the second premise: p. As p can only occur in the first model, the implicit alternatives are eliminated, leaving the conclusion q.

For MT, we are given the second premise, not q (written as ¬q). This eliminates the initial model. What happens next? According to Johnson-Laird and Byrne, that depends on the reasoner's ability to "flesh out" the implicit models, i.e. make them explicit. Doing so produces these two alternative models of what could be true:

$$¬p \quad q$$
$$¬p \quad ¬q$$

The second premise, ¬q, eliminates the first of these, leaving the last one, and hence the conclusion ¬p. Errors will thus result from a failure to flesh out the set of models: in particular, it is predicted that people will be likely to say that no conclusion follows, and indeed that is the most common error with this inference.

A final note about MT: there is at least one case in real life when it is readily understood. You sometimes hear this kind of statement:

If the Flatback 4 are a great band, then I'm a monkey's uncle

(or a Dutchman, or the Queen of Sheba, to name some variations I have heard). Or, more subtly:

If the Flatback 4 get to No. 1, then pigs will fly

(or I'll eat my hat, cats will bark, Hell will freeze over, and so on). Obviously, I would only say this kind of thing to you assuming that you believe the consequent (q) to be false; but for monkey's uncle conditionals to have their effect I also need to assume that you will go on to infer that I believe the antecedent (p) to be false. MT is quite transparent in these cases: perhaps the strong pre-existing belief that q is false is what does it, by the principle of relevance (see Chapter 5). They are a neat and forceful device for using a negative to deny a preconception, something we shall look at again in the next chapter.

Truth-table tasks

We can deal with studies using truth-table tasks fairly briefly, as there have not been that many of them. Even so, some important conclusions have emerged from using them. The basic structure of the task was outlined in Chapter 1. Systematic research tends to use abstract arguments containing meaningless material. The task is to judge whether a given instance makes a conditional true or false (alternatively, whether an instance conforms with or contradicts a conditional).

The basic experiment was reported by Johnson-Laird and Tagart (1969). They used letter-number rules such as:

> If there is a letter A on one side of the card, then there is a number 3 on the other side.

Subjects were given a pack of cards and were asked to place each one in one of three piles: cards truthfully described by the statement, cards falsely described, and cards to which the statement was irrelevant. Wason (1966) had previously argued on linguistic grounds that conditionals would be regarded as irrelevant to instances where the antecedent (p) was false, as in the case of, say, hairdressers to Clyde's claim about students earlier in this chapter; when p was true, the conditional would be seen as true given the p q case, and false given the p ¬q case. Wason called this the "defective" truth-table.

Johnson-Laird and Tagart found that 79% of their subjects evaluated the cards in exactly this way. However, logically equivalent formulations of the statement were not always treated the same. For example, a disjunctive of the following form, Not p or q, which is logically equivalent to If p then q (a person is not a student, or they are poor), received very few "irrelevant" judgements to any instance.

You might think that including an "irrelevant" pile invited subjects to use it. Of course, the results with the "not p or q" sentence go against this idea. So do the findings of Evans (1972), who had subjects construct instances rather than evaluate them. Given a conditional statement (about shapes and colours), subjects had to construct all possible ways of verifying or falsifying it. Any instances they did not construct could be inferred as being irrelevant to the subjects. Again, p q was seen as verifying, p ¬q as falsifying, and ¬p q and ¬p ¬q were most often not constructed, in line with Wason's defective truth-table and Johnson-Laird and Tagart's earlier findings.

The Evans study was important for a different reason: it also included conditionals with negated components. Most of the interest in the truth-table task has stemmed from what was revealed by using this factor, so we shall leave it for now and return to it in the next chapter, where we shall go into more detail about negation and reasoning.

Wason's selection task

This problem, as I have already mentioned, is now widely acclaimed as the most heavily used in research on reasoning, so the literature on it is vast. Over the years, it has turned up in many forms and been used for different purposes; it has been the pivot of far-reaching theories and the generator of intriguing findings; and has, more recently, been at the centre of fundamental arguments about human reasoning and how it may be researched.

One of the changes in perspective on this task that we shall deal with at first has been a shift from regarding it as an interesting research problem in its own right, to using it as a tool to investigate other problems—rather in the way that experiments using, say, the digit span or Stroop effect have done in other areas of cognitive psychology. In this chapter, we shall follow the theme of earlier sections and first consider the problem in its basic, original form; in later chapters you will see how its use has been generalised.

The basic selection task was set out in Chapter 1. We shall now have a brief recap of it, and an explanation of the supposed underlying logic of the task (you will see why this cautious wording is necessary later), then a summary of the experimental findings. It is when different kinds of selection task have been used that it really turns into an instrument for asking general questions about reasoning, and so we shall look more closely at them in the next chapter.

The standard abstract selection task presents you with an "if … then" conditional sentence, such as "If a card has a vowel on one side, then there is an even number on the other side". You are presented with four cards. You know that each shows an instance relating to the antecedent (p) on one side, and an instance relating to the consequent (q) on the other side. You can see one card showing p (E in the example), one showing not-p (K), one showing q (4) and one showing not-q (7). You are asked to select those cards which would have to be examined to tell whether the sentence is true or false of these cards. This presentation is summarised in Fig. 3.2.

Now for the solution. The cards you need to look for are those that could have a falsifying case on them, because one false case shows that the rule itself is false, whereas true cases do not prove the rule is true. As you have seen when we looked at truth-tables, a conditional is false when there is an instance of p ¬q (e.g. a rich student, following our earlier example), so you need to look for such possible cases among the cards. Going through each of the cards in turn, we can see that you therefore need to check the p card (showing a vowel), because it could have either q (an even number) or ¬q (an odd number) on the back, and the latter case is what we are looking for; you do not need to check the ¬p card, because whatever was on its other side, it could not add up to an instance of p ¬q; the same goes for the q card; and lastly, the ¬q card could have p or ¬p on the back, and if it had p then it would also be a falsifying card, so you need to check this one as well. The right answer is thus to select the p and ¬q cards. (Another way of looking at it is to realise that only the p and ¬q cards could support a valid inference, MP and MT respectively.)

correct

If you tried to solve the task, the odds are only about 1 in 10 that you actually made this choice: Wason and Johnson-Laird's review in 1972 found that fewer than 10% of subjects made this formally warranted selection, a figure that had not changed 20 years later, with a much larger sample of experiments to go on (Evans et al., 1993a). People are not simply guessing: most subjects select the p card alone or the p and q cards. The two findings that need explaining then are the needless selection of q, and the failure to select ¬q.

Two approaches have been taken to answer these questions. They have evolved in parallel. The first is to dissect the problem and try to find out (i) what elements of it seem to make it so hard, and (ii) what can be done to make it easier. One possible source of difficulty can be dismissed straight away: people are in no doubt about what constitutes a falsifying case, and will recognise the p ¬q case as such when they see it. We saw that in our brief look at truth-table tasks. This was reported in the first paper on the task (Wason, 1968) and has been amply confirmed since

FIG. 3.2. The standard abstract Wason selection task.

You are given the statement "If a card has a vowel on one side, then it has an even number on the other side" and four cards, each one with a single number on one side and a single number on the other, as follows:

| E | K | 4 | 7 |

Which of the cards would you need to turn over to test whether the statement is true or false?

(Dominowski, 1995). In fact, this difference between recognising and selecting the p ¬q case has great theoretical implications, and results in some amazing verbal contortions when people are confronted with it (see Chapter 4). Nor does it matter whether you ask subjects to test whether the sentence is true or false, or just to test whether it is false: the same selection patterns emerge (Griggs, 1995).

If people know what the falsifying case is, and are told explicitly to look for it, but do not select it, this appears to leave just their difficulty in finding the possible falsifying cases among the hidden values on the cards. There is some evidence that this can be made easier: if the p and ¬p cards are omitted, people are much more likely to select ¬q than q. This reduced array selection task (RAST) has been found to produce a far higher rate of logically sanctioned performance in both adults (Johnson-Laird & Wason, 1970a; Wason & Green, 1984) and children (Girotto, Light, & Colbourn, 1988). It is as if the p card, which is almost always selected, seduces people away from the ¬q card and towards the q card.

The abstract four-card selection task is a much more elusive beast though—that is why so much research has been devoted to it. Griggs (1995) describes some of the variations that have been found to make the standard task easier (in the sense of producing more p ¬q selections). There are three main families of factors: task instructions, sentence clarifications, and decision justification.

Task instructions depend for their effect on problem content. A variant on instructing subjects to try to prove the sentence false is to ask them to try to find instances that violate it. This has little if any effect on the standard abstract task, but does facilitate p ¬q selections in more realistic versions (which we shall deal with in Chapter 4).

Griggs himself, however, has reported striking results with instructions based on a theory of Margolis (1987). This theory points to a distinction between *open* and *closed scenarios* in hypothesis testing. In an open scenario, you have to choose how to go about testing; in a closed scenario, how to search is already determined. Margolis argues that the selection task is a closed-scenario problem that is sometimes presented as an open-scenario problem. There is also ambiguity as to whether the sentence is to be read as an implication conditional or a biconditional. Thus, if these ambiguities were removed, subjects would be more likely to get it right. Using instructions designed to do just this, Griggs reports that 74% of subjects chose the p ¬q combination, a huge facilitation effect.

"Sentence clarification" refers simply to removing the supposed ambiguity in the conditional sentence, i.e. whether it can be read as a conditional or biconditional. Inserting subclauses after the sentence to rule out the latter seems to have had significant effects in some studies but not others; again, the type of materials seems important, as Griggs's Margolis-inspired studies indicate.

Asking subjects to justify their decisions about the cards they are selecting seems also to have had mixed results, and to run up against the problem that subjects seem unwilling at least, and unable at most, to give think-aloud reports (of what they are thinking about when trying to decide what to choose) even when prompted. Evans (1989) reports abandoning such an experiment on these grounds. Asking for retrospective reports (of reasons for having chosen a card) is easier, and does indicate that some facilitation is possible, but again this only seems to emerge in combination with other variables such as problem content (note though that retrospective reports have been used to probe the very important theoretical matter of the difference between selection decisions and their evaluations: see Chapter 5).

You may be wondering what happens when you put all these three factors together. Griggs has done just that, and reports that high rates of p ¬q selections (up to 81%) are produced when a sentence clarification statement is used in place of the conditional sentence, when subjects are asked to find instances that violate the sentence rather than test whether it is true or false, and when they are asked to give reasons for their choices. This is a dramatic finding when you consider the p ¬q rate in the standard tasks of under 10%, and shows how powerful the demand characteristics of the task can be.

The second approach to accounting for abstract selection task performance will be dealt with in more detail in the next two chapters: that of putting forward theories of selection task behaviour. I shall therefore try to cut a long story short at this stage.

The earliest theory was advanced by Wason himself (1968; Johnson-Laird & Wason, 1970b) and centres on the idea of *confirmation (or verification) bias*. The subjects were said to be looking for verifying rather than falsifying cases, hence their omission of ¬q; whether they chose p or p q was attributed to their prior interpretation of the sentence as an implication conditional or a biconditional. The basic outline of this explanation has been revived by Johnson-Laird and Byrne (1991) in applying mental models theory to the selection task. Evans, however, noticed that verifying items also happened to be the items actually named in the sentence, and provided evidence that people were indeed simply "matching": picking up the named items (Evans & Lynch, 1973; see the section on negation and matching bias in the Chapter 4). In other words, they were selecting on the basis of what seemed relevant. This explanation has recently been given much greater theoretical depth by going further into what constitutes relevance, and has led, in the work of Oaksford and Chater (1994a), to the remarkable claim that selecting p and q is, after all, a rational response in the abstract task. Again, we shall return to these arguments in Chapter 5.

Before we leave the selection task for a moment, there is another way that may have occurred to you as a means of making it easier to solve: make it more realistic. This idea was first mooted in the early days of research on the problem and has been the source of a mountain of research. Chapter 4 is largely devoted to it. To round off this one, we shall have a slight break from *if*, and consider research on reasoning with *or*.

Disjunctive reasoning

I mentioned at the start of this chapter that *or* has not excited as much interest among researchers as has *if*, so we can be briefer in considering it. Some of the problems that have been raised and confronted are in any case quite similar, but it is also true that *or* presents issues of its own, so in the next sections we shall focus on them. First, we will look at its formal properties, then at the psychological research.

As with the implication and equivalence/biconditional readings of *if*, there are two formally distinct readings of *or*. These are known as inclusive disjunction and exclusive disjunction; they can be logically related to the implication and equivalence conditional, respectively. Here is a set of truth-tables for the two forms of disjunction:

p	q	Inclusive: Either p or q (or both)	Exclusive: Either p or q (but not both)
true	true	true	false
true	false	true	true
false	true	true	true
false	false	false	false

In both cases, then, the statement "p or q" is true when only one of its components is true, and false when neither is true; but when both are true the inclusive is true, whereas the exclusive is false in this case.

Clyde will explain. First, the inclusive form. He tells you a fascinating fact about his sister Janet: she keeps tropical fish, which are either angels or neons, he is not sure. Clearly he is right if she has just angels (p ¬q) or just neons (¬p q), and wrong if her tank instead contains only tetras and guppies (¬p ¬q); but he would not be wrong if she turned out to keep both angels and neons (p q). Now the exclusive form. Clyde looks concerned: his sister is expecting a baby, and she tells him the father is either her husband or his (formerly) best friend. Obviously it cannot be both of them (p q), and if it turns out to be someone else (¬p ¬q) she is also wrong; if she is right it must be the husband (p ¬q) or that snake he thought he could trust (¬p q).

Experiments with disjunctives

An obvious experimental move is to see the extent to which people assign truth values to the various instances when given a disjunctive sentence. This should show us two things: (i) how accurately (with respect to logic) people assess the truth conditions of "or", and (ii) whether they tend to go for the inclusive or exclusive interpretation. The second would be revealed by a preference for regarding the p q case as true, indicating inclusive, or as false, indicating exclusive.

On the first point, the set of studies using abstract materials, such as letter-number sentences, reviewed by Evans et al. (1993a) shows a mixed picture. The ¬p ¬q instance was always rated as false, which it should be under either reading, but the ¬p q and p ¬q instances were only rated as true about 80% of the time, which is strange, because this again is the rating required under both readings. On the second point, there was some inconsistency between the studies: sometimes there was a clear preference for rating the p q case as true (indicating an inclusive reading), whereas in other studies there was no clear preference, and in still others the preference was consistent with the exclusive reading. Some psychologists have in fact argued that the exclusive reading is more natural in ordinary usage (e.g. Fillenbaum, 1974). We shall return to this proposal shortly. Asking for truth-table evaluations is only one way of addressing these questions, of course: we can also look at disjunctive inferences.

As with the conditional, there are two *denial* inferences and two *affirmation* inferences: from p to q and from q to p in each case. Here are the denial inferences:

(1)	e.g.	(2)	e.g.
Either p or q	Angels or neons	Either p or q	Angels or neons
not p	Not angels	not q	Not neons
q	Neons	p	Angels

and here are the affirmation inferences:

(1)		(2)	
Either p or q	Angels or neons	Either p or q	Angels or neons
p	Angels	q	Neons
not q?	not neons?	not p?	not angels?

If we take the denial inferences, we can see from the truth-table given earlier that both should be judged as valid, under each reading: if you find out that p is false, you can safely conclude that q is true, and vice versa, whether the sentence is taken as inclusive or exclusive. An affirmation inference involves making an inference from p or q being stated as true. You can validly conclude that the other component is false only under the exclusive reading. With the inclusive, the other component could be true or false, so the affirmation inferences are invalid in this case (compare the cases of the sister's baby versus the sister's fish).

Studies have again not been entirely consistent, but Roberge (1976a, 1978) compared the denial inferences under both readings; he varied these by presenting sentences as "Either p or q (or both)" to indicate inclusive, or as "Either p or q (but not both)" to indicate exclusive. He found that endorsement of this inference was high (between 70% and 93%) but not universal; it was higher generally under the exclusive than the inclusive reading. With the affirmation inference, he again found that it was widely endorsed under an exclusive reading (92%: Roberge, 1976b). However, he also found that it was endorsed by over one-third of subjects under an inclusive reading (Roberge, 1974) when it is invalid, and so should have been rejected. If we regard this as an error, it again seems that logical accuracy was higher with exclusive disjunction and that overall, exclusives tend to be easier than inclusives (from a logical point of view).

Realistic disjunctives

We will anticipate some of the issues to be dealt with in the next chapter by briefly considering the effect of realistic content on disjunctive reasoning here.

The study of realistic disjunctives was pioneered by Fillenbaum (e.g. 1974). Strictly speaking, his studies were more about interpretation than reasoning, but his findings provided useful pointers to what would be discovered in later work using truth-tables and inferences. Fillenbaum points out that whereas in logic, *or* "is unordered, inclusive, and may connect any two propositions whatever, and its interpretation is completely specified" (p. 913), the everyday *or* has none of these features.

We have already seen evidence on the second and last points: *or* may be regarded as inclusive or exclusive, and the logically warranted inferences are not always made. On the third point, the linguist R. Lakoff disputed whether *or* can naturally be used to connect just any two propositions, and claimed that in everyday use there had to be a common topic to both components. Thus it is more natural to say that "Either it will rain tomorrow or it will snow" than "Either it will rain tomorrow or Clyde's sister keeps fish". Psychological researchers have sometimes appealed to this principle in their work (e.g. Newstead, Griggs, & Chrostowski, 1984; see later).

On the first point, ordering, Fillenbaum is referring to a particular kind of content that will figure large later in the book: deontic content. Deontic thinking is about actions you may, must, ought, should, etc. perform or not, so its main concerns are with permission, obligation, threat, promise, and so on. *Or* is often used in this sense, for instance in the case of a so-called "pseudoimperative", from Springston and Clark (1973):

Sit down or I'll scream.

Here, the two components convey a time order: sitting down (or not) will be followed by screaming (or not), and the sentence constitutes a threat. You can see the connection between disjunctives and conditionals quite clearly in such cases: the speaker could just as well have said:

If you don't sit down I'll scream.

Fillenbaum and Springston and Clark used such paraphrases between sentence types to explore the various natural interpretations of *or*.

Two more recent studies of realistic disjunctives have looked at reasoning with realistic *or* and turned up some interesting findings. Newstead et al. (1984) point out that it is not enough just to use ordinary words to make up disjunctive sentences, such as "The bird is in the nest or the shoe is on the foot", and call them realistic, because of aspects such as Lakoff's common topic principle. They produced seven types of disjunctive, as follows:

Threat: Either you eat your dinner or you go straight to bed.

Promise: I will either pay you back next week or mow the lawn for you.

Choice: You can either have ice cream or apple pie for dessert.

Qualification: A member must earn over £20,000 or be distinguished in his field.

Uncertainty: It was written either by Ian Jennings or Peter Lambert.

Abstract: In each pair, either the triangle is green or the square is red.

Concrete: My son will either turn out to be rich or he will be intelligent.

Using a truth-table task in which subjects judged whether each of the four possible instances (p q, ¬p q, p ¬q, ¬p ¬q) was consistent or inconsistent with each statement, Newstead et al. found a general preference for exclusive judgements (i.e. p q as false) in all contexts except Qualification, where there was a roughly evenly split choice. The same preference for the exclusive also emerged in a second experiment using an inference task, where, again with the exception of Qualification, subjects drew the affirmation inferences (given p, infer ¬q; given q, infer ¬p) as well as the denial inferences: the affirmation inference, as we saw earlier, is only valid with the exclusive form. Note how in this study the experimenters have been careful to maintain the common topic principle, and how many of these realistic contexts (the first four) are deontic.

Disjunctions expressing choice were further investigated by Ray, Reynolds, and Carranza (1989). They demonstrate how, in deontic contexts, there is more to *or* than the logician's distinction between inclusive and exclusive. These richer aspects derive from considering factors such as the speaker's goals in uttering deontic sentences in the first place. Using an evaluation task, they found that subjects would readily classify permission disjunctives in four, rather than two ways. These four ways come from considering, when hearing a sentence such as "You may either go swimming or play football," two questions: must I act? and, may I do both? Depending on the answers, yes or no, it seems that permission disjunctives can be classified as follows (using examples from Ray et al.):

Inclusive (must act, may do both)

Mother to son: For your chore you may either clean the house or mow the lawn.

Exclusive (must act, may not do both)
> Judge to delinquent son in custody case: You may either live
> with your mother in San Fransisco or live with your father
> in Chicago.

Free (need not act, may do both)
> Hostess to guest: You may have coffee or brandy.

Nand (need not act, may not do both)
> Father to child: For a snack, you may eat either a couple of
> cookies, or a piece of cake.

In a second experiment, Ray et al. found that subjects evaluated
disjunctive permission sentences consistently with this pattern when
asked to think about the intentions of the utterer, but that when asked
to think about what they would do as the receiver of the sentence, they
usually adopted the "exclusive" response: act but do not do both. Ray
et al. suggest that this is the polite thing to do in most cases, and that
in everyday situations we often ask ourselves the meta-question
"should I be polite?" before deciding how to respond.

This study shows that deontic content produces quite different and
richer patterns of thought compared to the sorts of non-deontic or
descriptive contents traditionally used in reasoning experiments. This
is an important matter which we shall return to in later chapters.

Wason's THOG problem

This section concerns another problem invented by Wason, designed
to see how people can reason with disjunctive alternatives. Note that
it is not simply a disjunctive version of the selection task. Wason (1977)
himself claims to have thought of it in 1976, but an earlier version
appears in Wason and Johnson-Laird (1972, Ch. 5); the first paper
reporting experimental results was that of Wason and Brooks (1979). It
is presented in standard abstract form in Fig. 3.3: as before, you will
learn a lot more if you have a go at it now, before reading on.

The answer is that the white square and the black circle cannot be
THOGs, while the white circle must be a THOG. If you find this answer
baffling, you are among the majority.

This is why the right answers are right. You were told that the black
square is a THOG, and that the example the experimenter is thinking
of can have either of these properties but not both. So the hidden rule
for THOGness could be (1) p ¬q: black and not square (i.e. circle) or (2)

In front of you are four designs:

Black Square, White Square, Black Circle, and White Circle

You are to assume that I have written down one of the colours (black and white) and one of the shapes (square or circle). Now read the following rule carefully.

If, and only if, any of the designs includes either the colour I have written down, or the shape I have written down, but not both, then it is called a THOG.

I will tell you that the Black Square is a THOG.

Each of the designs can now be classified into one of the following categories:

A.   Definitely is a THOG
B.   Insufficient information to decide
C.   Definitely is not a THOG

FIG. 3.3.   An abstract form of Wason's THOG problem.

¬p q: not black (i.e. white) and square. It cannot be black and square, as that contains both properties (p q), and it cannot be white and circle, as this contains neither (¬p ¬q), and both are prohibited under exclusive "or". Next, classify the shapes under each possibility. Given the first hypothesised rule, black and circle, you can rule out the black circle, as it contains both properties, and the white square, as it contains neither; the white circle contains just one (circle), so must be a THOG under this hypothesis. With the second hypothesis, white and square, you can rule out the black circle (contains neither property) and white square (contains both), whereas the white circle is OK as it contains one (white)—exactly the same as with the first hypothesis! So it does not matter which is the hidden rule: the white circle is a THOG and the black circle and white square cannot be.

You can see that the task asks you to reason using an exclusive disjunction statement (the 1972 prototype used an inclusive), which you should be quite familiar with by now. However, it is quite likely that you did not solve the problem. You probably came out with the opposite answer: that the white circle cannot be a THOG whereas the other two could be or must be. That is what most people do; Wason and Brooks call these intuitive errors. As with the selection task, much effort has been put into explaining why this happens, and into developing easier versions. This work has been recently reviewed by Newstead, Girotto, and Legrenzi (1995), so I shall summarise their main findings.

As with the selection task, understanding and using its logic do not in themselves seem to be the problem: Wason and Brooks had shown that when the task was unravelled, subjects were well able to construct possible cases using the THOG materials, and classify shapes accordingly. Rather, it seems that much of the difficulty stems from people being unable to separate the hypothesised properties derived from the experimenter's statement of the rule from the features of the actual exemplar that is given as a THOG (black square in the version we have been using). Newstead et al. call this idea confusion theory.

Confusion theory was supported in an experiment by Girotto and Legrenzi (1989), in which the original geometric THOG materials were embedded in a realistic content. This was called the pub problem. It concerned a character called Charles who plays a game with four friends in a pub. Charles tells his friends:

> I have brought a deck of cards. It contains only these four types of card [four cards showing shapes such as the ones in Fig. 3.3]. I deal one for myself from the deck, and I won't show it to you. Now, I'll deal each of you a card, and I will pay for a dinner for each person who has a card including either the colour of my card, or the shape of my card, but not both. [Now imagine that the four cards in Fig. 3.3 are given to Charles' friends, Rob, Tim, Paul, and John respectively.] Without showing you my card, I can tell you that I owe Rob a dinner. Which card do you think I could have? And do you think that I have to pay for a dinner for someone else? If so, for whom?

The answer to the last question, of course, is John, and 89% of people gave this answer, a considerable increase on the proportion who gave the right answer in the Wason and Brooks study (35%). You might think that what is important here is that a deontic element has been introduced: other realistic versions that lead to improved performance also have this property, whereas non-facilitating versions tend to be purely descriptive. However, Girotto and Legrenzi (1993) developed a purely abstract version that still resulted in improved performance. It involved giving subjects an actual name, SARS, to a hypothesised design, with THOGs defined as having either the colour or the shape of the SARS: 70% solved the problem when this was done.

To explain why people fall prey to this confusion in the first place, Newstead et el. draw an interesting parallel with research in other areas of thinking, such as decision making. In one such study (see also Chapter 9), Tversky and Shafir (1992) have demonstrated that people will withhold a decision when uncertain about which of two events might occur even though they would make the same decision whichever of the two events actually did occur. As an example, people who say they would prefer to go on holiday rather than stay at home if they pass or if they fail their exams, elect to withhold their decision when they do not know if they have passed or failed.

The difficulty common to this problem and the THOG problem (and possibly the selection task as well) is said to be due to having to keep several hypotheses in mind at once, and reason from them. People are defeated by the resulting cognitive overload. When people are overloaded, they resort to more primitive strategies that yield a plausible-looking answer: in this case, matching the values named in the exemplar with the values in the test cases, where possible. The middle two shapes in Fig. 3.3 have one matching value each, whereas the right-hand shape has none, so people make a judgement on that basis alone and give up on the logical analysis, hence the intuitive errors. We shall look more closely at response biases such as this in the next chapter.

Summary

1. In the cases of both *if* and *or* that there is not a complete meeting between their logical and psychological properties. In both cases, there are two possible general readings: implication or equivalence for *if*, inclusive and exclusive for *or*.
2. People's use of these connectives in language and in reasoning is not predicted even when these differences are taken into account: there is evidence for a "defective" conditional truth-table, endorsement of the fallacies, and lack of endorsement of the valid modus tollens inference with *if*; and a similar lack of acceptance of logically warranted denial inferences, together with a richer pattern of inference types, with *or*.
3. In reasoning tasks with abstract materials, there is evidence that although particular elements of the tasks may not in themselves be beyond people's competence, their combination may overload human cognitive capacities.

4. Examples are where people readily recognise a falsifying instance of a conditional, but fail to select a case that could reveal one in the selection task; and where people can recognise and form hypotheses about disjunctives, but fail on the THOG problem.
5. We have also begun to see the importance of problem content in determining success in reasoning: for instance, deontic content was found to lead to significant improvements in performance on disjunctive tasks, including THOG.

Deduction: Biases and content effects 4

We left the last chapter with a brief glance at the way in which performance on one reasoning problem, the THOG task, can be radically affected by the kind of content used in it, and by the way in which the task is presented. Historically, reasoning tasks have usually been introduced in abstract, (supposedly) content-free form with a view to assessing performance uncontaminated by pre-existing knowledge, beliefs, and motives. Underlying this approach is an assumption that there is some kind of "pure" reasoning ability that we can only access by using abstract tasks. This assumption is questionable on at least two grounds. First, performance on abstract tasks has been shown to be subject to a number of biases, the existence of which implies that such tasks do not tap directly into any human logical ability—unless that ability is fundamentally biased. Second, abstract contents are still contents, and an alternative possibility is that the form and content of problems are not psychologically separable, so that *how* you think cannot be divorced from *what* you are thinking about.

We can look at the development of reasoning research using different contents against the background of this shift in perspective, from regarding content as a contaminant to regarding it as central to the task of explanation. The study of the role of content in reasoning has been the foremost research issue for over 25 years partly as a result of this changing view. Also, there have been many new findings, along with deep theoretical questions, raised by exploring this issue. We shall devote Chapter 5 to theory; this chapter will review the major fields and studies of content and context in reasoning. The great bulk of this work has involved categorical syllogisms (see Chapter 2) and conditional reasoning, especially on the Wason selection task (see Chapter 3).

We shall begin with the experimental evidence for systematic biases in deductive thinking; biases in other areas will be considered in Chapters 6–9. Then we shall move on to research involving realistic or thematic task content, before considering a particular form of reasoning, which this kind of research has focused on: deontic reasoning.

Biases in reasoning

"Bias" is not, or should not be, the same loaded term in science as it is in everyday speech. When you say that someone is biased, you tend to mean that the person unreasonably favours or criticises, consciously or unconsciously, some view, conclusion, action, or person, over another. In the psychology of reasoning, the term "bias" can include this sort of partiality, but extends beyond it to encompass any systematic tendency which is independent of that a relevant normative theory would endorse.

Belief bias

This was one of the earliest biases to be identified, and comes from studies of Aristotelian syllogisms with thematic, or realistic, material. Try these examples; figure out which of these arguments are valid:

1. All the athletes are healthy
   Some healthy people are wealthy
   Some of the athletes are wealthy

2. All the students are poor
   No students are stupid
   Some poor people are not stupid

3. All the men are healthy
   Some healthy people are women
   Some of the men are women

4. All the monks are men
   No monks are women
   Some men are not women

If you concluded that 1 and 2 are valid and 3 and 4 are not, you have fallen prey to belief bias. Smart readers will have spotted the trick: 1 and 3 have the same structure, as do 2 and 4. Even smarter readers will have realised that 1 and 3 are invalid forms while 2 and 4 are valid. The conclusions are designed to be believable in the cases of 1 and 2, and unbelievable in the cases of 3 and 4.

As you have seen before, any deductive argument produces valid or invalid conclusions as a matter of its form: content is logically irrelevant. However, studies have shown that people do not respond to syllogistic arguments in this way. Belief and logic interact.

Belief-bias effects have been investigated for decades, but earlier studies suffered from methodological flaws, as recent authors have pointed out (Evans et al., 1993a; Garnham & Oakhill, 1994). Contemporary research, which dates from the early 1980s onwards, has focused on the interaction between belief and logic in experiments, and what this finding implies for theory. Table 4.1 gives some results from a study by Evans, Barston, and Pollard (1983), which clearly show this interaction. You can see that valid arguments were accepted more than invalid arguments, and that believable arguments were accepted more than unbelievable arguments, but the effect of believability was much stronger on the invalid arguments than the valid ones. This basic pattern of results has proved to be quite stable over a number of studies, although there have been problems with more subtle variables, as we shall see.

Evans et al. (1983b; see also Evans, 1989) give two possible explanations of their findings. One is called the *misinterpreted necessity* model, and applies to the reasoning process itself. It argues that people may not fully appreciate the idea of logical necessity, i.e. that an argument is only valid when a conclusion must—not may—follow from the premises. Hence the acceptance of believable but invalid arguments. This model is intended only to apply to invalid syllogisms, and is undermined by the finding that emphasising logical validity in the task instructions does not reduce belief bias (Evans et al., 1983b, Experiment 3; Newstead & Evans, 1993).

Their second explanation is called the *selective scrutiny* model. It states that people use an initial heuristic when approaching this sort of problem that tells them to accept believable conclusions straight away, and only attempt a logical analysis when a conclusion is unbelievable; how they go about this analysis is left open. Thus, it proposes that belief bias arises from a process that operates before any actual reasoning process.

Mental models theorists give a different account. You will recall from Chapter 2 that the theory proposes that syllogistic reasoning involves comprehension of the premises, the derivation of an integrated model of the premises to provide a possible conclusion, and an attempt to

TABLE 4.1

The belief-bias effect in syllogistic reasoning. (Data from Evans et al., 1983b, Experiment 2)

	Valid	Invalid
Believable	86	66
Unbelievable	62	13

Figures show the percentages of arguments accepted, pooling over the two moods of conclusion which subjects were given.

produce alternative models to see if that initial conclusion was the only one possible. If no such alternative conclusions are found, the argument is accepted as valid. Some arguments lead to only one model, and these arguments are obviously always valid. Some arguments have premises that can be interpreted in more than one way, and so permit more than one model; in some cases these models are consistent with only one conclusion, hence valid, whereas in others they are consistent with more than one, hence invalid. According to the theory, arguments that yield more than one model should be harder to reason with than single-model arguments.

Oakhill, Johnson-Laird, and Garnham (1989) applied the theory to belief bias by proposing that beliefs would affect the process of constructing initial models. If an initial model was believable, reasoners would not proceed to consider alternative models and would tend to accept it; they would go to the next stage only when the initial model was unbelievable. The problem with this explanation is the evidence for belief-bias effects on one-model syllogisms: beliefs cannot be affecting the search for alternative models because there are none. Oakhill et al. were forced to put forward a different process here, which they call conclusion filtering: people examine their conclusions and may withhold a valid one if it conflicts with beliefs.

We therefore have two kinds of selective scrutiny: that proposed by Evans and colleagues, which is supposed to apply before any reasoning takes place, and that proposed by the mental modellers, which has scrutiny occurring after reasoning. This is reminiscent of early and late selection models of attention, and perhaps a similar resolution will be put forward: that people can apply their "filter" early or late, depending on the task.

Some rapprochement of approaches is in fact taking place: Evans and his colleagues have recently also adopted a mental models orientation (Newstead, Pollard, Evans, & Allen, 1992), although there are disputes between this group and Oakhill et al. as to the exact way to make the theory work in this case. The picture is not helped by inconsistent experimental findings (Newstead & Evans, 1993) when tasks are designed with specific theoretical predictions in mind. Overall, then, it seems that although some version of mental models theory may be the best current candidate in explaining belief bias, its precise form has yet to be worked out.

Confirmation bias

We saw in the preceding section that belief bias results in a tendency for people to be less likely to accept deductive conclusions that conflict with their beliefs. A related phenomenon is called confirmation bias: the tendency to attend selectively to, or treat more positively, information favourable to your beliefs rather than to question them. We shall return to this bias in later chapters on induction and judgement, as many studies in those fields have addressed it. It is relevant now because it has also been invoked in the field of deduction, and because of its relation to belief bias.

These relations have been detailed by Evans (1989). He dismisses the idea that confirmation bias is motivational, arguing instead that it reflects people's inability to question beliefs rather than their desire not to, and that this cognitive failure is behind performance on a wide range of reasoning problems (we shall return to this point in Chapter 6).

Confirmation bias was initially proposed to account for the usual behaviour in the abstract selection task (see Chapter 3): to select the p and q cards rather than the potentially falsifying p ¬q combination. Wason (1966) proposed that people were using the "defective" truth-table, with ¬p regarded as irrelevant, and seeking to verify the target conditional sentence when they should be trying to falsify it. Experiments prompting people to consider the relevance and implications of the ¬q card led to the "insight" theory, which proposed that success on the selection task was largely a matter of appreciating the need to falsify rather than verify.

This explanation foundered on the discovery of *matching bias*: for instance, subjects who are given a conditional with a negative in it, such as "If there is an E on one side then there is not a 4 on the other side", should, if they are verifying, select cards showing an E and, say, a 7. They do not: they still tend to select E and 4 (Evans & Lynch, 1973), thus appearing not to do anything that might be called reasoning at all. Let us look further at this bias and then at a close relative.

Matching bias

Matching bias first emerged when Evans (1972) gave subjects truth-table tasks in which four abstract target conditionals were used, one for each way in which the two components, p and q, could be affirmed or negated. These are the four ways of doing this: p and q can both be affirmative (AA), p can be affirmative and q negative (AN), p negative and q affirmative (NA), or p and q both negative (NN). The example just given is in AN form: If E then not 4. When negatives are used in this way, the logical status of each instance changes, as we saw with the E 4 example. Using all four possible sentence forms enables this to be done systematically. Table 4.2a shows the logical status of each instance for each of the four sentences.

You will see from Table 4.2a that each instance also varies according to how much it matches the values named in the sentence. Instances may match only one of the items in the sentence (E 7 or K 4), both (E 4), or neither (K 7). Matching was found by Evans to affect how people responded to an instance. For example, take the TF logical case (p true, q false). This was correctly constructed as the falsifying item much more often with an AN sentence, where it would be the double matching item E 4, than on the NA form, where it would be the double mismatching item K 7. Similar effects were observed in a later experiment where subjects had to evaluate given instances rather than construct their own. The exception to this general pattern is the TT case (p true, q true), which was almost always constructed and evaluated as verifying, irrespective of matching.

Matching also generalises to different forms of the conditional: "p only if q", and "q if p" (Ormerod, Manktelow, & Jones, 1993), and was

TABLE 4.2

Matching and logical status of items in the truth-table task and selection task with negatives varied in the conditional sentence

Notation against the sentences:
AA: antecedent affirmative, consequent negative; AN: antecedent affirmative, consequent negative; NA: antecedent negative, consequent affirmative; NN: antecedent negative, consequent negative.

(a) The truth-table task

			Truth-table Cases		
		TT	TF	FT	FF*
AA:	If the letter is E then the number is 4	E4	E7	K7	K4
AN:	If the letter is E then the number is not 4	E7	E4	K4	K7
NA:	If the letter is not E then the number is 4	K4	K7	E4	E7
NN:	If the letter is not E then the number is not 4	K7	K4	E7	E4

(b) The selection task

			Logical Cases		
		TA	FA	TC	FC**
AA:	If there is an E on one side then there is a 4 on the other side	E	K	4	7
AN:	If there is an E on one side then there is not a 4 on the other side	E	K	7	4
NA:	If there is not an E on one side then there is a 4 on the other side	K	E	4	7
NN:	If there is not an E on one side then there is not a 4 on the other side	K	E	7	4

*TT, true antecedent, true consequent; TF, true antecedent, false consequent; FT, false antecedent, true consequent; FF, false antecedent, false consequent.
**TA, true antecedent; FA, false antecedent; TC, true consequent; FC, false consequent.

also found with the abstract selection task: here, subjects were more likely to select a card showing a matching item than one showing a mismatching item (Evans & Lynch, 1973; the finding has been replicated several times since), irrespective of its logical status. Table 4.2b shows how matching and truth are related to the selection task cards when negatives are introduced into a conditional. Again, though, the card showing the true antecedent value was less prone to the effect. These findings have been put to some interesting uses, as we shall see. We also saw in Chapter 3 how there is evidence for a similar tendency in the THOG problem, where people deny that the double-mismatching design is a THOG, when logically it is the only one that can be.

Several explanations have been put forward for matching bias; they are extensively reviewed by Evans (1998). It appears, on the face of it, to be a straightforward case of irrationality: people being deflected from the true path of logic by an irrelevant task feature. Indeed, some writers have taken this line. Others have attempted more subtle accounts though, and we shall look at three of them.

First, Evans himself (e.g. 1989) has argued that the effect comes from linguistically cued unconscious judgements of *relevance*. The two essential results in the matching bias literature are: (i) mismatching items tend to be classified as irrelevant (or not constructed) in the truth-table task, or ignored in the selection task; (ii) the effect is much reduced on antecedent (p or not-p) items. Evans links these effects to the linguistic functions of the connectives used in the target sentences: *not* and *if*. *Not* has a natural use in denying ideas that might have been taken as true; we typically do not assert simple truths by using negative sentences (Wason & Johnson-Laird, 1972). Thus, to take one of Wason's examples, suppose you truthfully announce to your friends next Monday, "I didn't go to Paris at the weekend." They will reply, "We didn't know you were going to!" *Not*, then, directs attention to the proposition it is denying, so a not-p or not-q case in a reasoning task directs attention to p and q. The sentence "If there is not an E then there is not a 4" will thus be seen still to concern E and 4; when you say "If it isn't sunny on Saturday then we won't go to the country", you are still talking about the relation between sunshine and country trips.

In a similar vein, Evans also appeals to a linguistic function of *if*, which is to focus attention on a *presupposition* expressed in the antecedent, p. Consider the last example: its focus is on the weather, and what will happen given one aspect of it, absence of sunshine. Thus the idea expressed in the antecedent will tend always to be relevant, whether it is expressed in affirmative or negative form, and so matching bias will be reduced in this case.

These proposals led to predictions that have been confirmed in experiments. For instance, the if-heuristic just mentioned is consistent with high rates of acceptance of the *modus ponens* inference (see Chapter 3). It should also lead to higher rates of acceptance of the fallacious Affirming the Consequent inference when the conditional is expressed in "p only if q" form—and that happens too (Evans, 1989; Evans et al., 1993a). The not-heuristic leads to the prediction that items that preserve the topic mentioned in the sentence should lead to a reduced matching bias effect. This can be arranged by having the mismatching cases contain explicitly negated matching items, instead of different items. For instance, instead of giving K as an instance of not-E, one could give "not E". Sure enough, when this is done, matching bias in the truth-table task is greatly reduced (Evans, 1983). Evans, Clibbens, and Rood (1996) have at last extended this method to the abstract selection task, and found that using explicit negatives abolished matching bias altogether.

Linguistically cued relevance should also explain why there is no matching bias with *or*. Evans (1989) argues that whereas conditionals invite us to consider whether the statement might apply at all, disjunctives do not: they invite us to consider which of two alternatives is actually the case. Thus, there is less of a sense in which any instance, affirmative or negative, could be judged to be irrelevant; irrelevance judgements should therefore be less frequent overall, and that is what has been found.

There will be more about the construct of relevance, especially as it applies to the selection task, in Chapter 5.

The second explanation of matching bias comes from the theory of mental models, set out by Johnson-Laird and Byrne (1991). Its elements are not all that far removed from those in Evans' account, but this theory does claim an advantage in that it specifies a reasoning process beyond the sort of heuristics Evans proposes.

The basic way in which the theory accounts for conditional inferences was shown in the preceding chapter. To account for matching bias, Johnson-Laird and Byrne make use of the idea (see earlier) that a negative invites the explicit representation of the positive instance which it denies. Thus a standard AA conditional "If the letter is E then the number is 4" is said to yield the following initial representation:

[E]   4
    …

The AN form is said to yield this:

[E]

    4

  ...

whereas the NA form yields this:

    4

[E]

  ...

No representation is given for the NN form. Because people are said to reason only about what is explicitly represented in models, they have to "flesh out" these initial models (i.e. fill in the unspecified values in each initial possible model, and make explicit the content of the implicit models indicated by the three dots) in order to reason correctly. Failure to do so will lead to reliance on the initial explicit content, hence matching bias.

The problem with this, as Evans (1993a) pointed out, is that the theory does not account for the lessening of matching bias on deductions involving the antecedent (p): in other words, there is no place for the if-heuristic in Johnson-Laird and Byrne's theory. To deal with this aspect of the data, Evans suggests a modification of the original theory so that initial models include explicit representation of the true-antecedent case (e.g. not being E, not being sunny), for instance in the NA form:

[¬E] 4
[E]

   ...

It should not take you long to work out what the revised initial representations for the NA form should look like as well. Johnson-Laird (1995) has gone some way to conceding this point (e.g. p. 137), although his revision of the mental models theory differs from Evans' proposals.

The third approach to matching bias comes from Oaksford and Stenning (1992), who argue that the observed effects are due to the procedure used in the experiments, which has prevented subjects from processing the negatives in the conditionals in the usual way. This implies that if steps are taken to remove these obstacles, matching bias should also be removed, and Oaksford and Stenning provide experimental support for this argument.

They present an interesting extension of the argument about the natural function of negatives as means of denying preconceptions: that negatives also specify a *contrast class*, i.e. a category of which the named item is a member. This is seen most clearly with realistic examples. For instance, suppose you say that you did not go to Paris at the weekend. The contrast class for this statement consists of an ad-hoc category (cf. Barsalou, 1983) comprising "things you could do at the weekend" minus "going to Paris". But what are the contrast classes for the letter E and the number 4? Oaksford and Stenning argue that it is difficulty in contrast class construction that leads to matching.

They used both truth-table and selection tasks. The truth-table experiment used an abstract task, which should make contrast-class construction difficult, and a thematic task with contents such as "If I finish my work, then I am home in time for dinner". Negatives were varied in the four ways you have seen. With the thematic task, contrast-class construction was made easy by eliminating the need for it: the logical items were (e.g.) "I do not finish my work"—an explicit negation. The results were not clear-cut, though. Evans' theory would predict that there should be an overall decrease in matching in the thematic task, and there was; however, there should not have been a difference in matching between the four forms of the conditionals, AA, AN, NA, NN (because each has the same number of matching and mismatching instances), but there was. On the other hand, the processing-negations theory would predict that the NN conditional would lead to most matching, because it contains the most negatives to process, but it did not: matching most often occurred with both NN and NA abstract conditionals.

In two selection-task experiments, the second one provided clearer results owing to the removal of some methodological problems with the first one. In short, they used conditionals containing binary materials—items that are either one thing or another—with the aim of making contrast-class construction easier. The materials harked back to some of the original contents used in Wason's early work, i.e. "If there is (not) a vowel on one side then there is (not) an even number on the other side". A letter that is not a vowel is obviously a consonant, the contrast class being "letters of the alphabet" minus "vowels", and a number that is not even is odd, the contrast class being "numbers" minus "even numbers". They also used a coloured-shapes condition, e.g. "If the square on one side is (not) yellow then the triangle on the other side is (not) blue", with the same aim, and a control condition with letter–number content such as "If the letter is (not) C then the number is (not) 2". Matching almost disappeared, as predicted, in the first two conditions: most subjects selected the confirming TA and TC instances (see Table 4.2b).

Evans et al. (1996) have not conceded this argument, however. They contend that binary materials may simply lead to subjects being able to label contrasting cases explicitly, turning them all into positive cases (cf. a similar effect with the SARS version of the THOG problem in the preceding chapter) and thereby preventing the not-heuristic from operating. Furthermore, you will recall that Evans et al. used instances in their negated selection task that were explicitly negated, such as "a letter that is not A", and found that matching disappeared. They contend that Oaksford and Stenning would expect such instances to make contrast-class construction more difficult, so that matching should not, on the processing-negations account, reduce; yet it does.

It appears, in summary, that although matching bias is a well-established empirical effect, its psychological basis has yet to be settled decisively. Evans (1998) concedes that no theory accounts for all the observed data satisfactorily, but favours his own relevance theory and that of Oaksford and Stenning over the others.

Conclusion bias

This is a similar sort of bias in two respects: it arises when people have to reason with negated conditionals, and it has been explored principally by Evans (although discovered by Roberge, e.g. 1971). In this case, the task is the conditional inference task, which was discussed in the preceding chapter (see Table 3.1 for the full set of conditional inferences). Here is a reminder of what an inference task looks like:

> If the letter is E then the number is 4
> The letter is E
> _____
> Therefore?

This task can, like the truth-table and selection tasks, be varied by negating the antecedent (E) or the consequent (4). Using negatives in this way changes the form of the possible conclusions.

For instance, the above is a *modus ponens* (MP) argument, and the valid conclusion is, obviously, "the number is 4". Negating the major premise like this:

> If the letter is not E then the number is 4
> The letter is E
> _____
> Therefore?

turns the argument into one of denying the antecedent (DA), as E is not not-E, and there is no valid conclusion (under implication). Inferences from the consequent are similarly affected. Here is the unnegated form:

> If the letter is E then the number is 4
> The number is 4
> Therefore?

This is affirming the consequent (AC), which is invalid, but when a negative is used in the consequent:

> If the letter is E then the number is not 4
> The number is 4
> Therefore?

we have a *modus tollens* argument (MT), which has the valid conclusion, "the letter is not E". You should now be able to go through the arguments when both parts of the major premise are negated.

When subjects were given these sorts of arguments, Evans (1977) found that they were more likely to endorse arguments which led to a negative conclusion. For example, an MT argument leads to the conclusion "not p" when the sentence begins "If p ...", but it leads to the conclusion "p" when the sentence begins "If not p ...". People draw the former conclusion more frequently. Once again, as with matching bias, the most "basic" inference is relatively unaffected: MP does not appear to vary in this way, being almost universally drawn irrespective of whether the conclusion is q or not-q. However, the other three inferences are significantly affected, as many studies have demonstrated (see Evans et al., 1993a; although see the evidence of Evans, Clibbens, & Rood, 1995).

Conclusion bias has not been as thoroughly explored as has matching bias. There is no indication that realistic material removes it, as it tends to with matching bias (Evans et al., 1995); and unlike matching bias, there is some evidence that conclusion bias is also found with disjunctive inferences (Evans et al., 1993a). Such observations led Evans to suggest that conclusion bias was a pure response bias, perhaps stemming from a "caution" heuristic. What this means is that an affirmative conclusion such as "the number is 4" is fairly bold: it can be falsified in many ways but verified in only one way. The opposite is true for "the number is not 4", so one is making a weaker, less easily falsified claim here. Evans' recent finding that the bias only reliably asserts itself with DA and MT inferences and not AC (Evans et al., 1995) has led to a modification of this view: he now refers to it as a "double negation effect", whereby people fail to deny negative propositions that lead to affirmative conclusions.

Evans et al. (1995) show how both mental models and mental logic theories could be adjusted to account for their findings, although at a price in each case. To account for the double-negation bias, mental models theory would have to propose that that the initial models for, e.g. the NA conditional would look like this:

$$[\neg p] \qquad q$$
$$\ldots$$

that is, lacking the automatic inclusion of a model for p, the affirmative proposition being denied by the negated antecedent, which the theory assumes in accounting for matching bias. The price is that when this set of initial models is proposed, the theory loses its ability to explain matching bias (see earlier and Evans et al., 1995, pp. 667–668), and would have to sacrifice the basic assumption that conditionals yield the same initial representation irrespective of the task they are embedded in.

Mental logic theories can also be made to account for conclusion bias, but they are held to be questionable because they have difficulty in coping with content effects, something that we shall look at more closely in the following section of this chapter, and in the next. Evans et al. come down in favour of the modified mental models theory, despite its difficulties, and argue that initial representation is indeed affected by task context, e.g. by the presence of instances in the selection and truth-table tasks, compared to their absence in inference tasks.

Having mentioned content effects at several points, let us now take a detailed look at them.

Content effects past and present

The study of deduction with different kinds of content has being going on for as long as any kind of psychological research into reasoning: one of the earliest examples was the study by Wilkins (1928) on syllogistic reasoning, which led to experiments on belief bias, reviewed earlier. In the modern era, there has been a focus on comparing performance with abstract content (e.g. letters and numbers) and thematic or realistic content; we saw an example of this in dealing with the THOG problem in Chapter 3. This has led to some subtle experiments and profound theoretical proposals. Two aspects of this work will loom large in the coming discussion: the preoccupation of researchers with the Wason selection task, and how the research has led to the exploration of a distinct form of thinking: deontic reasoning. These are not the only issues thrown up by research on content, as we shall see, but they are a good place to start.

Content and context in the selection task

People who first hear about the abstract (e.g. letter–number or shape–colour) version of the selection task usually get it wrong, and wonder why they and most other people do so. Perhaps, they ask, it has something to do with its abstract nature: we do not commonly go around thinking about such things in such ways. It is a short step from this idea to the strategy of attempting to make it more realistic by changing its content: instead of letters and numbers and suchlike, why not use more everyday terms?

This step was taken by Wason himself in the early days of selection-task research. Wason and Shapiro (1971) reported an experiment in which subjects were given either an abstract task, or a thematic version concerning journeys said to have been made by the experimenter. A claim was made about these journeys:

> Every time I go to Manchester I travel by train.

Four cards were presented, each known by the subject to show a town on one side and a means of transport on the other. The subject's task (in both versions) was to indicate which of the cards would need to be examined to tell whether the experimenter's claim was true or false. The two forms of the task are set out in Fig. 4.1; you might like to attempt it before carrying on.

Now, remember that to tell whether a statement is true or false you should try to falsify it; a conditional is falsified by an instance of p and not-q; the only cards that could contain this instance are the p card (which might have ¬q on the other side) and the ¬q card (which might have p on the other side). In this case, then, you should look for possible instances of B with a number other than 3 (the B and 5 cards), or instances of going to Manchester other than by train (the Manchester and car cards). If you got this answer with the journeys content but not the abstract, you have reproduced what Wason and Shapiro's subjects did: 10 out of 16 were right with the journeys content, but only 2 out of 16 were right with the abstract material.

More powerful evidence even than this was provided by Johnson-Laird, Legrenzi, and Legrenzi (1972). Again, they used a letter–number

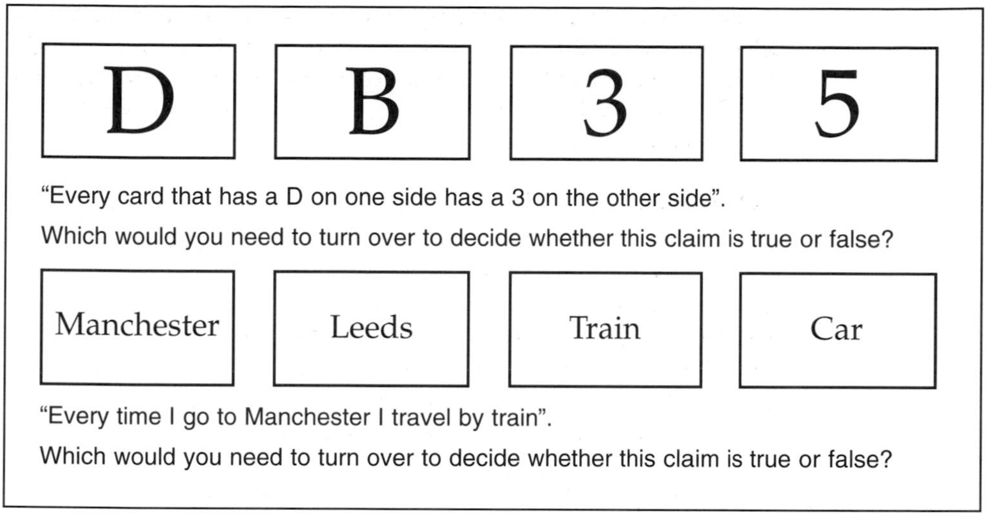

"Every card that has a D on one side has a 3 on the other side".

Which would you need to turn over to decide whether this claim is true or false?

"Every time I go to Manchester I travel by train".

Which would you need to turn over to decide whether this claim is true or false?

selection task, but compared it with performance on a thematic version where people had to play the role of postal workers, sorting the mail. They were given the following rule:

FIG. 4.1. Abstract and thematic versions of Wason's selection task. After Wason and Shapiro (1971).

> If a letter is sealed, then it has a 50 lire stamp on it

I have used the word *rule* here instead of statement or claim for a particular reason, which will soon become clear. Figure 4.2 shows the four "cards" in this thematic version; they were actually real envelopes. The task was to indicate those envelopes that would have to be examined "to find out whether or not they violate the rule" (Johnson-Laird et al., 1972, p. 397). Again, have a go at this task before proceeding.

The answer is in principle the same as before: look for the p ¬q instance, in this case a sealed letter with a lower-value stamp on it. Twenty-one of 24 subjects did so, compared to 2 out of 24 in the abstract condition, an enormous facilitation effect. You can try to anticipate some of the later research at this stage by noting down the differences between the postal task and the abstract task: they are important.

It appeared then, after these studies, that using thematic material did what it was predicted to do: "lead the subject to a greater insight into the logical structure of the task", in the words of Johnson-Laird et al. (1972, p. 396). But did it? This content effect, or *facilitation effect* as it came to be known, was called into question in a study reported by Manktelow and Evans (1979). They set out to test whether content would affect matching bias, by using negatives in sentences such as:

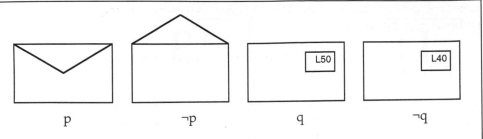

Johnson-Laird et al. (1972): "If a letter is sealed then it has a 50 lire stamp on it".*

Griggs and Cox (1982): "If a letter is sealed then it has a 15 cent stamp on it".*

Cheng and Holyoak (1985): "If a letter is sealed then it must carry a 20 cent stamp on it".

Which of these envelopes do you need to turn over to find out whether or not they violate the rule?

*These versions used a second ¬q envelope, one with no stamp.

FIG. 4.2.
The postal version of the selection task devised by Johnson-Laird et al. (1972) and some of its later adaptations. (After Johnson-Laird et al., 1972.)

If I (do not) eat pork, then I (do not) drink wine

and were surprised to find that there was no facilitation at all: performance was just as it was with abstract tasks. Not only that, but a replication of the Wason and Shapiro "journeys" task produced the same (non) effect. They therefore proposed that versions that had led to successful facilitation, such as the postal task, did so not by promoting logical reasoning, but by evoking people's memories for the correct counter-example: understamped letters, for instance. Such a rule had been in place in Britain around the time at which the postal experiment had been run.

This memory-cueing idea was tested by Griggs and his associates. They hypothesised that, if the facilitation effect was down to evoked memories, then a task such as the postal task should not work if it was run on people who had no experience of the relevant content; conversely, it should be possible to show a facilitation effect using a content that was known to be familiar to the subjects.

Griggs and Cox (1982) confirmed both these predictions in a series of experiments run in their home state, Florida, USA. Florida has never had a postal regulation of the type used by Johnson-Laird et al. Sure enough, Florida subjects did not produce the facilitation effect when given the postal selection task with American currency units (see Fig. 4.2). Griggs and Cox went on to survey their subject population for contents with which they were familiar, and came up with the drinking-age task. Here the rule was:

> If a person is drinking beer, then the person must be over 19 years of age.

Nineteen was actually the legal drinking age in Florida at the time. Subjects took the role of a police officer, checking for whether or not people were violating the rule. Cards showed what people were drinking on one side (beer or Coke) and their ages (16 or 22) on the other: clearly, the officer should look for underage drinkers, and select the beer and 16 cards. Now, as predicted, the facilitation effect re-emerged: 29 out of 40 subjects were correct, compared to none with an abstract task.

A strict memory-cueing hypothesis does not hold water for long: it will not even explain the original results of Johnson-Laird et al. This is because it posits that you are retrieving memories for counter-examples from your own experience. Some of Johnson-Laird's British subjects were given the task with Italian units of currency. Did they all remember posting letters in Italy? We are not told, but it does not seem likely. This crucial point can be made more strongly with a famous, unpublished experiment by D'Andrade reported in Rumelhart (1980), and known as the "Sears" problem. It is set out in Fig. 4.3.

Again, subjects had to look for potential violations of the rule, and most did so successfully: in this case, one should look for high-value receipts which have not been signed. It seems far-fetched to presume that everyone who does so has had experience of working in a department store where such a rule is in operation.

One of the issues first explored after the Wason and Shapiro paper was published was whether the facilitation effect was due to the *terms*

FIG. 4.3. D'Andrade's "Sears" version of the selection task. From Rumelhart (1980). Copyright © 1980 by Lawrence Erlbaum Associates Inc. Reprinted with permission.

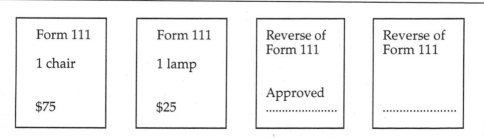

| Form 111

1 chair

$75 | Form 111

1 lamp

$25 | Reverse of
Form 111

Approved
.... | Reverse of
Form 111

.... |

"If any purchase exceeds $30, then the receipt must have the signature of the departmental manager on the back."

used in the task (towns and transport) or to the *relation* between them (journeys). In the case of the postal, drinking-age, and Sears tasks, we could ask whether these contents succeed because people know a lot about stamps and money, bars, and shops (which no doubt they do), or whether they know a lot about regulations in general: all of these versions concern looking for potential violations of rules whose status is not in question, as opposed to the standard abstract task where you have to search for instances that determine the truth value of a statement. Recent evidence strongly suggests that it is the understanding of regulations that was being tapped in the facilitating versions of the selection task. Understanding regulations is an aspect of deontic reasoning, and it is this issue that has become a major concern of selection task researchers in recent times, so we shall now turn to it.

Deontic reasoning

The first paper reporting an explicit test of the role of a deontic context, as opposed to thematic material, in facilitating performance on the selection task was published by Cheng and Holyoak (1985). This is one of the most important papers in the area: it is well worth reading the original.

Cheng and Holyoak, like Griggs and Cox before them, repeated the postal task with an American population, and found that it was possible to make it facilitate performance with the addition of a rationale for the rule, as follows:

> The rationale for this regulation is to increase profit from personal mail, which is nearly always sealed. Sealed letters are defined as personal and must therefore carry more postage than unsealed letters.

Note that this passage defines a benefit to the authority who lays down the rule, and a cost (and possible benefit) for the party who is its target: the user of the postal service. When the rationale was included, performance of American subjects was similar to that of Hong Kong subjects, who had experience of a two-tier postal regulation; without the rationale, performance declined significantly. So it seems that either cultural experience of a rule (as in the Hong Kong and 1972 British subjects) or a clear statement of a rationale will enable people to evoke their knowledge of regulations and reason correctly.

Cheng and Holyoak put forward an account of what "knowing about regulations" could consist of, psychologically: the theory of *pragmatic reasoning schemas*. A schema is a package of knowledge about a certain domain, similar to a concept, but unlike a concept it contains rules for thought and action. To explain facilitated performance on deontic selection tasks, they put forward a permission schema containing the following "production rules":

P1: If the action is to be taken, then the precondition must be satisfied.
P2: If the action is not to be taken, then the precondition need not be satisfied.
P3: If the precondition is satisfied, then the action may be taken.
P4: If the precondition is not satisfied, then the action must not be taken.

To explain how this schema would lead to facilitation of correct responding in the selection task, Cheng and Holyoak propose that a content or context that contained sufficient cues—such as a conditional rule that matched one of the production rules—would evoke the schema. Then, working through the four production rules, one can see that only two of them are determinate, i.e. specify what must take place: P1 and P4. These are the ones that dictate therefore which cards should be chosen: P1 for the card representing the action to be taken (sealing the letter: the p card) and P4 representing the precondition that has not been satisfied (a low-value stamp: the ¬q card). Each decisively rules out the case of p with ¬q.

They went on to test this theory with a new content, based on immigration regulations. These were like the Sears rule: it is unlikely that any set of subjects would have had actual experience of working as immigration officers. The rule was:

If the form says "ENTERING" on one side, then the other side includes cholera among the list of diseases.

Cards showed whether passengers were entering (p) or in transit (¬p), had cholera listed (q) or did not (¬q). Subjects were again asked to detect possible violations of this rule. When a rationale was provided ("to ensure that entering passengers are protected against the disease"), around 90% of both Hong Kong and US subjects selected the correct p ¬q combination. Without the rationale, performance was significantly lower, although still quite high for the selection task, at around 60% correct.

To establish that it was the deontic context that was the facilitating factor, Cheng and Holyoak ingeniously used a version of the problem in which the everyday content was stripped out, leaving just the following rule:

> If one is to take action "A", then one must first satisfy precondition "P".

This was embedded in a regulation and violation context, and produced a significant facilitation effect: 55% of subjects selected the p ¬q combination of cards with this deontic abstract problem compared with 30% with a non-deontic letter–number task (you will notice that this latter figure is quite high; this is possibly due to the use of explicit negatives on the cards, and of the word "must" in the consequent).

We thus have, in Cheng and Holyoak's results, strong evidence that a deontic context, not simply realistic content, leads to improved reasoning performance. However, not everyone is agreed that pragmatic reasoning schema (PRS) theory is the only way to account for this performance (see the next chapter for more on its theoretical implications).

An equally radical proposal was made by Cosmides (1989). She made an assumption contrary to Cheng and Holyoak on the question of where our deontic competence, revealed in selection-task experiments, comes from. They had proposed that deontic schemas are abstracted from our experience, along with other general knowledge structures; Cosmides proposed that deontic reasoning has an innate basis.

Put simply, Cosmides argues that people are equipped with innate rule structures, which she labels "Darwinian algorithms". These are necessary, she contends, because *social exchange* is fundamental to human survival. One of the bases of social exchange can be captured in the following generic rule:

> If you take a benefit, then you pay a cost.

She claims that we are innately able to understand this rule, and its corollary, that we will be innately sensitive to the possibility of *cheaters*: people who break the rule. A cheater is clearly someone who takes a benefit without paying a cost. Cosmides applied this framework to the deontic selection task and proposed that facilitating versions used rules that embodied this knowledge: sealing a letter or entering the country are benefits for which one pays the costs of a dearer stamp or a cholera injection, and you are cheating if you take the former without the latter.

Cosmides gets round the memory-cueing problem by using some elaborate contents involving imaginary tribes and their codes of privileges. She used her experiments to make a novel prediction. Turn the social exchange rule round, and you get a "switched" version:

If you pay a cost, then you take a benefit.

This enabled her to test her theory against others that refer only to the usual facilitation effect of choosing the p ¬q cards. For if people are responding according to her theory, then they should still look for cheaters: those who take a benefit without paying a cost. In the case of the "switched" rule, such a possibility would be represented by the ¬p and q cards, the reverse of the "logical" combination. And that is exactly what she found, the first time this response had been predicted or observed—a very different kind of facilitation effect.

An interesting and important aspect of research on deontic reasoning is that children have been shown to be very good at it, in contrast to their (and adults') performance on "pure" reasoning about truth and falsity. Girotto and his colleagues are chiefly responsible for demonstrating this (see the summary of this work in Girotto & Light, 1991). In one representative experiment (Girotto, Blaye, & Farioli, 1989), they used a deontic version of the RAST (see Chapter 3), in which only q and ¬q items are presented. Seven-year-old children were given a task concerning bees inside and outside a hive, presented as a kind of computer game. They were given the following rule, said to have been laid down by the queen bee:

If a bee buzzes, then it must stay outside.

An accompanying rationale saying that the queen wanted not to be disturbed by buzzing was also given, and the children were asked to check whether the rule was being obeyed. The screen showed a hive with some bees inside it and some outside; children used a light pen to point to a bee which then either buzzed or stayed silent. The correct answer is to check all and only the ¬q items: bees inside the hive, in case they buzz. Seventy per cent of the subjects did just this, a success rate comparable to that found with adults in deontic selection tasks.

You might think that this is impressive enough evidence for early competence in deontic reasoning, but recent research has pushed back the age threshold even further. Cummins (1996a) used an essentially similar task to that employed by Girotto et al., only this time the potential offenders were mice given this rule by Queen Minnie Mouse because of the threat from a marauding cat:

> It is not safe outside for the squeaky mice, so all squeaky mice must stay in the house. Yes, all squeaky mice have to stay in the house.

Startlingly, Cummins found that 68% of 3-year-olds were correct at this task; the figure rose to 85% with 4-year-olds. Similar research using the same age group but with different tasks, and coming to the same conclusion, has been reported by Harris and Nuñez (1996). Cummins uses such findings to argue, like Cosmides, for an innate facility at deontic reasoning.

The two schema theories, PRS and social exchange theory, have had an enormous impact on the psychology of reasoning, but have not gone unchallenged. Two alternative approaches, mental logic and information gain theory (mentioned in Chapter 2 in the context of syllogistic reasoning) will be dealt with in the next chapter, which reviews the wider issues raised by the various theories of deduction. Another, arising from mental models theory, will be considered briefly here in the final part of this section, as well as in the next chapter.

Mental models theory was applied to deontic reasoning by Manktelow and Over (1991, 1995). They point out some problems with the two major schema theories. First, PRS theory contains in its production rules terms it is designed to explain, "must" and "may", and gives no account of why a deontic statement should be uttered in the first place; furthermore, the "permission" rule Cheng and Holyoak used in their experiments is in fact a conditional obligation ("if you p then you must q": a true permission rule would take the form "if you p then you may q"). Social exchange theory, on the other hand, has problems with studies where facilitating rules have been found that do not fit the generic form proposed by Cosmides. The Sears rule earlier is one such: being a high-value receipt does not seem like a benefit, and a signature does not seem like a cost. The same can be said even more firmly for a precautionary rule that Manktelow and Over (1990a) devised:

> If you clear up spilt blood, then you must wear rubber gloves.

It is difficult to regard clearing up blood as a benefit for which you pay the cost of wearing gloves! And yet people readily detected the possibility of violations of this rule—clearing up blood without wearing gloves—in an experiment.

Manktelow and Over propose that deontic statements such as permissions are made by one party (called the agent) with the aim of regulating the behaviour of another (the actor). In other words, this form of thought is goal-directed. This point had been made by Cheng and Holyoak, but for Manktelow and Over goal-directedness was linked to the notion of a party's *preferences* for one kind of situation (or mental model) over another. An example from their 1991 paper should make this clear. Consider a permission rule given by a mother to her son:

If you tidy up your room, then you may go out to play.

This rule would only be uttered by the mother when (i) she prefers a tidy to an untidy room and (ii) she assumes that the boy prefers going out to play to staying in. Looked at in this way, two new aspects of deontic thought emerge: (i) there can be more than one kind of violation, and (ii) both the agent and the actor can violate the rule—a phenomenon that has become known as a *social perspective effect*. Here are the ways in which the two parties can consider the rule to have been broken, with their relevant instances in a selection task:

1. The agent sees that p is true but does not do q (p, ¬q) [room is tidy but boy is not allowed out—we might say mother is unfair]
2. The agent sees that p is not true but does q (¬p, q) [room is not tidy but boy is allowed out—mother is weak]
3. The actor sees that p is true but does not do q (p, ¬q) [room is tidied but boy does not go out—son is self-denying]
4. The actor sees that p is not true but does q (¬p, q) [room is not tidied but boy goes out—son cheats]

Subjects were shown to be sensitive to all these four cases of violation in an experiment, again designed to avoid the memory-cueing objection, involving shops offering gifts. Two further cases are possible, consisting of instances where neither party performs the actions set out in the rule (i.e. ¬p, ¬q), but these have not been tested in an experiment. Perspective effects involving cases 1 and 4, the ones that fit Cosmides' notion of cheating, have been independently confirmed by Gigerenzer and Hug (1992) and Politzer and Nguyen-Xuan (1992) with adults and Light, Girotto, and Legrenzi (1990) with 11- to 12-year-old children. Utility was shown to be open to subtle manipulations by Kirby (1994), using the drinking-age problem given earlier. He found that it was possible to change selection behaviour by emphasising the benefits of detecting an offender or the costs of either missing an offender or falsely accusing a non-offender.

One further consequence of this approach is that this kind of reasoning begins to resemble decision making, in the application of the construct of subjective utility in referring to preferences, benefits, and costs. As you will see in Chapter 9, decision making makes use of the more elaborate construct of *subjective expected utility*. This means that you make a decision on the basis not only of how much you prefer one situation over another, but how probable that situation is. Subjective expected utility is thus seen as a combination of subjective utility and subjective probability. So, if deontic reasoning can be seen as a form of decision making, then it too should be affected by probability as well as utility.

This hypothesis was first tested by Kirby (1994). He manipulated the probability of someone breaking the drinking-age rule by varying the ages of the imaginary drinkers: two new ¬q cards showed "12 years of age" and "4 years of age" alongside the usual "19 years of age" ¬q item. In the context of detecting offenders of a beer-drinking rule, Kirby assumed that people would regard 12-year-olds as being less likely offenders than 19-year-olds, with 4-year-olds less likely still, and select fewer and fewer cards accordingly. That is exactly what he found.

The effects of probability were investigated more extensively in a series of experiments by Manktelow, Sutherland, and Over (1995). They introduced a probabilistic variable into an adaptation of Cheng and Holyoak's immigration task by using a large array selection task (LAST) in which each kind of card was portrayed several times instead of just once, as is done in most other selection-task studies. Subjects were given a similar rule about entering and cholera, with the following rationale:

> You are particularly concerned that people infected with cholera should not be allowed to enter the country. It is well known that cholera is particularly common in tropical countries.

The first sentence establishes the utility of complying with the rule, the second establishes the probability variable. In one experiment, the latter was represented on the p and not-p cards by adding information about whether the passengers had arrived from a tropical or a European country, in another this information was added to the q and not-q cards. People should, of course, check for possible instances of a passenger entering the country without cholera among their vaccination list wherever they come from. In the first case, however, fewer "European" than "tropical" p cards (passengers entering) were selected, and in the second the result was repeated with the not-q cards (passengers without cholera on their vaccination list). Further experiments showed that this was a suppression effect: people seemed to regard the less likely violation as less relevant to the task of detection.

We shall deal with suppression of inferences in more detail later, and return to the idea of relevance in the next chapter. The concluding point to be made in this section is to emphasise how experiments on a statistical effect in the selection task have led to a series of studies that have revolved around a previously neglected area of human thinking, although one that is obviously commonplace in everyday life: deontic reasoning.

Deduction and uncertainty

Evans and Over (1996a) have recently made the point that the great bulk of psychological research on reasoning has, following logic, concerned inferences made from premises that are to be assumed true or false. However, real life is not like that: few things are believed or disbelieved with utter certainty, and in many cases we must make inferences from premises about which we are less than 100% sure, one way or the other. The deontic experiments reviewed earlier have begun to explore the role of uncertainty by manipulating probability, and other recent investigations have done the same. We shall look at two such areas: causal inference, and suppression effects.

Causal inference

Thinking about the relations between a cause (C) and an effect (E) has a long history in psychology, although not in the psychology of reasoning: you will not find an index entry for it in many of the recent textbooks. The field can be broadly split into two areas: causal attribution (reasoning about whether E was caused by C), and causal inference (making deductions from causal statements). We shall touch on these again in Chapter 6; for now, we will look briefly at some recent work on some interesting aspects of causal inference, which can be related to studies of deontic thinking. Research on causal attribution is often covered in social psychology texts.

Causal reasoning "pervades everyday discourse" (Cheng & Nisbett, 1993), and is bound up with two essential constructs: *necessity* and *sufficiency*. C is necessary for E when E cannot occur without C, although C may occur without E; for instance, yeast is necessary for bread to rise, but yeast may be present and the bread still does not rise (in my experience). C is sufficient for E when C cannot occur without E, although E is possible without C; for instance, leaving bread uncovered is enough to make it stale, but not using it for a week does the same. Obviously, it is also possible for C to be both necessary and sufficient for E: adding hot water to tea unfailingly produces a cup of tea (black, no sugar).

Causal inferences are often made using "If p then q" conditionals, and this leads to an immediate complication, because conditionals have their own necessity and sufficiency relations independent of whether they express causality. Logically, for any conditional, the antecedent (p) is sufficient for the consequent (q), whereas the consequent is necessary for the antecedent. To use an example from Chapter 3 (If someone is a student then he or she is poor), knowing that Alex is a student is sufficient to conclude that she is poor (by MP); and if she is not poor, she cannot be a student either (by MT). This kind of truth-functional necessity and sufficiency can cut across causal necessity and sufficiency. Sorting out these and other relations has been the subject of several recent studies.

Cheng and Nisbett (1993) point out that causal inference must involve at least one additional principle besides necessity and sufficiency: that of *contingency*. This was hinted at in the examples of necessity and sufficiency. Contingency is needed because knowing that E is always present whenever C occurs does not entitle you to infer that C is causally sufficient for E—because E may occur without C. For example, whenever you bake bread there is oxygen in the air; but there is anyway, so baking cannot be seen as a cause of oxygen in the air. "C is a sufficient cause of E" implies not only that E occurs whenever C does, but also that E is less likely to occur when C does not occur.

Cheng and Nisbett explored this principle in an experiment, comparing people's responses to causal and non-causal conditionals. Using abstract materials, they carefully set out to one group that A was causally sufficient but not necessary for B (i.e. B may occur without A), whereas another group was given the same information—that A always appeared with B, but B could appear without A—in a non-causal context. Subjects performed all the four inferences (MP, DA, AC, MT) and there was no difference between groups. However, as predicted, there was a difference between the groups when questioned about their assumption of contingency, i.e. whether the conditional could still be true given that B occurred without A. More than half in the causal condition made the assumption, compared to only 7% in the non-causal condition.

The idea of contingency in causal reasoning is important in everyday life. Imagine that you see an advert for a new cold cure, Snuffo. The ad features a parade of smiling people declaring how they got better (E) within a couple of days of taking Snuffo (C). Will you go and buy some when you start sneezing? You should only do so if you have information about people who did not take Snuffo (a control group, in other words): if they all got better within a couple of days as well, then you cannot infer that Snuffo gets rid of colds. Cheng and Nisbett's results seem to indicate that we are generally well aware of this factor, but common experience tells us that this might be a slightly optimistic view.

These elements of causal inference lead to further issues. One is the distinction between *causes* and *enabling conditions*. Cheng and Novick (1991) in a study of causal attribution give the example of a plane crash "caused" by an engine fault: the plane hits the ground owing to the gravitational pull of the earth, although this will not be cited as a cause when the investigation team files its report. The engine fault is a cause, whereas gravity is an enabling condition. Cheng and Novick present a "probabilistic contrast" model to account for this distinction. To use their example of a forest fire: people are said to contrast occasions when the forest catches fire with occasions when it does not. Suppose that lightning is a feature of the former but not the latter (i.e. lightning covaries with fire): lightning will be seen as a probable cause of forest fires.

Besides enabling conditions, there can also be *disabling conditions*, and these were investigated by Cummins and her colleagues (Cummins, 1995; Cummins, Lubart, Alksnis, & Rist, 1991). In fact, she explored two kinds of factor that could disrupt the inference from C to E: disabling conditions and alternative causes. Disabling conditions disrupt causal sufficiency, whereas alternative causes disrupt causal necessity. Here is an example of how these two factors operate, taken from Cummins (1995):

If the brake was depressed, then the car slowed down.

There are many possible alternative conditions for the car slowing down: the engine cuts out, the car runs into sand, and so on. Equally, there are many possible disabling conditions: the brakes do not work, the road is icy, etc. Causal conditionals vary according to the possible numbers of each factor, which can either be specified or retrieved from general knowledge, and Cummins showed that they affect the degree to which conditional inferences are accepted in causal contexts: inferences were suppressed to the extent that these two factors were present.

Recently, parallels have been drawn between causal and deontic reasoning, because similar effects have been been proposed in the latter as well as the former. Consider the mother–son rule mentioned earlier: perhaps the son regards tidying the room as sufficient for being allowed out to play, whereas the mother regards it as a necessary condition. If so, then a context that suggests one or the other should produce the "perspective" effects described earlier; similar effects should occur in causal contexts. Fairley, Manktelow, and Over (in press) have made just such a case, and found the predicted results. Thus, when causal sufficiency was questioned, subjects focused on possible cases of p without q, while when causal necessity was questioned, they focused on possible cases of q without p. Thompson (1995), focusing on subjects' perceptions of necessity, has used this principle for a general critique of PRS theory, and we shall return to this point in the next chapter.

We have seen how it is possible to inhibit, or suppress, conditional inferences in both causal and deontic contexts. Suppression effects have also been observed in other kinds of conditionals as well, and we shall look at these studies in the final section of this chapter.

Suppression of inferences

Suppression effects can take two forms: reducing the fallacious inferences that should not occur (DA and AC), and reducing the valid inferences that should occur (MP and MT). In the former case, this amounts to an increase in logical accuracy, in the latter to an increase in error. Remember that DA and AC are fallacies when a conditional is read as an implication, but not when it is read as an equivalence or biconditional; Geis and Zwicky (1971) argued that conditionals would tend to "invite" inferences such as DA unless the context dictated otherwise. So the first kind of suppression should be observed when equivalence interpretations are blocked.

This was demonstrated by Staudenmayer (1975) in an early study using the strategy of providing conditionals assumed to have many or few alternative conditions. Those with more alternative conditions led to lower rates of acceptance of DA and AC. Markovits (1984) compared responses of subjects who had to write down possible alternative conditions before performing an inference task: those who could imagine many such alternatives accepted fewer fallacies than those who could imagine few. Rates of acceptance of MP and MT were largely unaffected: they are, of course, valid inferences under both implication and equivalence interpretations.

Recently, suppression effects have been revived because of their wider theoretical implications. Mental logic theorists have regarded the relative immunity of valid inferences from the sort of manipulations just mentioned as evidence for mental rules for valid inference. However, Byrne (1989) demonstrated that valid inferences could also be suppressed in a similar way, this time using additional rather than alternative conditions. Here is an example, taken from Byrne, to illustrate the technique.

Given the following conditional and a minor premise:

> If she meets her friend then she will go to a play
> She meets her friend

most people (96% in Byrne's study) concluded, by MP, that she goes to a play. However, when given an additional premise:

> If she has enough money then she will go to a play

only a minority (38%) now drew the conclusion. Similar effects occurred with MT, but DA and AC were unaffected—the mirror image of what happens when alternative conditions are presented. This is a troublesome finding for mental logic theories, because they all assume that we possess a mental rule for MP, which should apply irrespective of context. However, Byrne claims that the mental models theory can explain the finding because the extra premise leads to different model representations in the two cases. This is reflected in the ways in which the two uses of extra premises can be paraphrased (see Byrne and Johnson-Laird, 1992). Here is an example of an alternative condition in the form of an extra premise:

> If she meets her friend then she will go to a play
> If she meets her family then she will go to a play.

This can be paraphrased as "If she meets her friend *or* her family then she will go to a play", which leads to the blocking of the fallacies (e.g. "she does not meet her friend" cannot rule out that she went to a play because she may have met her family) leaving the valid inferences in place. On the other hand:

>.If she meets her friend then she will go to a play
>If she has enough money then she will go to a play

asserts an additional condition, and the pair can be paraphrased as "If she meets her friend *and* she has enough money then she will go to a play". Now, the valid inferences are blocked because, for instance, only one part of the compound antecedent has been affirmed (see earlier). The fallacies are not blocked: denial of one part of the antecedent still casts doubt on the consequent.

More on the theoretical implications of such findings in the next chapter. For now, it is worth pointing out that standard mental models theory is not the only way of addressing suppression effects. Stevenson and Over (1995) argue that the effect is due to additional premises lessening belief in the initial premise. They tested this idea by throwing the argument into reverse: a manipulation that casts doubt on the extra information should lead to the restoration of, for instance, MP. They did this by supplying a third premise, as in this example:

>If John goes fishing then he will have a fish supper
>If John catches a fish then he will have a fish supper
>John is always/usually/rarely/never lucky when he goes
>   fishing
>John goes fishing
>_____
>Therefore, John has a fish supper

Subjects tended not to endorse this MP inference when only the first two premises were presented (the usual suppression effect), tended to do so when the third premise said "always", and tended to suppress it again according to the varying degrees of doubt cast by the qualifications expressed in the third premise. This sort of behaviour is hard to explain in the purely interpretational sense of mental models theory used by Byrne and Johnson-Laird. Stevenson and Over argue that such evidence means that the theory will have to be supplemented with weighting components representing degrees of belief in the contents of models.

Summary

1. There is a large volume of evidence for non-logical biases in reasoning experiments, although their interpretation is still a matter of debate: confirmation bias, matching bias, and conclusion bias have all been the subject of recent reinterpretations.

2. Similarly, there is a huge literature on content effects in reasoning. Belief bias results when content appears to deflect subjects away from conclusions with which they disagree. Other content effects result in realistic tasks producing a higher level of logically accurate answers compared to similar tasks using abstract material.

3. One productive consequence of the focus on content effects has been the opening up of enquiry into hitherto neglected but important areas of reasoning: this chapter looked in particular at deontic reasoning, causal reasoning, and reasoning from uncertain premises.

4. With this enrichment of areas of enquiry has come an expansion of theory, a theme continued in the next chapter.

Theories of deduction 5

In the preceding three chapters, a host of ideas and experiments on human reasoning have been discussed, with brief accounts both of how these studies may help us explain deductive thinking, and of how the explanations have led to further experiments. In this chapter, we return to these explanations in more detail. We shall consider five main types of theory in three ways: (i) their structure and content, (ii) their successes and limits in accounting for the research data, and (iii) points on which they agree and differ. The contest between theories has been a feature of reasoning research since the early 1980s, and is still in full swing.

The five theoretical families are: Mental Logic and Inference Rules, Reasoning Schemas, Mental Models, Relevance and Heuristics, and Information Gain. All except the first have been developed since the early 1980s, and even the first has been recast in the 1990s.

Mental logic and inference rules

The idea that the untutored human mind carries within it some kind of logical system that enables us to make deductions goes back to Aristotle, and was not seriously questioned until very recently. In psychology, it forms the basis of Piaget's account of the growth of intelligence (see Manktelow & Over, 1990b, for a review of Piagetian theory as a theory of reasoning). For some people, possession of a mental logic seems unarguable, and for others it is an empirical question. In this section, I shall consider two modern theories that take the latter course, and which argue that their mental logic approach is simply the best way of accounting for the data.

Rips' PSYCOP theory

You have already met this theory in Chapter 2, in dealing with syllogisms. The name PSYCOP is derived from the words PSYChology Of Proof, and the theory is presented in detail by Rips (1994). It is a technically complex and wide-ranging theory that aims to do more than just explain the outcome of reasoning experiments, and I shall only be able to outline it here. Further details are given in Chapter 2.

The theory

Here is the basis of the theory as set out by Rips (1994, p. x):

> According to [PSYCOP], a person faced with a task involving deduction attempts to carry it out through a series of steps that take him or her from an initial description of the problem to its solution. These intermediate steps are licensed by mental inference rules, such as modus ponens, whose output people find intuitively obvious. The resulting structure thus provides a conceptual bridge between the problem's "givens" and its solution.

These inference rules, in other words, are used to construct and verify a *mental proof*. Rips does not argue that such attempts at proof are always successful—otherwise he would predict that reasoning would be infallible—but that such an attempt is always made. Factors that might cause an error would be those that hinder the application of an appropriate inference rule, such as working memory restrictions, or perhaps the lack of a requisite rule, or possession of a non-standard rule.

The inference rules are said to construct mental proofs in working memory. In the case of an argument that a person has to evaluate according to whether it follows or not, the person tries to prove that the conclusion follows from the premises. The argument is entered into working memory and the premises are scanned to see if any inferences are possible from the battery of rules. If so, any new sentences are added to memory, the updated set is scanned for further inferences, and so on until a proof is constructed or until no more rules can be applied (in which case the answer is that the conclusion does not follow). A syllogistic example is worked through in Chapter 2.

There are two types of inference rule: forward and backward. Forward rules draw implications from premises; an example is the rule for *modus ponens* (MP), with which you should be familiar (see Chapter 3 if you need reminding). MP is known as the rule for forward if-elimination in PSYCOP. This terminology simply means that execution of the rule results in the elimination of *if* in the conclusion. And-elimination is similar: given that there is a dog in the garden and a cat in the garden, you can conclude that there is a dog in the garden: the *and* has gone. Forward rules thus generate sets of new sentences, or assertions. Backward rules work on conclusions, working back to find assertions that are necessary for the argument that the reasoner is trying to prove. PSYCOP's backward rules contain the family of introduction rules. For example, and-introduction is where you conclude that there is a cat and a dog in the garden when it has been proved that there is a cat, and that there is a dog. Backward if-introduction involves proving a conditional sentence by seeing whether, when p is assumed, q is also present: if there is always a q when there is a p, then we can introduce "if" and assert "if p then q".

The system makes use of a principle derived from problem-solving theory: that of subgoals. This means that in trying to find a proof of the argument as a whole, the system will set up intermediate goals for proof that are necessary for the argument. Table 5.1 gives an adapted version of an example from Rips (1994, Ch. 4) to show how the following rules are applied to prove a deductive argument: forward and-elimination, backward and-introduction, and backward if-introduction. This example also shows how one of the basic control assumptions of the theory is applied: PSYCOP applies its forward rules first and, if these are not enough to secure a proof, goes on to apply the backward rules.

The evidence

The PSYCOP theory can be evaluated both against the tests that Rips designed for it, and against research data from elsewhere. Rips (1994,

TABLE 5.1

Proving a deductive argument using the PSYCOP system

IF Betty is in Little Rock THEN Ellen is in Hammond
Phoebe is in Tucson AND Sandra is in Memphis

IF Betty is in Little Rock THEN (Ellen is in Hammond AND Sandra is in Memphis)

The conclusion is the goal to be proved.

1. PSYCOP notices that the second sentence is a conjunction and applies forward and-elimination, generating two new sentences which are entered in working memory:

2. Phoebe is in Tucson   Sandra is in Memphis

3. No other forward rules apply.

4. [Because the conclusion (i.e. goal) is a conditional, backward if-introduction can be applied (see text).]
   Subgoal: prove Ellen is in Hammond AND Sandra is in Memphis
   Make the supposition: Betty is in Little Rock
   Assume: If Betty is in Little Rock THEN Ellen is in Hammond
   Conclude: Ellen is in Hammond [by forward if-elimination; see text]

5. Ellen is in Hammond AND Sandra is in Memphis [by backward AND-introduction from 4 and 2; see text].

6. IF Betty is in Little Rock THEN (Ellen is in Hammond AND Sandra is in Memphis) [by backward IF-introduction]

Ch. 5) gives as an example of the former an experiment using materials similar to those in Table 5.1, along with some about imaginary machines. Subjects were given whole arguments and asked to judge whether the conclusion was necessarily true or not. Thirty-two such problems were presented involving various rules, and predictions were made as to their respective difficulty using assumptions about the likely availability of rules to subjects, plus a guessing factor. The predicted and observed performance correlated closely; other possible factors such as number of premises in the argument, or number of atomic sentences (the conclusion in the argument in Table 5.1 has three, for instance) did not predict performance at all.

As an example of the second type of test, Rips (1994, Chs. 5, 9) outlines PSYCOP's explanation for the observed behaviour on Wason's selection task. On the abstract task (see Chapters 1 and 3), Rips points out that the theory predicts that subjects should elect to examine only the p card, which is what about a third of subjects do. This is because there is no conclusion to evaluate, so PSYCOP can only use its forward rules; in this case the only one applicable is forward if-elimination (or MP), and that can only be applied to the p card. However, an equally common response is to select both the p and q cards; Rips argues that this will happen when subjects assume that the target conditional can be read as a biconditional, i.e. as implying If q then p as well as If p then q; forward if-elimination can then also be applied to the q card. In the case of subjects who carry out the task correctly, the explanation is in terms of their being able to project possible values on to the hidden sides of the cards.

On the question of the facilitation effects (see Chapter 4), Rips uses a memory-cueing argument in both deontic and non-deontic contexts. This and the other explanations for selection-task performance cannot be taken as powerful evidence for PSYCOP, however, as they have all been advanced before: in the case of the abstract task, by Wason himself in the earliest days of selection-task research. None of them are novel explanations particular to PSYCOP. The theory is clearly on its weakest ground here, although whether the selection task could give it, or any other mental logic theory, a fair test in the first place is a question we shall ask again later.

Braine and O'Brien's theory

An alternative recent mental logic theory was presented by Braine and O'Brien and their colleagues (1991; see also O'Brien, 1993, 1995). In some respects it is similar to the Rips theory, as it is also based on *natural deduction* rather than textbook logic and includes many of the same rules. It does not have a name, so I shall call it the BO'B theory for short.

The theory

The BO'B theory has three major components: a set of *inference schemas*, a *reasoning program* that implements these rules, and a set of *pragmatic principles* to explain constraints on their application in various contexts (i.e. a comprehension component). It has been most fully worked out in the area of conditional reasoning (Braine & O'Brien, 1991), but general accounts are also available (e.g. Braine, 1990) and it has been applied to text comprehension as well as reasoning (Lea, O'Brien, Noveck, Fisch, & Braine, 1990). The last two references present extensive listings of the theory's main components: the inference rules and the reasoning program.

The inference rules take the form of reasoning schemas, not simply mental versions of the rules of text-book logic: an important starting point in answering the critics of mental logic theories, as we shall see. These schemas are further subdivided into core schemas and feeder schemas. The core schemas "describe a set of inferences that people make routinely and without apparent effort" (O'Brien, 1993), including *modus ponens* and or-elimination (the disjunctive denial inference: see Chapter 3); there are also *incompatibility* rules, which are used in making "false" judgements, such as when an argument leads to the inference of both x and not-x. Feeder schemas are auxiliary: they are only applied when their output provides propositions that are included in further inferences using the core schemas; and-elimination and and-introduction are among this set.

The reasoning program controls when these inference rules will be applied in a line of reasoning. There is a direct-reasoning routine and an indirect-reasoning routine, along with an inference procedure (for deriving conclusions from premises) and an evaluation procedure (for assessing the validity of given conclusions). The direct-reasoning routine applies the core and feeder schemas automatically when appropriate propositions are considered together: for instance, when "p or q" and "not-p" are jointly held in working memory, the conclusion "q" is supplied. This aspect of reasoning is therefore considered basic to human deductive competence, and so it is predicted that tasks that require the exercise of these processes will be carried out accurately.

The indirect-reasoning routine applies to problems that lie outside the province of the direct-reasoning routine. The BO'B theory allows that people may acquire complex schemas through learning, or that the application of such schemas may be facilitated (or inhibited) by certain contexts or problem domains. Thus, problems that demand complex schemas for their solution will be less likely to be solved.

The pragmatic principles help to determine which routines are called for. These principles can come from the natural-language meanings of connectives such as *if* and *or*, which, as we have seen in Chapter 3, differ from their meanings as logical particles. One kind of pragmatic principle is that of the invited inference, which was described in the preceding chapter. According to Braine and O'Brien (1991), the basic meaning of a connective is supplied by its basic inference schemas. This is known as its lexical entry. In the case of *if*, for instance, the basic meaning is given by two schemas: *modus ponens* and a schema for conditional proof (this is similar to PSYCOP's rule of backward if-introduction; PSYCOP also has a third inference rule for "if": backward if-elimination). In addition, however, a reasoner may be invited by context to infer that "if p then q" also implies "if not p then not q", for instance in the case of a conditional promise. Similarly, a conditional obligation such as "if you p then you must q" may invite the inference that if you did not q, then you should not p (so to speak). Inferences of a non-logical kind are also allowed, e.g. from "scripts", which are schemas for stereotyped social situations (Lea et al., 1990). O'Brien (1995) also includes the Gricean implicatures (see Chapter 2) among the list of pragmatic principles.

The evidence

Evidence has been provided for the BO'B theory along similar lines to that for PSYCOP: direct tests by its advocates, along with accounts of other observed findings in the literature, including the data on the selection task. In addition, the theory has been tested in distinctly different ways, as we shall see. As far as the basic inference data are concerned, the BO'B theory and PSYCOP make very similar predictions, as Rips (1994) confirms, with one or two exceptions, so the data can be marshalled in support of either approach. The main set of such data was provided by Braine, Reiser, and Rumain (1984).

With the selection task, O'Brien (1993, 1995) takes a subtly different line from Rips. O'Brien argues that the abstract task is an example of one that simply falls outside the range of normal human deductive competence. He gives the lines of reasoning the BO'B theory dictates would be needed to solve the task: not only is there more than one possible line for each card, but they are long and complex, ranging from 9 to 16 steps. The same argument applies to the THOG problem. Facilitation effects are put down to deontic problems being categorically different from standard, non-deontic problems, and logically simpler. Thus, they may fall within people's natural reasoning range. Manktelow and Over (1991, 1995) made a similar point in their research on deontic reasoning: the deontic selection task asks for judgements of possible violations of regulations whose truth status is not in question, as opposed to the standard selection task, which asks for judgements of cases that could potentially falsify descriptive statements whose truth status is uncertain—a very different activity. O'Brien sums this up by contending that there has been no reliably observed facilitation of the non-deontic selection task, as the BO'B theory would predict; hence, selection task research does not call the theory into question.

Two different sorts of tests to which the BO'B theory has been subjected involved *intermediate inferences* and *text comprehension*.

Intermediate inferences are those made while you work your way to a solution of a reasoning problem; presumably, they would be consistent with Rips' idea of subgoals, although neither camp has made this connection as far as I know. O'Brien (1995) gives this example. Imagine you have been asked to supply the conclusion to this set of premises:

n or p; not n; if p then h; if h then z; not both z and q; ?

According to O'Brien, this is a simple problem, which is solved by direct reasoning as follows: the first two premises yield p by or-elimination; p together with the third premise yields h by *modus ponens*; this in turn yields z by *modus ponens*; and not q is then concluded by a schema to eliminate "not both". When subjects were given such problems and asked to write down everything that occurred to them while they solved the problem, most subjects wrote down the intermediate inferences in the predicted order—even when the premises were presented the opposite way round. The BO'B theory predicts that they will do this because of the way in which the inference schemas must be applied to solve the problem, which is independent of the order of presentation of the premises.

The theory has also been applied to text comprehension, by Lea et al. (1990). They presented subjects with story vignettes such as the following:

The Borofskys were planning a dinner party.
"Alice and Sarah are vegetarians," Mrs Borofsky said, "so if we invite either one of them, we cannot serve meat."
"Well, if we invite Harry, we have to invite Alice," Mr Borofsky said.
"And if we invite George, we have to invite Sarah."
"We already made up our minds to invite either Harry or George, or maybe both of them," said Mrs Borofsky.

These were the premises of the problem. You should be able to decode where inference rules are called for. The last line of the story was the conclusion, and the subjects had to judge whether it made sense. It took one of two forms:

> "That's right," Mr Borofsky replied, "so we can't serve meat." [valid]
> "That's right," Mr Borofsky replied, "so we can serve meat." [invalid]

After the experiment, the subjects were given a recognition test involving judging whether sentences had occurred in the story: the test sentences were either paraphrases of actually appearing sentences, sentences inferrable according to the BO'B theory, or sentences inferrable only by standard logic, not by BO'B.

Subjects were overwhelmingly accurate on the validity judgements, and they were good at recognising the paraphrases as paraphrases. However, they also thought that the BO'B recognition items were paraphrases, i.e. rewordings of sentences that had actually appeared; they did not do so with the non-BO'B inference items. Thus, the inferences made according to mental logic theory, but not standard logic, were so straightforward that subjects were unaware of having made them.

Such experiments provide powerful evidence for the theory, as its proponents have not been shy of claiming. Another attractive feature of it is the energy which the BO'B group has allotted to locking horns with its rivals, particularly pragmatic schemas and mental models. A case of "the empire strikes back", perhaps. We shall return to this contest as we consider the latter two kinds of reasoning theory.

Domain-specific reasoning schemas

The discovery of the effects of content in reasoning experiments poses a serious problem for any theories which hold that reasoning is achieved by the application of abstract inference rules such as those found in logic textbooks. Reasoning competence can hardly be said to be content-independent if it is influenced by content. Piagetian theory was an example of this difficulty: even his abstract system was modified so that formal competence was assumed only to be exercised within a person's particular areas of expertise. This seems a reasonable common-sense proposal. The problem with this theoretical manoeuvre, though, is that it makes such a theory untestable: any deviation from logical competence could always be put down to a performance factor like this.

We have seen that one way by which mental logic theory can escape both from the content problem and the testability problem is to propose, as do Rips and Braine and O'Brien, that mental logic is not the same as textbook logic, using general psychological principles and empirical findings to construct a theory of what a mental logic could contain. This has the benefit of producing testable predictions, but, as we have seen, mental logic theories still tend to be at their weakest in accounting for content effects, especially in the selection task. Evans and Over (1996a, Ch. 6) make a similar point about errors and biases in general.

Another way out of the content problem is to reject the idea of general, abstract inference rules in favour of systems specific to particular domains of thought. We have already covered two such theories in Chapter 4, so we shall look at them again: pragmatic reasoning schemas and social contract theory. Both are mainly concerned with deontic reasoning and both have appealed largely to the selection task for experimental tests. They have already been described in detail, so I shall go straight to the theoretical arguments for and against them.

Pragmatic reasoning schemas

The original statement of PRS theory by Cheng and Holyoak (1985) had such an impact that it is perhaps not surprising that the theory has had its back to the wall ever since. It has been assailed by conceptual critiques from both mental logicians and mental modellers, and by experimentalists. We shall look first at the theoretical problems, and then at the troublesome experiments.

Theoretical problems

The first point against PRS theory which critics tend to make is that although its scope is intended to be wide, its experimental base is narrow. That is, PRS theory is intended to outline a set of inference schemas specialised for a range of domains of thought, the implication being that it should be possible to do this, eventually, for all domains. At present, we only have schemas for permission (Cheng & Holyoak, 1985) and obligation (Cheng, Holyoak, Nisbett, & Oliver, 1986; Politzer & Nguyen-Xuan, 1992), but in principle there could be others, such as causal schemas, as PRS theorists argue. The critics often point out that the experimental evidence for PRS theory comes only from a few selection-task experiments (although note that Cheng & Holyoak also used a paraphrasing task). PRS theory is therefore vulnerable on a number of fronts: (i) it does not provide a general account of reasoning competence, but there are other theories that do, and they could account for the results predicted by PRS theory; (ii) the methodology of the crucial experiments could be called into question, undermining its supporting evidence; and (iii) the theory's predictions might not be upheld outside the selection task. There are examples of all these objections in the literature.

The two general accounts of reasoning that we have met most often so far are the theories of mental logic and mental models. Both have argued that the effects predicted by PRS theory are also consistent with their approaches, making PRS theory redundant. O'Brien (1995) mainly concerns himself with demolishing the empirical base of PRS theory, which I shall come to later. As to why selection task performance seems to improve in deontic contexts, we have seen that he considers that form of the selection task to be a categorically different problem in any case. Successful performance could be attributed to pragmatic principles such as an invited MT inference with permission rules (O'Brien, 1995, p.200).

Rips, as we have seen, resorts to memory cueing to explain results such as Cheng and Holyoak's. Strangely, he does allow that "Cheng and Holyoak are probably right about the existence of rules for permission and obligation, even if these rules aren't responsible for selection-task performance" (Rips, 1994, p.323)! He arrives at this conclusion owing to the way in which it is clearly possible to infer "it is permissible to do p having done q" from "it is obligatory to do p having done q". Thus, there seems to be a place for additional deontic inference rules such as these in his system, to explain such ready intuitions.

Neither of these factions proposes a detailed account of the PRS results, but Johnson-Laird's mental models theory does. We shall go further into this theory later. In the present context, here is an outline of how deontic reasoning is carried out, from the perspective of mental models theory, as set out by Johnson-Laird (1995). Briefly, the argument follows from the theory's basic principle that reasoning proceeds from what is explicitly represented in models. Thus, in the case of the selection task for instance, correct solutions demand that the not-q case be explicitly represented, and so any manipulation that achieves this should produce the facilitation effect. Johnson-Laird thus argues that specific contents produce facilitation effects by making violating cases salient, either by memory cueing or a "framework" that causes violations to be highlighted. In the case of permission rules, he also invokes invited inferences, in a similar way to Rips, to account for perspective effects.

Empirical problems

As we saw in Chapter 4, the most powerful evidence for PRS theory is the observation that selection tasks arranged to evoke a pragmatic schema such as permission produce facilitated responding even when they consist of abstract letter–number content. Several writers have wondered about this evidence, and have argued that Cheng and Holyoak's results can be explained without reference to their reasoning schemas. The most extensive such criticism has come from O'Brien (e.g. 1995; Noveck & O'Brien, 1996).

O'Brien points out that Cheng and Holyoak's "abstract" permission problem contains a number of features that make it difficult to judge whether it was the evocation of the permission schema that enhanced performance relative to a control (non-permission) problem. Among these are the fact that the permission problem had subjects assume the perspective of an authority checking for violators whereas the control problem did not; an inconsistent use of explicit negatives on the cards; an additional paraphrase of the target conditional in the permission but not the control problem; a greater number of words used to set out the permission problem; and an inconsistent order of presentation of sentence and cards between the two problems.

In a series of experiments designed to control for these confounding variables, Noveck and O'Brien found, in sum: "a permission rule by itself does nothing to elicit solution … Adding explicit negatives … increased the proportion of subjects solving the problem … further adding enriching features increased the percentage to … the same value reported by Cheng and Holyoak". Furthermore, Noveck and O'Brien found very little evidence for facilitation using an obligation problem, when the confounding factors were controlled for, contrary to the predictions of PRS theory.

An additional empirical point against PRS theory comes from some failed attempts to confirm its predictions when tasks other than the selection task are used. For instance, Markovits and Savary (1992) presented a version of the postal selection task (see Chapter 4) in a conditional inference format, and found that it did not lead to performance consistent with a standard logical pattern. On the other hand, a selection task did yield improved performance. There is nothing in PRS theory to predict that its effects should be task-specific.

Thompson (1995) also used an inference task to test PRS theory against her own Contextual Cuing theory. Contextual Cuing theory posits that "inferences will vary as a function of the necessity and sufficiency of the conditional relation" (Thompson, 1995, p. 1). Necessity and sufficiency were explained in the section on causal reasoning in Chapter 4; Thompson uses the notion of conditional, rather than causal, necessity and sufficiency. Thus, for Thompson a necessary relation is where p can only occur when q occurs, and a sufficiency relation is where the occurrence of p guarantees the occurrence of q. Which relation is held to apply will be influenced by the availability to the reasoner of counter-examples. These take the form of alternative antecedents to q (which reduce perceived necessity) or alternative consequents (which reduce perceived sufficiency). Thompson's argument is that the availability of these cases is cued by the content and context of a conditional, hence the theory's name.

Using a task in which subjects had to paraphrase "if p then q" sentences into "p only if q" forms, Thompson found that rated necessity was a better predictor of the degree to which this was done than was schema type: there was no difference between permission and causal sentences when necessity was controlled for, contrary to PRS theory. The same pattern emerged in an inference experiment: the perceived necessity of p for q predicted inferences far better than schema type. With necessity controlled for, there were no differences between permission, obligation, causal, definition, and contingent conditionals. In other words, Thompson contends, such differences between contents as have been observed can be put down to the differences in perceived necessity that these contents bring about, for instance in their tendency to make counter-examples available.

Social exchange theory

This theory (see also Chapter 4) was introduced by Cosmides (1989; Cosmides & Tooby, 1992). Its aim, like that of PRS theory, was to use general principles to explain specific reasoning data. In this case, as we saw, the core idea is that evolution has equipped us with a reasoning module that enables us to co-exist efficiently. This module governs our interpersonal transactions involving benefits and costs, and is summed up in the generic contractual rule that *If you take a benefit, then you pay a cost*. We are said to be equally sensitive to the possibility of cheating: taking a benefit without paying a cost.

To account for the range of deontic selection-task findings, the idea of social exchange had to be generalised to that of social contracts, because nothing is actually exchanged in, say, the drinking-age problem. So instead of paying a cost, Cosmides allows that benefits may be contingent on meeting a requirement, such as attaining a minimum age. Cheng and Holyoak (1989) contend that this change undermines the essentially social nature of the contract: you do not pay anything to anyone by waiting until you are 19.

Cheng and Holyoak go on to argue that Cosmides' theory only makes sound empirical predictions when it is equivalent to PRS theory. To account for perspective effects, for instance, Holyoak and Cheng (1995) underpin PRS theory with complementary notions of rights (conferred by permission statements) and duties (conferred by obligation statements) imported from American legal theory. They prefer PRS theory, not surprisingly, on the grounds that it makes more predictions than social contract theory; they regard the latter as a subset of PRS theory.

Rips (1994, Ch. 9) takes a similar view, although he is, of course, against both of these domain-specific approaches. He also questions the evolutionary rationale that motivates Cosmides' view, arguing that evolutionary theory provides no justification for preferring domain-specific mechanisms to domain-general mechanisms such as mental logic. His specific explanation of the results of deontic experiments, in terms of memory cueing and underlying constructs of what "obligatory" and "permissible" mean, are consistent with Thompson's arguments in terms of perceived necessity and sufficiency. Thus "p is obligatory given q" could be expressed as "p is necessary given q", and "p is permissible given q" could be expressed as "q is sufficient for p".

Cummins (1996b), however, writes in favour of an innate deontic reasoning module, on the basis of observations not only from reasoning experiments, but from developmental psychology (see her "squeaky mice" experiment in Chapter 4), primatology (where chimpanzees and baboons appear to make some kinds of deontic inferences), and neuropsychology (where some brain injuries have been found to lead to a selective impairment of social/emotional thinking). She does not present such a theory in detail, but does indicate that Cosmides' theory will not suffice, because it fails to predict some of the data in deontic experiments.

Mental models

The theory of mental models was first set out in full by Johnson-Laird (1983), when it was applied mainly to syllogistic reasoning and linguistic inference. It was extensively revised by Johnson-Laird and Byrne (1991), when its applications were extended to propositional reasoning (a recent summary of this approach, with further modifications of the theory's notation, is given by Johnson-Laird, 1995). Since then, it has continued to develop and has been extended further, for instance into inductive and probabilistic thinking. We saw how the theory has been used to explain syllogistic reasoning performance in

Chapter 2, and propositional reasoning in Chapters 3–4; inductive thinking will be dealt with in Chapter 7.

Johnson-Laird has always regarded the model theory as fundamentally distinct from inference rule theories (see Johnson-Laird, 1995), although not all theorists agree. Some allege that at a deep level both mental model and inference rule theories can be regarded as logical (e.g. Stenning & Oaksford, 1993). The basis of Johnson-Laird's contention is that inference rules describe syntactic processes, whereas mental models are semantic. Syntax is the set of rules concerning the form of expressions: the grammar of a language is an example, as is logic. Semantics, on the other hand, concerns the relation between, for instance, the terms in a language and what they relate to outside the language: the real, or even the fictional, world. Thus, in the case of a logical argument, syntax can tell you whether the argument is valid, but not whether it is true: you need semantics for that. Mental models are fundamentally semantic, as the tokens in them, and the relations between the tokens, are derived directly from the world outside the models.

We have seen in preceding chapters how the theory can be applied to draw inferences and determine validity and invalidity. It has been applied to a wide range of areas of thinking, not just the ones illustrated: obviously, I cannot do full justice to this enterprise here. However, the theory has also been subjected to some serious criticisms, especially from the mental logicians.

The hostile press

Some of the critiques of mental models theory are intricate and quite technical, so for clarity I shall summarise mainly those that refer to experimental results. There is a nice volley of criticism and reply in this vein in *Psychological Review* (Bonatti, 1994; Johnson-Laird, Byrne, & Schaeken, 1994; O'Brien, Braine, & Yang, 1994), and the précis of the theory given by Johnson-Laird and Byrne (1993) is followed by a set of critical notices, and their reply. Both sets of articles are well worth reading for the level of detail they contain. We shall focus on the 1994 set.

Much of the argument from Bonatti and O'Brien et al. concerns how to derive the predictions made and not made by the model and rule theories, and how they stand up in the face of the experimental evidence. Johnson-Laird (e.g. 1995; Johnson-Laird & Byrne, 1991) has always emphasised that one of the most basic predictions of the model theory is that the difficulty of a reasoning problem should vary according to the number of mental models needed for its solution.

One-model problems should be easier than more complex problems, and a task which requires more than two models should be impossibly difficult (see the syllogistic examples in Chapter 2). This is because of the demands placed on working memory. It is clearly vital then to say how "number of models" is to be counted.

Bonatti (1994) points to three different ways in which this might be done, which he argues means that the model theory can be shaped to fit any possible findings. Johnson-Laird et al. (1994) assert that the relevant number is that involved in constructing and evaluating conclusions, rather than in encoding premises. This enables the model theory to escape from a result obtained by O'Brien et al. (1994). They gave subjects arguments such as the following, the task being to decide whether the conclusion followed or not:

> If S or X or B or C or K or R or N or L or D or F then not both
>   I and G
>
> X
> ———————————————————————————————————
> not both I and G

Subjects found such problems easy, yet the string of "or" clauses in the first premise seems to call for a ridiculously large number of models: the model theory conveys the meaning of *or* by three models if it is inclusive or two if it is exclusive. Johnson-Laird et al. (1994) reply that people will not build models for the sake of it, but that the second premise and an understanding of disjunctives establish that the antecedent of the first premise is true, irrespective of the number of its other parts. In other words, these other parts form an implicit model. The problem can thus be expressed in the following terms:

> p
> ———————————
> If p or ... then q
> q

where q stands for "not both I and G" and the three dots as usual stand for the implicit models. This fits a standard *modus ponens* argument, well within people's predicted capacity.

O'Brien et al. (1994) also point to a prediction they say is made by their mental logic theory but not by mental models: the phenomenon of intermediate inferences, which we met in the section on mental logic earlier in this chapter. Johnson-Laird et al. concede that their theory has not been applied to this effect before, but offer an interpretation of it based on the application of the model theory to text comprehension (set out in Johnson-Laird, 1983). This dictates that people will start with the most informative piece of information (e.g. the second premise in the example just given), maintain co-reference (i.e. keep to the topic), and draw informative intermediate inferences. Therefore, problems will not always be addressed in the order in which the premises are presented, an effect which, as we saw, was taken as strong evidence for the BO'B theory.

There is a class of observations the model theory does not cope with so slickly, mainly involving biases and content effects. Bonatti, O'Brien et al., and a number of other critics, have pointed out that the model theory's claim to coping readily with content effects is based on some as yet unspecified processes of how perception, language, and what model theorists call "world knowledge" lead to models. The point that rule theories cannot cope with such effects for the same reason is a good one, and although the BO'B theory has pragmatic principles to deal with this, it is at the price of reducing its testability. As far as biases are concerned, Evans and Over (1996a) have recently criticised the model theory's ability to explain them. We have already seen how it had difficulty with belief-bias effects on valid syllogisms, and how its account of conclusion bias succeeds only at the expense of its account of matching bias (Chapter 4). These writers also argue that the theory will need to be supplemented by components expressing both uncertainty, to enable it to be extended to decision making and reasoning from uncertain premises, and utility, for deontic thinking (Chapter 4 again).

Evans and Over emphasise a quality of the model theory that at present places it a cut above the rest: the tremendous range of cognitive activities to which it has been, and continues to be, applied. Apart from the various areas of reasoning which we have considered so far, the theory has also been extended to inductive reasoning, which we shall look at in Chapter 7, and even to creativity, which we shall not. This scope is beyond even the possible, not just the actual, application of mental logic theories. Part of Evans and Over's case is that, in being more precise about "world knowledge", the model theory will need to be supplemented by extensive heuristic and interpretative processes if it is to succeed in these applications, and we will now turn to their account of such processes.

Heuristics and relevance

The idea that reasoning is a multi-stage activity is included in all reasoning theories, for instance in the proposals for comprehension processes providing the input to rules or models. However, the idea of stages has been applied in greatest detail in the work of Evans and his colleagues. In short, Evans argues that many of the data from reasoning experiments can be explained by the operation of what he calls heuristic processes. You can find this view set out by Evans (1989) and in updated form by Evans and Over (1996a).

Dual process data

The earliest evidence for different kinds of reasoning associated with different stages of reasoning came from a study of the selection task reported by Wason and Evans (1975). They used the technique of inserting negatives into the target conditional sentence to test whether people who got the task right were really doing so on the basis of insight into the logic of the task (as Wason had originally proposed), or on some other basis. One possible explanation was matching bias. You will recall from Chapter 4 that matching bias in the selection task largely concerns the q and not-q cards: irrespective of their logical significance, people tend to select one or other of these cards if it has been mentioned in the sentence, and ignore it if it has not.

Thus, in the standard "if p then q" (AA) sentence, the two cards mentioned are p and q, and they tend to be selected. However, in the "if p then not q" (AN) sentence, the values mentioned are still, of course, p and q, and these still tend to be selected, only this time the q card is a falsifying instance. So subjects get the task wrong with an AA sentence but right with an AN sentence, for the same apparent reason: matching. Wason and Evans asked what kind of explanation people would give for this behaviour. They found that subjects did not say "I was selecting the cards named in the sentence". When given the AA task and selecting p q, they would say that they were trying to prove the sentence true, but in the AN task, they would say they were trying to prove it false—which is what they should have been doing all along.

As the same subjects were given both versions of the task, it seemed unlikely that they were slipping in and out of logical insight (the effect was mainly observed among subjects who were given the AN task first). Wason and Evans' radical proposal was that the subjects' explanations were not accounts of the thought processes they had used in making their choices, but post-hoc *rationalisations* of choices already made. It was as if they had said to themselves "Why must I have done that?".

A striking recent demonstration of essentially the same effect was provided by Evans (1996). Selection tasks of various forms were presented by computer, and subjects were asked to point with the mouse to the cards they were considering, before clicking to confirm their choice. Chosen cards had much longer inspection times than unchosen cards. It seems, in other words, that subjects made their choices and then spent time considering, perhaps justifying to themselves, what they had done: they decided before thinking, as Evans puts it (note that Roberts, in press, has recently criticised this study; his article is followed by a reply from Evans).

Some serious implications flow from these findings. First, it looks as if asking subjects for reports of their mental processes may be of doubtful use. Second, these results suggest a non-logical and unconscious decision process followed by a conscious and logically accurate justification process. Third, if selection task choices do not reflect an attempt at reasoning, then at least the standard form of the selection task may not be a useful way of studying reasoning. This is a position Evans holds (e.g. 1995) and which has been happily endorsed by mental logic theorists such as O'Brien (1995), although for rather different reasons. The idea that the selection task may not produce even an attempt at logical reasoning (until people are asked to explain themselves) is also consistent with the information gain approach, as we shall see in the final section of this chapter.

Heuristic processes

Evans has called the two proposed elements of reasoning reflected in the Wason and Evans experiment *heuristic* and *analytic* processes. He has not devoted much time to the latter, but has recently endorsed mental models theory as at least forming a basis for it (e.g. Evans & Over, 1996a). He has, however, provided some detail on the heuristic component. Heuristic processes are largely selective and attentional: they extract from the environment the data on which the analytic processes are to operate. As the selection task only calls for judgements of what might be relevant to a test of a sentence, Evans concludes that card choices depend entirely on heuristic processes.

Relevance

In recent writings, Evans has linked the heuristic stage of reasoning to the construct of relevance (see Evans, 1995, 1996; Evans & Over, 1996a). As Evans and Over put it: "explicit or conscious thinking is focused on highly selected representations which appear "relevant" but ... this relevance is determined by preconscious and tacit processes" (p. 48). Evans equates this focusing with the process of forming explicit representations in mental models theory, as proposed by Legrenzi, Girotto, and Johnson-Laird (1993).

We have seen in Chapter 4 an example of these processes in the shape of the if- and not-heuristics proposed to account for matching bias, which led to the idea that matching is not a pure response bias after all, but a product of language understanding. Responses to realistic problems are also held to depend on relevance, although in this case the cues are pragmatic rather than linguistic. For instance, responses on deontic problems can be cued by considerations of utility and goals.

Other theorists have also offered relevance-based accounts. The most widely known relevance theory was presented by Sperber and Wilson (1986, 1996) as an account of language understanding. They developed the Gricean idea that natural linguistic communication must go beyond syntax and semantics. One of Grice's conversational maxims was "be relevant": keep to the point. Turning this maxim round: when two apparently unrelated utterances occur, it will be presumed that they are about the same topic. Thus, every utterance carries with it a guarantee of relevance. So if your friend says to you "I'm going to watch TV tonight. You can borrow the car", you can make a number of inferences about why the first sentence leads to the next, even though they are semantically unconnected.

Relevance is defined cognitively in terms of *effect* and *effort* (on a person's beliefs): relevance of a piece of information is greater the more effect it has, and the less cognitive effort is involved in processing it. The effect part of this formula is similar to a construct employed by Evans and Over: that of epistemic utility, i.e. the usefulness of some information in revising beliefs. Sperber has recently applied relevance theory to reasoning in an analysis of the selection task (Sperber, Cara, & Girotto, 1995). Alongside the principle of the guarantee of relevance (which they call the communicative principle), they also propose the "cognitive principle" that cognitive processes are aimed at processing the most relevant information in the most relevant way (p. 48). They turn these principles into predictions for the selection task, and successfully test them.

Sperber et al. argue that people will automatically attempt to compute relevance. Thus, when cues to relevance happen to coincide with the prescriptions of logic, experimental subjects will appear to be reasoning logically, but they will not if cues do not coincide. In applying this account to the typical responses observed in selection-task research they make several proposals.

First, the conditional sentence leads to what Sperber et al. call a "preferred conjunctive implication". This means inferring which values you expect to occur together. In the case of the abstract task, this will be that p leads to the inference of q: hence the p card will be selected or, where subjects adopt the biconditional interpretation, the p and q cards (as such subjects will also infer p from q). The p q combination will also be selected when subjects make what was called the existential presupposition in Chapter 2: that, given the sentence "If p then q", there will be actual cases of p and q. Subjects will select p and not q (the "logical" response) when they presume that the conditional sentence is a denial of cases of p ¬q.

From these proposals, and the effect/effort formula mentioned earlier, Sperber et al. devise a "recipe" for constructing easy selection tasks, i.e. ones that will produce a high rate of p ¬q choices. First, make the p ¬q case easy to represent (low effort), or at least easier than the p q case. Second, make knowing that there may be p ¬q cases have greater cognitive effects than knowing that there may be p q cases. Third, use a "pragmatically felicitous" (not too artificial) context. An example of these factors in an experiment is where they used the concept of a *bachelor* as a lexicalised, hence readily available, p ¬q case: a man (p) who is not (¬) married (q). This case was invoked in a task involving the detection of possible cases of bachelors in a context in which doubt is cast on a claim about married men. In this experiment (Sperber et al., 1995, Experiment 2), 65% of subjects selected the p ¬q combination, a significantly "facilitated" result. In further studies where effect and effort were systematically varied (high or low), this performance was only found in the condition where effect was high and effort low, as relevance theory predicts.

Two points are worth making about Sperber's relevance theory. First, Sperber et al. deny that they are simply restating Evans' construal of the term. They consider relevance to be an inferential process, whereas, as we have seen, Evans considers relevance to consist of attentional and selective heuristic processes. Thus, for Sperber et al., the selection task does involve inference, which Evans rejects. However, they concur with Evans that the task does not involve conditional inference in a logical sense. They use this conclusion to arrive at a strong condemnation of the usefulness of the selection task as a tool to explore human thinking (other similar conclusions were described earlier).

Just in case you imagined that this latter theory settles things as regards the selection task, and possibly human reason in general, we shall consider in the last part of this chapter a general approach to reasoning that in turn claims to account for the relevance results, and much else besides: the information gain theory.

Information gain theory

This general theory has already been discussed in Chapter 2, where it was applied to Aristotelian syllogisms. However, it first saw the light of day in reasoning research as an explanation of the selection task, has also been applied to the RAST version of it (see Oaksford, Chater, Grainger, & Larkin, 1997), and one can expect the approach to be extended more widely as time passes.

Information gain was applied to the selection task by Oaksford and Chater (1994a). It is based on the technique of "rational analysis" developed by Anderson (1990, 1991) and applied by him to other areas of cognition such as categorisation and memory. The central insight of the information gain approach to reasoning, which you may have grasped when reading the preceding sections of this chapter, and earlier chapters, is that experimenters may invite their subjects to work their way through logical rules in solving their tasks, but the subjects might be doing something else. Perhaps they are just looking for the best information.

What is meant by "best information?" According to Oaksford and Chater, the selection task invites people to judge what would be the best kind of test to decide between two competing hypotheses: (i) that the target sentence is true, so that p is always followed by q (which they call the dependence model: p depends on q, because p cannot occur without q), or (ii) that p and q occur independently (the independence model). They assume that the prior probability of each hypothesis is .5, i.e. they are equally likely. This can be combined with knowledge about the probabilities of p and q in the task context to provide an estimate of the expected gain in information as a result of examining each card: information gain is defined as the difference between a person's uncertainty about competing hypotheses before and after receiving some data, in this case, examining a particular card. Beliefs about the probabilities of p and q will thus affect a person's estimates of which will be the most informative data to select.

Uncertainty is measured using information theory, which was originally developed in communications engineering. Information is equated with reduction in uncertainty. Subjective probabilities are calculated using Bayes' theorem (which we shall encounter again in later chapters). Bayesian formulae require all alternative hypotheses to be defined, in this case the dependence and independence models. If you are interested in the technical details, the basic formulae are set out in Table 5.2.

As a selection task subject does not know what is on the other side of the cards, information gain is reckoned up with respect to all possible

TABLE 5.2

1. Information before receiving data D:

$$I(H_i) = -\sum_{i=1}^{n} p(H_i)\log_2 p(H_i)$$

[This is the information theory formula for reducing uncertainty, hence the minus sign. n is the set of mutually exclusive and exhaustive hypotheses, H_i, p = probability, I = information.]

2. Information after receiving data D:

$$I(H_i \mid D) = -\sum_{i=1}^{n} p(H_i \mid D)\log_2 p(H_i \mid D)$$

[The expression (Hi | D) translates as "hypothesis H given data D".]

3. Information gain:

$$Ig = I(H_i) - I(H_i \mid D)$$

[Information gain is the outcome of the second formula subtracted from the first.]

$p(H_i \mid D)$ terms are derived using Bayes' theorem:

$$p(H_i \mid D) = \frac{p(D \mid H_i)p(H_i)}{\sum\limits_{j=1}^{n} p(D \mid H_j)p(H_j)}$$

[This gives the posterior probability of a hypothesis H_i given data D in terms of the prior probability of each hypothesis H_j and the likelihoods of data D given each hypothesis H_j.]

alternatives: q or ¬q for the p and ¬p cards, and p or ¬p for the q and ¬q cards; hence the truer measure is that of expected information gain (EIg). Oaksford and Chater also include a "noise" factor to the EIg measure for each card, to allow for genuine error, and scale each EIg measure against the average value for each card, to reflect the perceived distinctions between cards. These factors yield scaled expected information gain estimates, or SE(Ig). Thus, individual card selection is determined by the proportion of total SE(Ig) it possesses. Underlying the SE(Ig) estimates is the assumption that the prior probabilities of p and q are low, in other words that p and q are rare in the world. When p and q are rare compared to not-p and not-q (which is what the rarity assumption entails), then cases of p and q will be relatively informative.

When all these factors are combined mathematically, the following ordering of SE(Ig)s for each card emerges: p > q > ¬q > ¬p. This, of course, is exactly the order almost always observed in studies of the standard abstract selection task. Note that on these calculations, selecting q ahead of ¬q is seen as a rational response—if subjects are approaching the task as one of searching for the data most likely to reduce their uncertainty, rather than following through the logic of implication.

But what about the classic facilitation effect, where subjects select ¬q more than q? This is held to be due to task features that overturn the rarity assumption, i.e. that lead the subject to suppose that the probability of p or q is high rather than low. For instance, if q (or p) is assumed to be common rather than rare, the informational value of a case of not-q will increase; hence there will be a preference for ¬q over q, which is what we find in facilitated problems. To account for performance, including perspective effects, in deontic tasks, where it is easy to get subjects to choose the ¬p q combination (see Chapter 4), Oaksford and Chater add a factor for subjective utility as well as probability—in all other cases it will be, as they put it, "probabilities all the way down" (Oaksford & Chater, 1995b).

They also use their calculations to predict the matching bias results with negated sentences (see Chapter 4), and account for the effects of Sperber et al.'s "recipe" for facilitating selection tasks by showing that these manipulations act by overturning rarity (Oaksford & Chater, 1995a). For instance, in the "bachelors" experiment mentioned earlier, the q value is "married": this violates rarity since there are more married than unmarried men. Thus the not-q value, "bachelor", becomes potentially more informative than the q value.

Critiques

Naturally, such a radical theory has become subject to a certain amount of questioning. A set of three such critiques appears in *Psychological Review*, together with Oaksford and Chater's reply (Oaksford & Chater, 1996). One is largely concerned with the formal properties of the calculations of information gain (Laming, 1996), which Oaksford and Chater dispute on every point, so I shall not go into details here.

Evans and Over (1996b; see also 1996a, pp. 89–91) question the very basis of information gain as reduction in uncertainty. They give as an example the case where someone might believe a hypothesis with $P(H)$ = .25 and then, after some information, that value changes to $P(H)$ = .75 (i.e. the belief changes from something like probably false, nearly zero, to probably true, nearly 1). Uncertainty is the same in either case: .25 from an absolute value (0 or 1) and so there is no information gain, yet clearly there is a change in belief. Oaksford and Chater (1996) concede this point, and adopt a different way of measuring change in degree of belief to account for it; surprisingly, this does not affect their calculations, so their predictions and explanations remain the same. This does not satisfy Evans and Over (1996a), who argue that information gain is still too narrow a measure of how people's beliefs may change in the light of their goals and preferences. What is gained by new data, they say, is *epistemic utility*, meaning data that are useful in revising one's knowledge. Oaksford and Chater also concede another of Evans and Over's points, which is that the model does not seem able to account for experiments in which subjects know in advance that there are exceptions to the conditional sentence. They say that the information gain model could cope with such experiments by including an "exception parameter" (p. 382), but do not spell it out.

Almor and Sloman (1996) question whether the information gain theory can account for facilitated responses in non-deontic contexts. This was an objection raised by Sperber et al., and we have seen that Oaksford and Chater have an answer: overturning rarity will make the ¬q card more informative in any context. Almor and Sloman provide other kinds of tasks that produce high levels of p ¬q selections, but Oaksford and Chater dismiss all these as either deontic, in which case their adapted theory including utilities applies, or as "definitional", in that case the theory would not apply. This is because a definitional rule is one that must be true, as in Almor and Sloman's "If a large object is stored then a large container must be used". If this sentence must be true, the P(H) of the dependence model is 1: p is always associated with q. Thus, "there is no uncertainty, and so no data (no card selections) can reduce it" (Oaksford & Chater, 1996, p. 389).

The information gain theory is an exciting development, both because it is such a radically different approach, and because of the challenges it lays down for other large-scale theories. Its originators have successfully fended off some of the criticisms that have already been levelled at it. It remains to be seen how successfully it can be applied beyond its current areas, and how the main players in the mental logic and mental models camps will respond. One continuing point against the theory is that although it provides a formal account of the data, it does not offer a truly psychological account of the cognitive processes that lead to the data (Evans & Over, 1996a, b). We shall return to these two forms of theory, which are known as computational-level and algorithmic-level theories, in the final chapter.

Summary

1. In a few years explanations for human deductive reasoning have proliferated, from one, mental logic, to many. Even the mental logic approach has been revised, expanded, and filled out in great detail by contemporary theorists.

2. The mental models theory has offered the most coherent and wide-ranging alternative to mental logic. It has the advantage over mental logic of having been applied to a broad panorama of areas of cognition, both within and beyond reasoning.

3. However, the theory is subject to reliance on some as yet unspecified processes, such as how models are derived from knowledge, language, and perception, and what leads to elements being explicitly rather than implicitly represented.

4. The heuristic-analytic or relevance theory makes predictions about representation that the other theories do not. However, this approach needs an account of inferential processes if it is to succeed as a general explanation; Evans has suggested the model theory as a candidate.

5. There is a new approach to reasoning in the shape of the information gain theory. This proposes that experimental subjects may be trying to acquire information to benefit their beliefs, rather than attempting some kind of logical analysis, and offers a Bayesian account of expected information gain.

Hypothesis testing 6

The deductive reasoning reviewed so far is, of course, not the only kind of reasoning that has been studied. In this chapter and the next we shall look at two important, and closely related, forms of thinking: hypothesis testing and induction. Hypothesis testing is also related to the forms of deductive thought we have considered in the preceding chapters: for instance, a scientific, medical, or other hypothesis could be put into conditional (if p then q) or quantified (all A are B) form, and its implications checked against the observed facts. Thus, some authors consider the selection task as a hypothesis-testing problem. Hypothesis testing is also related to causal reasoning, and to the philosophy of science.

However, the study of hypothesis testing has not been restricted to deductive tests of existing statements. Part of the activity also consists in finding out what the hypothesis is in the first place. Deriving plausible rules on the basis of information is the subject matter of induction, and we shall consider this in detail in the next chapter; such rules are not always treated as testable hypotheses. In this chapter we shall review studies where hypotheses are both derived and tested. Although some of these studies have used quite simple and artificial experiments, they have often been seen explicitly as laboratory analogues of the real activity of scientists, doctors, lawyers, weather forecasters, stock-market analysts, and so on. We begin with one of the most productive of such experiments, originated by a familiar name.

Wason's 2 4 6 task

This task grew out of Wason's interest in the early studies of concept formation in the 1950s, which we shall return to in Chapter 7. Wason was concerned about the way in which people could arrive at false hypotheses by what he called *simple enumeration*: the compiling of positive, confirming cases.

Wason (1960) gave subjects the following set of numbers: 2 4 6. Subjects were told that this number triple conformed to a rule he had in mind, and that the subject's task was to find out what it was. To do this, the subjects were to generate more triples, to which the experimenter would respond "yes" if they conformed to the rule and "no" if they did not. When subjects were sure that they had figured out the experimenter's rule, they were to announce it. If it was not the right one, they were told so and invited to carry on with the task by generating more triples, announcing more rules, and so on.

If you think this is a rather trivial sort of puzzle, imagine this real-world analogue. You are working for a health education authority and want to set up a publicity campaign aimed at reducing smoking among teenagers. You think (i.e. your hypothesis is) that short advert-like messages in TV commercial breaks will be the most effective. In fact, although you do not know it yet, advert-style messages in any medium—TV, radio, magazines, etc.—will be just as effective. How can you test whether you are right or wrong about the TV ads? This problem is formally identical to the 2 4 6 task.

Here is how: your hypothesis (TV ads) is narrower than the real rule (ads in any medium). Now return to the 2 4 6 task. The obvious sort of hypothesised rule that subjects would be likely to form would be one that was about regular series, or perhaps even numbers. This was a deliberate trick: the real rule was simply "increasing numbers". Note that simple enumeration based on an "obvious" hypothesis will lead to the generation of triples that will be consistent with both this hypothesis and the real rule, even though such a hypothesis is not the "right" one. To find the right one, subjects need to devise tests that could falsify their original hypotheses. Because subjects were asked to write down their triples, hypotheses, and announced rules, it was possible to record not only whether they figured out the rule correctly and how many announcements it took to do so, but also the kinds of tests that had gone into this effort. It was this pattern of behaviour that was the real interest in the task.

In the first reported 2 4 6 experiment (see Wason & Johnson-Laird, 1972, pp. 207–208), only 21% of subjects announced the correct rule first time; 28% never announced it at all, and "the majority" (presumably the remaining 51%) made at least one incorrect announcement before coming up with the right rule. You can see examples of two protocols, from a first-time success and from one that got there in the end, in Table 6.1; as mentioned earlier, the real interest is not so much whether the subjects hit on the right rule but how they did so, and some important features of their performance can be seen in these records.

According to Wason, there are three ways of going about the task, and you can see instances of them in the protocols. The first is to *verify*:

to generate confirming instances of your hypothesis and then announce it as the rule. Protocol (b) is an example of this strategy. The second is to *falsify*: to generate an instance inconsistent with your current hypothesis. Neither protocol has a clear example of this. The third is to *vary the hypothesis*. Protocol (a) shows this being done at an early stage,

TABLE 6.1

Sample protocols from the 2 4 6 task. (After Wason & Johnson-Laird, 1972)

(a) Correct first announcement.

Instances		*Hypotheses*
2 4 6	yes	(given)
3 6 9	yes	three goes into the second figure twice and into the third figure three times
2 4 8	yes	perhaps the figures have to have an LCD
2 4 10	yes	same reason
2 5 10	yes	the second number does not have to be decided by the first one
10 6 4	no	the highest number must go last
4 6 10	yes	the first number must be the lowest
2 3 5	yes	it is only the order that counts
4 5 6	yes	same reason
1 7 13	yes	same reason

"The rule is that the figures must be in numerical order" (correct: 16 minutes).

(b) Four incorrect announcements.

Instances		*Hypotheses*
2 4 6	yes	(given)
8 10 12	yes	two added each time
14 16 18	yes	even numbers in order of magnitude
20 22 24	yes	same reason
1 3 5	yes	two added to preceding number

"The rule is that by starting with any number two is added each time to form the next number" (incorrect).

2 6 10	yes	the middle number is the arithmetic mean of the other two
1 50 99	yes	same reason

"The rule is that the middle number is the aritmetic mean of the other two" (incorrect).

3 10 17	yes	same number, seven, added each time
0 3 6	yes	three added each time

"The rule is that the difference between two numbers next to each other is the same" (incorrect).

12 8 4	no	the same number is subtracted each time to form the next number

"The rule is adding a number, always the same one, to form the next number" (incorrect).

1 4 9	yes	any three number in order of magnitude

"The rule is any three numbers in order of magnitude" (correct: 17 minutes).

whereas in protocol (b) the "variations" only occur later; interestingly, the second, third, and fourth announcements are simply re-wordings of each other, indicating the tight grip people can keep on their hypotheses. Both protocols show a pattern of generated triples and candidate hypotheses that has been found to be typical with these numbers (see e.g. Kareev, Halberstadt, & Shafir, 1993, for a recent case): even numbers evenly spaced. The number of generated triples that do not conform to this pattern was found to predict success at the task by Vallée-Tourangeau, Austin, and Rankin (1995), and you can see that happening here.

Confirmation and positivity

Wason's early ideas on the behaviour revealed by the 2 4 6 task were couched in terms of a confirmation bias: people were said to seek out information that was consistent with their hypotheses and avoid inconsistent information. There was an apparent coincidence with performance on the early versions of the selection task, which appeared a few years later: as we saw in Chapter 4, subjects here tend to select the p or p and q cards, and thus seem not to be looking for the critical falsifying values. Of course, we now know that confirmation bias is an unlikely mechanism in explaining the selection task, and that the bases of subjects' responses can be subtle and varied. The same goes for the 2 4 6 task. (Evans, 1989, considers this aspect of the relation between the two tasks in more detail.)

The most important subtlety in considering research on hypothesis testing in general, and the 2 4 6 task in particular, is the distinction between *confirmation* and *positivity*, and their corollaries, *disconfirmation* and *negativity*. This was first pointed out by Wetherick (1962). A confirmatory strategy is not the same thing as a positive test strategy, although the terms sound similar. For example (cf. Gorman, 1995a), imagine that you are a subject in a 2 4 6 experiment, and your initial hypothesis is "numbers ascending by two". You generate the next triple: 3 5 7. This is a positive test, because the triple is an instance of your hypothesis. But it can only be called confirmatory if you expected that you would get the answer "yes" to show that it is consistent with the target rule (which, remember, you do not know at this stage). You might actually have expected it to get a "no", perhaps because you suspect, as we saw, that your initial hypothesis might apply only to even number series. Thus a positive instance may have been intended as a disconfirming case. Similarly, if you generate a negative case that you believe will get a "no", then you are actually confirming.

This insight was extended by Klayman and Ha (1987). They point out that conclusions about confirmation bias and irrationality in the 2 4 6 task ignore a crucial aspect of the testing situation: the relation between the subject's hypothesis and the target rule. There are in principle five such relations:

1. The subject's hypothesis (H) and the target rule (T) are *the same*: you think that the rule is "ascending by two" and it is, so all triples which are instances of H are instances of T, and vice versa.
2. H is *less general* than T: your H is "ascending by two" and the rule T is "ascending numbers". All triples consistent with H are also T triples, but some in the T set are not in the H set.
3. H is *more general* than T: your H is "ascending by two" but T is "even numbers ascending by two". The set of triples consistent with T is a subset of those in H, so although all T triples are in H, some H triples are not in T.
4. H and T *overlap*: your H is "ascending by two" but T is "three even numbers". Some triples in the H set will also be in the T set, but each set will contain triples that are not in the other.
5. H and T are *disjoint*: your H is "ascending by two" but T is "descending numbers". No triple in the H set is in the T set.

These situations are set out in diagram form in Fig. 6.1.

The original 2 4 6 task is an example of the second of these relations: the target rule T was deliberately designed to be more general than the "obvious" H invited by the given triple. In this situation, positive testing (generating triples from the H set) can never lead to the discovery of T; in the example of the health campaign, this would mean looking only at the effectiveness of TV ads, ignoring other media. This is because such instances cannot absolutely verify the hypothesis: they will generate a "yes" from the experimenter even if the hypothesis is false—which in this case it is. This in turn is because there are no triples that are in H but not in T.

In this situation, you can only truly test your H by negative testing: looking for cases that you think are not in the H set. When you produce one, it will either get a "yes" or a "no". For instance, you say 6 4 2 (or test the leaflets left in doctors' surgeries): this gets a "no" (they are found not to be effective). This case does not tell you anything about the relation between H and T as it is not in either set. However, what about 3 6 9 (or ads on the radio)? This is outside your H, but is called "yes" (they work): it is in the T set. So your hypothesis must be false. A bias towards positive testing will lead to permanent "yes" feedback, and therefore look like confirmation bias.

FIG. 6.1.

Possible relations
between the set of
items consistent with
a hypothesis and a
target rule in
hypothesis-testing
tasks.

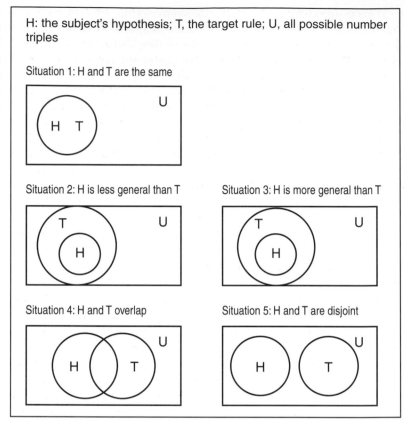

However, this is not the case for all the H–T relations given earlier. Consider situation 3, the mirror image of the standard 2 4 6 task, where you have been given the triple 2 4 6, told that it is an instance of T, and have formed your H that the rule is "ascending by two". However, the "true" rule T is actually "even numbers ascending by two"—you do not know this yet, of course. In the health campaign, imagine that only TV ads shown during late-night "youth" programmes are effective. You have the usual bias for positive tests, so produce the triple 3 5 7 (daytime TV ads). This is in H but not, of course, in T, so gets a "no": you have achieved instant falsification! In fact, if you were to attempt just negative tests, you would simply confirm: instances such as 3 6 9 or 6 4 2 (peak-time TV, or magazine ads), besides not being in H, are also never in T, unlike the standard task from situation 2.

So in the second case, a bias towards positive testing will lead to falsification of hypotheses, hence rule discovery, whereas in the first case it cannot. Klayman and Ha go on to argue that positive testing is generally a rational strategy even in cases where one cannot know what the exact relation between H and T is. Using some detailed mathematical analysis, which I shall not go into, they show that positive tests are more likely than negative tests to lead to falsification, given two reasonable assumptions: (i) that the probabilities of an instance being in H and in T are roughly equal (as one can place little trust in an H that deviates too widely from the target set), and (ii) that the probability of an instance being in T is less than it not being in T; in other words, the T set is rare. A *rarity assumption* is also made by Oaksford and Chater (1994a) in their "rational analysis" of the selection task (see Chapter 5) and in their Probability Heuristics model of syllogistic reasoning (see Chapter 2); they also have a theory of hypothesis testing, although of a rather different kind, as we shall see shortly.

Klayman and Ha argue that both assumptions hold in many real-world situations, such as reasoning about the causes of a disease: the disease will be relatively rare in the population, and it is likely that you will not know absolutely nothing nor almost everything about its causes before testing. They also show that the positive test strategy works in more realistic contexts when one is searching for the most likely T rather than the "true" T, which is what the real world is really like: as Gorman (1995a) remarks, scientists cannot ask God whether their hypotheses are right. Evans (1989) questions whether people have a strategy for positive testing so much as a bias. The difference is between a kind of conscious, deliberate way of working compared to a cognitive limitation: he argues that people fail to conduct potentially useful negative tests not because they do not want to but because it is difficult.

Poletiek (1996) extends the argument against the idea of adopting a disconfirmatory strategy as the route to success in hypothesis testing: she contends that disconfirmatory testing is psychologically impossible, because of the paradoxical relation between testing behaviour and the correctness of the hypothesis. We have already seen how negative testing is not the same thing as disconfirmation: if you conduct a negative test expecting a "no" answer you are in fact confirming. Whether a negative test disconfirms depends on the correctness of the hypothesis, i.e. whether it gets a "yes" even though you expected a "no".

Poletiek argues that your hypothesis is your "best guess" about the truth, integrating all the knowledge you currently have about the situation. Selecting a test from all those available with the intention to falsify your hypothesis must mean that it is not your best guess: you expect it to be false. So if your hypothesis is your best guess you cannot try to falsify it, and if you can, it is not your best guess. The only possible disconfirming tests are therefore positive tests that you expect to receive a "no" and negative tests which you expect to receive a "yes". In a 2 4 6 experiment, Poletiek found that very few such tests were offered, irrespective of instructions to confirm or disconfirm. The latter led to a higher rate of negative tests, but these were mostly expected to get a "no", and were hence confirmatory tests: "Subjects expect their best guess to be confirmed, regardless of the tests they propose" (Poletiek, 1996, p. 455).

Facilitating hypothesis-testing performance

As with many other of the reasoning problems given to subjects over the years, psychologists have looked at ways in which performance on the 2 4 6 task might be improved, usually with a view to overcoming confirmation bias. Of course, analyses such as Klayman and Ha's cast doubt on whether there is such a bias in the first place, but that is beside the point: attempts to facilitate 2 4 6 task performance have thrown up some interesting findings in their own right. We shall look briefly at three such manipulations, before going on to some alternative theoretical arguments that relate to them, and then passing from the laboratory study of hypothesis testing to some research that more closely approaches the real world of scientific enquiry. The three manipulations are instructions to disconfirm, task contents, and alternative-rule studies.

Instructions to disconfirm

An early prediction following Wason's pioneering research was that, if subjects seemed to avoid attempting to falsify their hypotheses, they could be made to adopt what was assumed to be the more rational falsifying turn of mind by specific instructions to do so. Once again, the outcomes of such studies have shown that there was more to this variable than had been expected, and Poletiek's recent argument gives us a nice hindsight view as to why this should be.

Gorman (1995a) reviews studies of the effectiveness of instructions on performance in the 2 4 6 and similar tasks. For example, Gorman and his colleagues studied a problem called New Eleusis as well as the 2 4 6 task. New Eleusis involves trying to work out the rule governing how playing cards are placed in order. Cards that fit the rule are laid out in a line, and cards that do not fit it are placed at right angles to this line, so players have a complete record of their actions. With both this and the 2 4 6 task, Gorman's group found that instructions to disconfirm hypotheses improved performance.

However, other researchers have failed to obtain this result. Tweney et al. (1980) used the 2 4 6 task and found that instructions to disconfirm made no difference to the number of subjects who eventually hit on the right rule, although there was some suggestion that there were more first-time solvers (those whose first announcement was of the correct rule) with disconfirming instructions.

To explain why disconfirming instructions sometimes worked and sometimes did not, Gorman (1995a) looked closely at the methods of the two sorts of study. Tweney et al. had used the usual procedure, with each rule announcement getting a "yes" or "no" response from the experimenter. Gorman's group on the other hand had subjects write down guesses without their being told whether they were right or wrong, then carry on testing: they were only given feedback about their suggested rules when the whole experiment was finished. As Gorman (1995a) puts it: "eliminating the option of asking the experimenter [for feedback about rule announcements] altered the task in a way that made disconfirmation essential".

Perhaps Gorman's version of the task brought it closer to real-life hypothesis testing, where you cannot ask a god-like authority how right your hypotheses are. The effect seemed to be related to the increased number of triples called "no" that were generated by subjects with the disconfirming instructions. This cannot, as we have seen, be taken at face value as evidence that subjects actually were pursuing a disconfirming strategy, but it does imply that they recognised the implications of negative evidence when they saw it. This would not conflict with Poletiek's impossibility thesis: Gorman's subjects may not have been striving to find "no" items but simply stumbled on them. Tukey (1986) had also noted that subjects sometimes generated triples without any apparent system motivating them, perhaps just to see what happened. Note also that, as Evans (1989) has pointed out, Gorman's instructions were not general ones to disconfirm, but specifically to test negative predictions, which is the means by which disconfirmations can be obtained. All this goes to show how you need to read the method sections of research papers very carefully.

Realistic content

The 2 4 6 task was designed all along as a laboratory analogue of real-world hypothesis testing, to assess people's appreciation of the logic of confirmation and disconfirmation. We have seen, using the health campaign example, how it is possible to construct realistic scenarios that are formally identical to the 2 4 6 task. Some investigators have experimented on versions of the task designed to look more like a piece of real science; we shall consider studies of real scientists' reasoning later in the chapter.

Mynatt, Doherty, and Tweney (1977) created a computer-game version of the 2 4 6 task (quite a novel thing in the 1970s) in which "particles" were fired from the top left-hand corner of the screen at various shapes (circles, squares, or triangles) that were at one of two brightness levels (high or low). The dim shapes had a kind of invisible circular "force field" around them which caused the particle to stop, and the subjects' task was to discover the rule relating shapes to particle motion: it was, clearly, "dim shapes". However, the subjects were given a display in which the dim shapes were a triangle, and a circle behind a bright triangle, which in turn was inside this circle's force field. This would make it look as if the bright triangle was also stopping the particle, inviting the hypothesis "triangles" (equivalent to the invited "numbers increasing by two" hypothesis in the 2 4 6 task). This display is shown in Fig. 6.2.

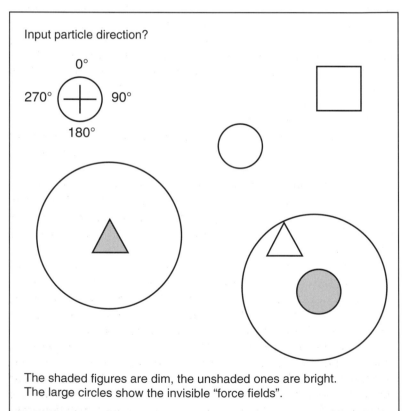

FIG. 6.2. Screen display used in the computerised hypothesis-testing experiment of Mynatt et al. (1977). Copyright © 1977 by The Experimental Psychology Society. Reprinted with permission.

The shaded figures are dim, the unshaded ones are bright. The large circles show the invisible "force fields".

Subjects were then given choices between pairs of displays they could use to test their hypotheses. To conduct potentially informative negative tests, they should choose displays without triangles in them. The 20 subjects (out of 45) who formed the initial "triangle" hypothesis conducted positive tests of it on around 70% of occasions, irrespective of whether they had been instructed to confirm, disconfirm, or just test their hypotheses. However, 11 of these subjects made negative tests at some stage and of these, 10 went on to announce the correct hypothesis, indicating once again that they were able to use negative evidence logically when it occurred. Overall, performance with this "realistic" task was not greatly different from that on the standard task.

In a follow-up study, a more complicated form of the task was used, but with much stronger falsifying instructions: subjects had to read a philosophical paper on the subject (Mynatt, Doherty, & Tweney, 1978). In fact, these subjects did not respond appropriately to negative evidence at all, and held on to inconsistent hypotheses. No subject actually solved the task. This relation between success and testing behaviour led the authors to the interesting idea that confirmatory and disconfirmatory strategies were useful at different stages of hypothesis formation and testing: confirmation is useful when you are trying to develop a hypothesis, and disconfirmation is useful when you have developed a hypothesis that now needs to be evaluated.

Alternative-hypothesis tasks

In contrast to the two manipulations described earlier, there is one that has proved reliable in facilitating performance on the 2 4 6 task and its derivatives: reframing the task as one of trying to decide between two competing hypotheses, rather than trying to decide whether one hypothesis is right. This was suggested by Wetherick (1962), but the first test of the idea only occurred years later, in the fourth experiment reported by Tweney at al. (1980); they credit Wason himself with the inspiration.

The idea is a simple one: instead of instances being called yes or no with respect to the target rule, they would be classified as examples of one of two named hypotheses: DAX, for a triple comprising ascending numbers, or MED, for any other kind of triple. Subjects now had to guess which rule the experimenter had in mind: 2 4 6 was given as a DAX triple. Of 20 subjects, 12 (60%) in this form of the experiment announced the correct rule first time, and only three failed to solve it, a far higher success rate than is normally observed. Tukey (1986) pinned the effect down to first announcements rather than overall solution, and Gorman, Stafford, and Gorman (1987) found the same facilitation when the target rule was even more general (three different numbers), which usually makes the task much more difficult. You may be reminded here of similar manipulations producing a similar effect in the THOG problem (Chapter 3), and in reasoning with negated conditionals (Chapter 4).

Positivity bias explains why this should happen: testing the MED hypothesis reverses the relation between hypothesis H and target rule T, so that T cases are now a subset of H cases. This is situation 3 described earlier: now, positive testing leads to disconfirmation, which in turn leads to solution. Subjects are not trying to disconfirm the DAX rule and are not simply doing more tests, though. Wharton, Cheng, and Wickens (1993) claimed that positive testing of complementary rules (i.e. two alternatives that exhaust the possibilities) was the critical factor, but the role of complementarity was questioned by Vallée-Tourangeau et al. (1995). They used conditions in which DAX and MED were not complementary categories, e.g. by introducing the possibility of a third kind of triple, ones that were both DAX and MED. They also had subjects generate exactly the same number of triples before announcing what they thought the rule was. All of these conditions produced higher rates of success than is usual with the traditional 2 4 6 task, indicating that it was the dual categories, irrespective of complementarity, that were important: if you have more than one hypothesis to consider, you are more likely to discover a rule. More on this idea in the next section.

Counterfactual theories

A development of the idea behind the DAX/MED task was suggested as a theory of hypothesis testing by Farris and Revlin (1989). They proposed that successful hypothesis testing depended on having alternative hypotheses. Say you have formed the initial hypothesis "numbers increasing by two". You need to frame an alternative, such as "numbers increasing by other than two" and test that. If you do so, you will produce a triple such as 3 6 9, which might look like an attempt to disconfirm the initial hypothesis but is in fact a positive test of the alternative.

Oaksford and Chater (1994b) point out a problem with this analysis. Call your original hypothesis H and the complementary (or counterfactual) hypothesis H'. You generate H (e.g. "numbers increasing by two") on the basis of the first instance (2 4 6: "yes"), then generate H' (e.g. "numbers increasing by other than two") and give it a positive test, say 3 6 9. If this gets a "no" response then H may still be correct, so the process is repeated with a new H'. If it gets a "yes" response then H must be false and H' may be correct. However, H' cannot be correct, as it is by definition inconsistent with the original instance, which you are told at the outset fits the experimenter's rule.

The problem may be due to Farris and Revlin's rather vague conception of the counterfactual hypothesis, H', as the *complement* to H: in their paper, H' is also allowed to be an "opposite" of H, and opposites are not always complements. For instance, given an initial H of "ascending by two", you may generate an H' of "ascending by equal intervals". This is not a truly complementary hypothesis, because there are other possibilities, covering the cases of numbers ascending by even intervals, any interval, and so on.

Oaksford and Chater suggest a modification of the counterfactual strategy to get round this logical problem. They argue that the instances generated by "yes" responses in the counterfactual strategy may provide important information which enables the reasoner to derive increasingly appropriate hypotheses and their complements (in Farris and Revlin's sense of the term). Say you have been given 2 4 6 and 3 6 9 as "yes" items, the latter in response to your H'. So both H and H' can be ruled out, for the reasons given earlier. However, you now know that both these triples are instances of the target rule T, so now you can go back, look for a property common to both triples, and refine your hypothesis. For example, each triple has equal intervals: your new H is "ascending by equal intervals" and a new H' is derived: "ascending by any intervals". A positive test of the latter would be 2 5 9: this gets a "yes", and so on. In the case of a "no" response to a positive test of H', announce H as the target rule.

This is called the *iterative counterfactual strategy* by Oaksford and Chater, and is set out in full, using a flow diagram, in their paper; a simplified version is presented by Gorman (1995a). The main advantage of this model over the positive test strategy is theoretical rather than empirical (both models predict similar behaviour): the iterative counterfactual strategy suggests one means by which new hypotheses may be created, by allowing a place for reasoners' use of all the positive instances that have been generated. Oaksford and Chater concede that they have not proposed a mechanism for how this is done beyond suggesting that subjects look for common properties in the "yes" instances. However, in general the processes of hypothesis creation are poorly understood, and no theory currently has much to offer about this crucial aspect of human thought. We shall look at related issues in the next chapter, when considering inductive thinking.

Pseudodiagnosticity

A different but related way of assessing people's hypothesis-testing behaviour was explored by Mynatt, Doherty, and their colleagues in a series of studies, beginning with Doherty, Mynatt, Tweney, and Schiavo (1979). It asks people to select evidence that they think will be useful in deciding between two related hypotheses, as in the DAX/MED version of the 2 4 6 task. They do not have to generate the evidence themselves and obtain the experimenter's feedback though, so in some respects the pseudodiagnosticity task is a closer relative of the selection task than the 2 4 6.

The task is one of deciding which information, from the range available, will provide the best way of deciding between hypotheses. Information that could do so—in other words, that is more likely under one hypothesis than the other—is called *diagnostic* information. Here is an example, adapted from a recent study by Mynatt, Doherty, and Dragan (1993).

You have been speaking to your rather well-off aunt Jane on the phone: she has just bought a car and has told you lots about it—except its make. You know that she was trying to decide between a Honda and a VW. However, she did tell you that it does over 25 miles per gallon, and that it has had no major mechanical problems in the two years since it was new. You are a regular reader of *Wide Wheels* magazine, which gives a rundown of used cars in each issue, and it tells you that 65% of Hondas do over 25 mpg (which I shall call information (a), for reasons that will become clear). You now have to decide which one bit of further information to seek to help you decide what kind of car Aunt Jane has been bragging about. Will it be :

(b) The percentage of VWs that do over 25mpg?
(c) The percentage of Hondas that had no serious
    mechanical problems in their first two years?
(d) The percentage of VWs that had no serious mechanical
    problems in their first two years?

Make a note of your decision before reading on.

Using a number of structurally identical problems as well as the car one, Mynatt et al. found that (b) was chosen by 28% of subjects, (c) by 59%, and (d) by only 13%. Thus, most subjects elected to find out more about Hondas, or their equivalent. But was (c) diagnostic: did the majority make the right choice? To work this out, we can use a Bayesian analysis (which has been briefly described in Chapter 5 in the section on information gain theory, and will feature again in Chapters 7 and 8). Before doing so, though, it is possible to give the general answer in outline: when deciding between two hypotheses, you should obtain information about both. Most of the subjects in the Mynatt et al. study, and probably you too, opted for further information only about the first one considered: that it is a Honda. This information is therefore not diagnostic, although you think it is: this is the pseudodiagnosticity effect.

Now for the analysis. The various bits of data in the problem of Aunt Jane's car are presented in Fig. 6.3. You can see that each cell shows the theoretical relation between the alternative hypotheses (Honda or VW), and the two kinds of information (fuel consumption and reliability). The data you are given at the outset, that 65% of Hondas do over 25 mpg, appears in cell (a). This can be represented as a conditional probability, $p(D1|H1)$, which translates as "the probability of data 1 given hypothesis 1"; in this case "the probability that the car does over 25 mpg given that it is a Honda". You should be able to translate the probability expressions in the other three cells fairly easily, bearing in mind that D2 is "no serious mechanical problems in two years" and H2 is "it is a VW".

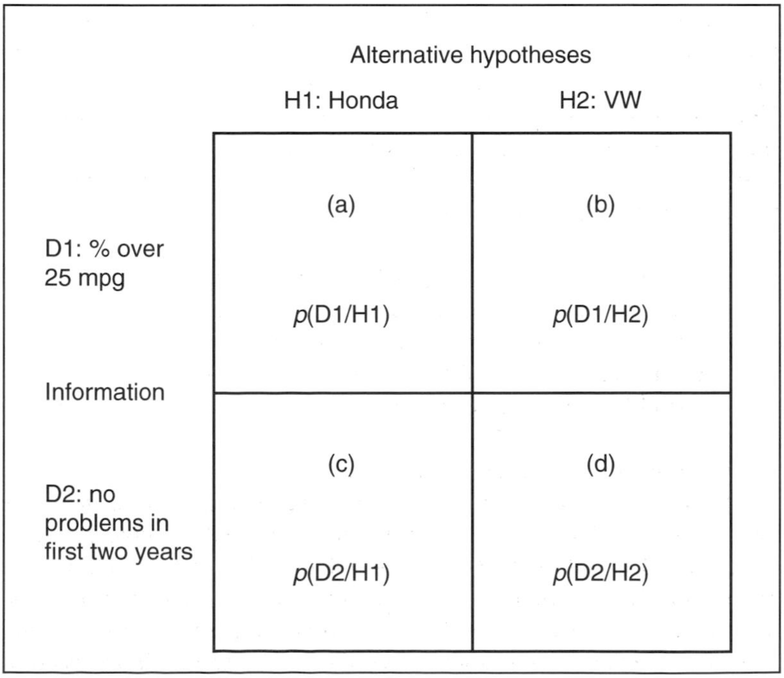

| | Alternative hypotheses | |
	H1: Honda	H2: VW
D1: % over 25 mpg	(a) $p(D1/H1)$	(b) $p(D1/H2)$
Information		
D2: no problems in first two years	(c) $p(D2/H1)$	(d) $p(D2/H2)$

FIG. 6.3. Matrix of relations between data (D) and hypotheses (H) in the pseudodiagnosticity paradigm. After Mynatt et al. (1993). Copyright © 1993 The Experimental Psychology Society. Reprinted with permission.

What Bayesian analysis delivers is a *likelihood ratio*. This is a comparison of the probability (likelihood) of finding a certain piece of data under a hypothesis H and its complement ¬H; in the example we have been using, H1 and H2 are the only possibilities, so we need to compare the probability of data D1 (or D2) under H1 or H2. You have already been given D1 under H1, so you need to compare D1 under H2. The likelihood ratio in this case is therefore:

$$\frac{p(D1 \mid H1)}{p(D1 \mid H2)}$$

You thus need to look for fuel consumption data for VWs; further information about Hondas, p(D2|H1), tells you nothing about the alternative hypothesis and so is not diagnostic. If you knew Aunt Jane was really concerned about economy and reliability, you would be fairly sure that she would choose the best car on these two measures, and VWs might be even better than Hondas.

Why do subjects go for the pseudodiagnostic option? According to Mynatt et al. (1993), the major reason is that people are incapable of evaluating more than one hypothesis at a time. The problem presentation encourages you to entertain the notion that the car is a Honda (H1), so you are limited to data that only concern that hypothesis. Mynatt et al. point to the similarity between this performance and "confirming" behaviour in the 2 4 6 task; note also the success of the DAX/MED problem in reducing this, by inducing subjects to conduct positive tests on first one hypothesis and then another. In Evans' terms, we would say that cell (c) is more subjectively relevant (see Evans & Over, 1996a, pp. 65–67). This explanation is also consistent with mental models theory, which posits a limit to the number of models that can occupy working memory at one time and a tendency to focus on what is explicitly represented.

Mynatt et al. found two ways of reducing the pseudodiagnosticity effect. First, they reduced the percentage given for cars doing more than 25 mpg (i.e. D1) to 35% in one condition. This lowered subjects' reliance on cell (c): 43% now chose this, with 47% going for cell (b). The explanation given is that a probability of less than .5 (or 50%) implies to subjects that the hypothesis is false, leading them to consider the alternative. Second, they found that the pseudodiagnosticity effect was greatly diminished when subjects were asked to reason about *actions* rather than inferences. An action in this context would be to think about the information you would need to help you decide whether you (or Aunt Jane) should buy a Honda or a VW. With an inference, you are trying to figure out which it is, so only in this case will you need to evaluate alternative hypotheses and hence run up against the "one at a time" restriction. A majority of subjects chose cell (b), the "Bayesian" cell, rather than the non-diagnostic cell (c), when asked to think about the task in terms of action rather than inference. There is a clear parallel here with work on the deontic selection task (see Chapter 4), which, as we saw, brings about a very different, and apparently more rational, pattern of responding compared with the standard task. Deontic reasoning is also fundamentally about actions.

Scientific reasoning

I mentioned earlier that many laboratory hypothesis-testing tasks had been designed to reflect the kind of reasoning followed in real science. To judge whether this claim is justified, we would need information directly about real-world scientific reasoning. There are three ways of going about this: set up a realistic but artificial science environment in the laboratory; embark on a closely monitored longitudinal "field" study of an actual scientific research programme; or analyse case histories of scientists' work retrospectively. The first has already been looked at: the work of Mynatt, Doherty, and colleagues on adaptations of the 2 4 6 task is an example. The second has only recently begun to be reported (see Dunbar, 1995); Gorman (1995b) gives an outline of some ways in which it might be done, and acknowledges the scale of effort that would be needed. The third requires an archive of scientific notes and records detailed enough to enable psychological analysis. Fortunately, such records do exist.

Tweney (1985; see also Tweney & Chitwood, 1995) for instance has worked on the archive of the 19th-century British physicist Michael Faraday, and Gorman (1992, 1995b; Carlson & Gorman, 1990) has similarly analysed the notes and records of the American inventors Thomas Edison and Alexander Graham Bell. Both these sets of investigators have taken their cue from the experimental work on hypothesis testing reviewed earlier, focusing particularly on matters concerning confirmation and disconfirmation.

This is in many respects the most important issue in the study of scientific reasoning. It was raised initially by philosophers of science, and it is fair to say that philosophical ideas provided much of the impetus for the psychological work. The most famous contribution to this enterprise was that of Popper (e.g. 1962). He attacked the long-standing assumption that because the stuff of science was empirical observation, scientific laws could only be based on generalisations from these observations. This is a form of inductive inference. The problem with this is that inductive conclusions are, logically speaking, always invalid: they are not guaranteed to be true. You may have observed that dogs chase cats, but that does not mean that every dog does: that would be like concluding that, because you have not died yet, you are going to live for ever.

Popper pointed out that, although an inductive generalisation can never be proved true, it can be proved false: just one counter-example will do. His prescription for science was therefore based on deduction rather than induction. Take some assumptions from a theory, frame a prediction (p) from them that should lead to some observation (q)—if p then q. If you fail to observe q, then, by *modus tollens*, p must be false. Observing q does not necessarily imply p: that would be affirming the consequent, which is a fallacy. The object of science is therefore to advance conjectures that are open to possible refutation.

Do scientists actually behave in this way? The data from observational studies of scientists at work are unclear: some groups have been found to run on confirmation, whereas others seem to have been more open to disconfirmation (Gorman, 1995b; Tweney & Chitwood, 1995). Alexander Graham Bell provides a fascinating record of the interplay of testing and confirmation in the work of one especially eminent person.

Because Bell was an inventor, and contemporaneous notes can be used to resolve disputes over patents, he left an extensive archive of notes of his ongoing work, his hypotheses, and his general aims. Some of this evidence was used in court, and so appears in court records, and Bell also described his ideas and progress in letters to his family. Bell was working on a device for transmitting speech: a telephone. His records date from the mid-1870s.

Bell initially used an analogy with the mechanics of the human ear as the basis for his transmitting device. The ear has a membrane, the eardrum, connected to the cochlea (the organ of the inner ear, from which nerves conduct information to the brain) by three bones (the ossicles). These bones amplify the vibrations of the eardrum by lever action into a wave-like pattern on the cochlear membrane. Bell's model was therefore to construct a device that would convert sound into an undulating, or wave-like, electrical current, and in 1876 he embarked on a series of experiments on the most effective way of doing this.

Bell went through each component of his device, changing one aspect at a time to see if it resulted in greater or lesser efficiency. Some of these changes were based on knowledge gained in previous experiments, and provide clear examples of positive and negative tests in Klayman and Ha's sense: tests that were expected to work or not work. On the basis of such a run of experiments he considered that he had the basis for a telephone, even though he did not yet have a properly functional device, and successfully applied for a patent. Following this, he learned of a similar patent with a slightly different design, using a liquid rather than an electromagnet to vary electrical resistance. This opened up a whole new series of experiments on the properties of liquid in regulating resistance, which in turn led to a successful, improved design: the first intelligible telephone message was relayed to Bell by his assistant Watson on 10 March, 1876.

Although the liquid devices were at least as good as his earlier electromagnetic resistors, Bell reasoned that the medium was not, so to speak, the message: what was really important was the efficient control of an undulating current. From then on, he abandoned liquid devices and returned to electromagnetic ones, filing for another patent the following year, after wowing the crowd at a public demonstration in June 1876. Bell's success in March with a liquid resistor did not count, for him, as disconfirmation of the utility of the electromagnetic type, but rather served to confirm his wider ideas about undulating currents.

Bell considered himself a "theoretical" inventor rather than a practical one: he was most concerned with establishing the principles behind, for instance, the telephone, rather than with building commercial models (that was left to Edison). To that extent, he was as much a scientist as an inventor. Note that this potted history of a brief phase in his career shows what looks like confirmation bias: Bell stuck with his ideas about undulating current and electromagnets even though he had found good results with liquids.

Gorman (1995b; see also Tweney & Chitwood, 1995) proposes, on the basis of such records, that confirmation bias might not be such a discredited idea after all. Whereas the notion of positive and negative testing (either through a strategy or as a result of cognitive limitations) might be a useful way of describing behaviour at the "molecular" level (i.e. single tests), confirmation bias, or a confirmation heuristic, might better describe activity at the "molar" level, i.e. the strategies that influence how large-scale series of experiments are conducted. Confirmation bias may even be necessary for progress, at least at the early stages of a research programme: an experiment that does not "work" may simply have been poorly designed or conducted, so one would need stronger grounds for concluding that a theory was false. Confirm early and disconfirm late was a strategy supported by Mynatt, Doherty, and colleagues in their artificial science studies based on the 2 4 6 task (see earlier). Refutation bias is also possible, for instance when testing someone else's theory that you think might be wrong. Perhaps that is how science, as a whole, can claim to be objective: individual scientists themselves might seek to confirm their own ideas but are just as keen to disconfirm others', setting up a ruthless Darwinian environment where only the strongest theories survive.

There is a wider range of studies into scientific reasoning than I have been able to portray here: a good review, classifying the families of studies into traditions springing from several major approaches, is given by Tweney and Chitwood (1995), and there is a wide-ranging historical account in Lovie (1992), whose perspective is deeply influenced by sociological approaches. The relation between laboratory experiments such as the 2 4 6 and other approaches to studying real scientific practice psychologically is fascinatingly brought to life by Gorman (1992); this book is unique in looking closely at the experiences of scientists, especially Gorman himself, at the hands of the editors of the learned journals in which research results are published.

Summary

1. Much of the study of hypothesis testing has been inspired by Wason's 2 4 6 task, which was designed to test people's ability to discover rules by generating potentially confirming and disconfirming instances.
2. Early work seemed to indicate a bias towards confirming hypotheses, but later experiment and theory have shown that instead there seems to be a bias for positive testing, and that this has a cognitive rather than a motivational basis.
3. Positive testing is not the same as confirmation: in some situations, positive testing is the most effective way to disconfirm a hypothesis.
4. The most effective way found to improve hypothesis-testing performance is to encourage alternative hypotheses; direct instructions to disconfirm and use of realistic content have had only mixed success.
5. Studies of pseudodiagnosticity have shown that people find it difficult to hold more than one hypothesis in mind at a time; the effect can be reduced by making the initial hypothesis less credible, and by reasoning about actions rather than inferences.
6. Studies of the archives of practising scientists have shown that a tendency to confirm at the level of whole research programmes, rather than single studies, may be useful and even necessary for the development of scientific theories.

Induction 7

Inductive thinking is a vast topic, which connects with several areas normally considered to be outside the psychology of thinking, such as learning, problem solving, semantic memory, and psycholinguistics. Within the field of thinking, there are relations with deduction and scientific reasoning and with their associated theories, which we have considered in preceding chapters; and also with judgement and decision making, which we shall come to. Probably the most extensively researched area of induction within the psychology of thinking is that concerned with judgements of frequency and probability: the next chapter is devoted to that subject. In this one, we shall consider some other important aspects: generalisation, specialisation, categorisation, analogical thinking, and two types of theory: rule-based and model-based. There is no single normative theory for induction in general, although there is for that part of it concerned with probability judgement, as we shall see; thus we shall be less concerned in this chapter with the comparison between normative standards and human performance. Most of the relevant theoretical proposals about induction have come from psychology or artificial intelligence.

Definitions of induction

There is a rather clichéd distinction between deduction and induction: that deduction is reasoning from the general (i.e. rules) to the particular (i.e. instances), whereas induction is the other way round: reasoning from the particular to the general. There is some truth in this, inasmuch as some inductions can be defined as reverse deductions leading to generalisations, but there is much more to induction than that.

Holland, Holyoak, Nisbett, and Thagard (1986, p. 1) define induction as including "all inferential processes that expand knowledge in the face of uncertainty". Garnham and Oakhill (1994) are uneasy about such a general definition, because it would lead to almost any thought process, even deduction, being included as a form of induction. They prefer a similar but tighter definition due to Johnson-Laird (1993, p. 60; also

1994a, p. 11). This is that an induction is "any process of thought yielding a conclusion that increases the semantic information in its initial observations or premises". Deduction does not increase semantic information: it merely makes explicit what was already implicit in the premises of the argument.

To make sense of this definition, and to see how it enables induction to be broken down into its subfields, we need to know what is meant by the term *semantic information*. We have met the technical idea of information in reviewing the information-gain approach to deduction (see Chapters 2 and 5): a statement or proposition is informative to the extent that it reduces uncertainty. To put it another way, the information content of a proposition depends on the number of states of affairs that it *rules out* as false. As an example, imagine you turn on your CD player, insert a disc, and press "play", but no sound comes out. You think to yourself, "I have forgotten to turn on the amplifier or left the selector at the tape setting"; alternatively, you might just think "I have left the selector at the tape setting". The second of these statements has more semantic information, because it rules out an extra state of affairs compared to the first: the one in which you may also have forgotten to turn on the amp.

We can use this example to point up the distinction between deduction and induction. There is no sound from your stereo, and your initial premise, based on your previous history of absent-mindedness, is:

The amp is off or the selector is at the wrong setting (or both).

You notice that the amp's power light is in fact on (this becomes your second premise), and conclude that the selector is wrongly set. This is a deduction, and it is valid: it must be true given the truth of the two premises (your hypothesis and your observation of the on-light). The conclusion rules out the same states of affairs as do the premises: in both cases, they leave only the situation where the amp is on but the selector is at the wrong setting.

Now imagine that you start with the same thought, but this time observe that the amp's power light is not on, showing that the amp is in fact still switched off. You conclude that the selector is OK, go to switch on the amp, and anticipate some music. This conclusion does not follow validly: it might be true, but you could in fact have made both mistakes. The premises (hypothesis and observation) rule out all but two states of affairs: (i) the amp is off but the selector is at the right setting, or (ii) the amp is off and the selector is at the wrong setting. Your conclusion has ruled out the second of these, and hence has increased semantic information compared to the premises: it is an induction. The example also reveals an essential property of inductive conclusions: they are logically invalid. That is an inevitable consequence of a process that increases semantic information; the conclusion is plausible, but not necessarily true.

General and specific induction

The most fundamental distinction in the study of induction is between *general* and *specific*. An inductive generalisation occurs when several pieces of data lead to the production of a conclusion that contains them, such as when you keep failing to make sound emerge from your stereo, repeatedly forget to feed the cat, and conclude that you are becoming an absent-minded person. This is the classic case of reasoning from the particular to the general. Specific inductions are where you go from a particular observation to a particular conclusion, as when there's no sound from your stereo, so you conclude that the amplifier is not switched on.

Inductive generalisations can be *explanatory* as well as *descriptive* (Johnson-Laird, 1993, 1994a). The aim of radical behaviourism, for instance, was to derive a set of laws that would *describe* the relations between stimuli, responses, and schedules of reinforcement. Explanatory induction is sometimes known as abduction; it is the process underlying the production of scientific hypotheses (see Chapter 6). Thus, for instance, your episodes of memory failure lead you to conclude that over-work is causing you to become absent-minded: your inductive conclusion takes the form of an explanation for the observations that prompted it. Specific inductions can also be explanatory as well as descriptive: the amp is off because you forgot to switch it on, owing to your increasing scattiness. There is a clear relation here to the area of causal inference (see Chapter 4).

General induction

Holland et al. (1986) split generalisation into two classes: *instance-based* and *condition-simplifying*. The latter has been the concern more of artificial intelligence researchers than psychologists: there is little if any experimental work reported on it. A condition is part of a rule for an item, A, being included as an instance of a concept, C (we shall look at concepts and categories in greater detail later). The relation can be expressed as a conditional:

If something is A then it is a C

The A part can contain more than one element, as in this example:

> If it quacks and waddles, then it is a duck
> [If Q and W then D]

Condition-simplifying generalisation occurs when the A part is relaxed, perhaps as the result of some new information, so that one of its constituent conditions is dropped:

> If it quacks, then it is a duck [If Q then D]

You can see that this is an induction in Johnson-Laird's sense (see Johnson-Laird, 1994a), because the generalised and simplified rule is more informative than the original rule: it eliminates an extra possible state of affairs. The original duck rule is consistent with a set of models that includes the case:

> Q ¬W ¬D [something that quacks but does not waddle
> and is not a duck]

In generalising from this rule, we are eliminating this case, e.g. by observing things that quack and do not waddle but are still ducks. Johnson-Laird considers other forms of rule-based generalisation besides this: condition-simplifying is not the only one.

Instance-based generalisation is, as we have seen, the kind that is commonly recognised as a standard form of induction: you make a series of observations and form a rule, or a concept, that contains them. This has produced some intriguing questions that have puzzled researchers since the time of Aristotle. The one that has been of greatest concern is the question of how an induction can be justified: in some cases, a single instance seems enough to yield a general rule (one of mine is "eating seafood in the tropics is risky": you should be able to induce fairly easily what single instance led to this). However, in others, there may be many pieces of data available, and yet we still do not generalise, at least not confidently, from them. Which factors lead to the production and acceptability of an instance-based generalisation?

Both Holland et al. and Johnson-Laird propose that one important factor is the number of instances that are A and also C and, conversely, the absence of things that are A but not C. Thus, we will confidently generalise from our encounters with quacking birds that things that quack are ducks, because whereas there are many instances available of quackers that are ducks, there are few if any instances available of quackers that turn out not to be ducks. The situation is different with waddling: we can recall instances of things that waddle that are not ducks (penguins, for example).

The use of the word "available" is deliberate here: at least for Johnson-Laird, a crucial constraint on induction is the ease with which instances can be brought to mind, which is how Tversky and Kahneman (1973), who introduced the term "availability", defined it. We shall look in detail at the work of these two theorists in the next chapter. Johnson-Laird's use of the availability construct marks the introduction of a probabilistic component, and it is this idea that enables us to explain how induction sometimes proceeds from few observations, whereas in other cases it requires many (Johnson-Laird, 1994b, contains an extended discussion of the application of the model theory to probabilistic thinking). Holland et al. also include such a component, which they specifically link to knowledge of the variability of the *reference class* of the events in question. The reference class is that part of knowledge that is most relevant in making assessments of an event: birds, in the case of data about quacking and waddling, for instance. Here is a famous experiment, which they quote, which shows how variability affects induction.

The experiment was reported by Nisbett, Krantz, Jepson, and Kunda (1983). Subjects were asked to imagine that they were exploring a little-known Pacific island, on which new minerals, animals, and people had been discovered. They were invited to generalise about each class on the basis of the cases they encountered. Samples of a new mineral called "floridium" were said to conduct electricity and burn with a green flame; birds called "shreebles" were found to have blue feathers and nest in eucalyptus trees; and members of a tribe called the "Barratos" were observed to have brown skins and be obese. There were three experimental conditions, according to the size of the sample in each case: subjects were told they had either seen one, three, or twenty examples of mineral, birds, or people. Their task was to estimate what proportion of the total population in each case could be inferred to have the specified property.

The results are shown in Fig. 7.1, and show strikingly the effects of knowledge of the variability of the reference class (remember, the subjects were dealing with imaginary items, so could not be using knowledge of actual cases). Subjects were quite prepared to generalise about minerals from even single samples; indeed, size of sample had no effect here. Properties of minerals are known to be largely invariant. The same was true of skin colour in the new tribe. At the other extreme, not only were subjects' inductions about the body size of the Barratos

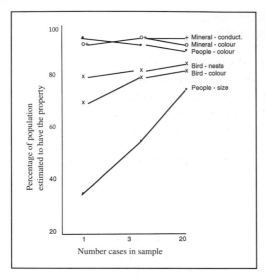

FIG. 7.1.
Results from the study of Nisbett et al. (1983) showing the influence of perceived variability of a reference class on inductive generalisation in three categories. Copyright © (1993) by the American Psychological Association. Reprinted with permission.

greatly affected by variability (as revealed in subjects' explanations), but sample size had a marked effect, as it should: larger samples are statistically more reliable. As Thagard and Nisbett (1982) note, reference-class variability allows one to explain a well-known observation in social psychology: that people tend to generalise more about groups of which they are not members (out-groups) than groups of which they are members (in-groups). You have more knowledge about in-groups than out-groups, and so the former will seem more variable than the latter.

Specific induction

As with certain aspects of generalisation, there has been little experimental work by psychologists on specific induction. A great many specific inductions are abductive: their conclusions are explanatory. The most detailed theoretical consideration comes from Johnson-Laird (1993, 1994a), where specific induction follows naturally from his perspective of induction as yielding models of states of affairs, as opposed to linguistic statements. Other theories, such as that of Holland et al. (1986), depend on language-like rules even though they propose a form of the mental model construct in explaining induction, and so would have more difficulty than Johnson-Laird's theory does in dealing with both general and specific induction. This issue will be referred to again later.

Availability seems to play a crucial role in specific induction: the conclusion you produce depends on the knowledge you have and the ease with which it is invoked. Johnson-Laird uses the example of a car which will not start: the starter does not turn the engine over. What is your immediate induction as to the cause? It is likely to be:

The battery is flat

This may be true or it may not, and it depends on your having at least some knowledge of the relation between batteries, starter motors, and car engines. Johnson-Laird proposes that you are likely to represent this simple knowledge in the form of a model (he uses symbols instead of letters), such as:

[b   s]   [t]
     ...

with b = battery, s = starter, t = engine turns; the three dots signify an implicit model with as yet unspecified content (see Chapters 2 and 5). Johnson-Laird does not specify that these models are mentally represented as lines on a page: models represent entities, their properties, and the relations between them, and so could take a variety of forms.

When the engine does not turn, the initial model is eliminated and the implicit model is fleshed out to yield:

    ¬[b   s]   ¬[t]

from which you can infer that there's something wrong with the battery, the starter, or the connection between them: exactly what will depend on further information and an updating of the model. Johnson-Laird rejects the idea that this kind of conclusion could depend on rules, on the grounds that it would involve committing the fallacy of affirming the consequent (see Chapter 3). Suppose you have an existing rule such as "If the battery is flat then the car will not start" and observe that "the car will not start". The conclusion that "the battery is flat" does not follow validly. However, it still seems possible that people could form such a conclusion and be aware that it does not necessarily follow: it would be a useful pointer to a possibility that could be investigated. Such an inference is allowed as plausible, hence informative, in some theories (e.g. Collins & Michalski, 1989).

Categorisation and induction

Categorisation, unlike some of the other areas we have looked at so far, is an extensively researched form of induction. It is a special case of inductive generalisation, although study of it has been extended beyond this parallel to include induction not only of categories, but also induction based on categories. A great deal of the research has been on developmental processes, but we shall only be able to touch on these studies here.

Categories are central to our ability to think economically and hence efficiently about the world. They enable us to make reliable predictions, and hence adapt to our environment effectively (Heit, 1998). You know that dogs (a category) chase cats (another category). You discover that your uncle has acquired something called a borzoi. On learning that a borzoi is a dog (a sort of giant, hairy greyhound), you can infer, until told otherwise, that a borzoi chases cats; and you can predict that your uncle's borzoi, Boris, will chase your cat, Clarence. Without this ability, you would have to learn separately, for each instance, what its properties were: not just borzois (a lower-level category), but each individual borzoi. It would take for ever.

Categorisation and induction are related in two ways, leading to two general psychological questions. First, how are categories induced and category membership decided? Second, how are categories used in making inductive inferences?

Categories, concepts, and membership

Category and *concept* are related terms; indeed some authors use them interchangeably, but others argue that they can be distinguished. Concepts are sometimes seen as more general than categories, in that they can be very simple, abstract, and basic to all forms of coherent thought, including categorisation. Thus in the borzoi example, you need a concept of "chasing" in addition to category knowledge about cats and dogs in order to infer what Boris will do to Clarence. For simplicity, I shall not pursue this distinction here.

How are concepts formed? The earliest major study of this question was reported by Bruner, Goodnow, and Austin (1956). They investigated the ability of people to acquire concepts in what is known as a Boolean domain (after George Boole, the 19th-century logician): Boolean concepts are those made up of elements that can be joined conjunctively (by *and*), such as "brother": male and same father and same mother; disjunctively (by *or*), such as "parent": mother or father; or negatively (by *not*), such as "stepmother": mother not biological mother. The materials used by Bruner et al. were abstract, consisting of shapes and colours. Subjects chose various instances and were told that they either were or were not instances of the concept. They carried on sampling until they were sure that they knew what the concept was. If this reminds you of Wason's 2 4 6 task (see Chapter 6), it should: it was its inspiration.

Subjects were found to use different strategies involving varying hypotheses in terms of the number of common elements that differed between the items chosen. Disjunctive concepts were found to be particularly difficult to acquire in this way. There are two problems with this approach to concept learning, besides the obvious one of its artificiality. The first is, as Johnson-Laird (1994a) points out, that there is more to real-world concepts than Boolean relations. Your mother is more than just female-and-parent to you. Second, it can be demonstrated by argument that concepts are not necessarily based on common elements (although note that, for instance, disjunctive concepts lack common elements by definition).

The argument against common elements was put forward by the philosopher Wittgenstein, and taken up by psychologists in the 1970s. What do cats have in common? They are furry, of a certain size, they miaow, have retractable claws, are friendly, and so on. So to be a cat, you have to have these properties? In fact, you do not: there are specially bred bald cats, huge cats, silent cats (I used to have one: it opened its mouth as if to miaow, but made no sound), nervous cats and cats that have been de-clawed. They are all still cats.

If category members can be members without there having to be any elements common to them, what is the alternative? One answer takes the form of *prototypes*: you have in memory a representation of a standard cat (either a particular, superb example or an abstract, ideal but not actual cat; theorists differ on this point: see Eysenck & Keane, 1995, Ch. 10), and something that resembles this standard sufficiently will be recognised as a cat. The idea of prototypes was emphasised largely through the work of Rosch and her colleagues (e.g. Rosch, 1978).

Evidence for categorisation as prototype induction originally came from anthropology, e.g. Berlin and Kay's (1969) classic work on colour perception and naming. They found that there were 11 basic colour terms (red, blue, etc.), which differed in the frequency with which they occurred in languages, and which could be distinguished from non-basic terms, such as turquoise or beige, on several principles. English has all 11 basic colour terms. Rosch showed that even people speaking languages that had only two of the possible 11 terms could remember the basic colours better than the non-basic colours, and learn new names for them more easily. She and others went on to investigate, and demonstrate, this apparently automatic tendency to respond to prototypes across a wide range of concepts.

Prototypicality implies typicality: an instance should be more readily classified as belonging to a given category to the extent that it resembles the prototype. There is a mass of evidence that this is indeed the case. For instance, it takes reliably less time to agree that "a robin is a bird" than that "a chicken is a bird" (Smith & Medin, 1981): robins are more typical birds than chickens. Typicality also affects judgements about artificial categories such as "furniture", and even definitive categories such as "odd number": some odd numbers are seen as more typically odd than others (Armstrong, Gleitman, & Gleitman, 1983).

Categories are also related to each other, and on different levels. Rosch, Mervis, Gray, Johnson, and Boyes-Braem (1976) found evidence that categories were organised in a hierarchy: superordinate (e.g. musical instrument), basic (e.g. piano) and subordinate (e.g. electric piano). The basic level was so called because it appeared to be optimally informative: people can list far more attributes for pianos than for musical instruments, but not many more for grand pianos than for pianos. The basic level is also where categories are maximally distinct from one another: there is little overlap between them.

An important point made by Rosch and her co-workers was that this kind of organisation of knowledge, with optimal levels of information both within categories (prototypes) and between them (basic-level categories) is not arbitrary or accidental, but rather reflects the objective structure of the environment. Feathers, beaks, and tweeting just do tend to go together, and so the cognitive system would be expected to reflect this natural correlation in the way in which it represents knowledge. The idea that cognition adapts to the structure of the environment underlies the technique of "rational analysis" pioneered by Anderson (1990, 1991), and which we saw applied to reasoning in Chapters 2 and 5. It has also been recently applied to category-based induction, which is the subject of the next section.

Category-based induction

Induction and categorisation can be related in ways other than those we have just considered: it is possible to base inductive inferences on category information. When induction is based on categories, you are inferring that what is true of one member of a category will be true of another. How confident are you in the following arguments?

[1]	[2]	[3]
Alsatians chase cats	Alsatians chase sticks	Alsatians guard scrapyards
Borzois chase cats	Borzois chase sticks	Borzois guard scrapyards

As with syllogisms, the premise is above the line and the conclusion is below it. Each argument seems decreasingly strong, from [1] to [3]. The first is, strictly speaking, not a true induction but an *enthymeme*: an inference that is valid if certain unstated premises are taken into account (alsatians are dogs; all dogs chase cats; borzois are dogs). The other two are clearly inductions (because you know that chasing sticks and guarding scrapyards are not generally true of dogs), and [2] seems stronger than [3]; but why?

This question has only recently attracted the attention of researchers. Part of the answer lies in the construct of reference-class variability, as in the work of Nisbett et al. (1983) referred to earlier: you probably assume that dogs are relatively invariant as regards cat-chasing, but more variable with respect to stick-chasing, and more still in guarding. However, category-based induction has more interesting features than this. Here are some similar arguments which will make the point:

[4]	[5]
Alsatians guard scrapyards	Alsatians have sesamoid bones
Rottweilers guard scrapyards	Rottweilers have sesamoid bones
Dobermanns guard scrapyards	Borzois have sesamoid bones
Borzois guard scrapyards	

Argument [4] gives more instances of types of guard dogs: you may know that each is a case of a big dog, and that borzois are also big dogs, and yet you may still not draw the conclusion confidently. Argument [5] shows how variability of the reference class can only be a partial factor: you have never heard of sesamoid bones, and yet may draw the inference with at least some confidence.

There is a difference here between properties that you know something about (e.g. guarding) and those that you do not (sesamoid bones). The latter are called *blank* properties (Osherson, Smith, Wilkie, Lopez, & Shafir, 1990). Blank properties are useful in the study of category-based induction because they remove one source of variability: inductive inferences involving blank properties can only be affected by the content of the categories and the relations between them, and not by the content of the properties. Non-blank properties complicate matters, although there have been some attempts to explain their influence on induction, as we shall see.

Categories and features

Osherson et al. (1990) produced a general theory of category-based induction, which they called the similarity-coverage model. It builds on the original research in the area, reported by Rips (1975). He had proposed that there were two psychological variables operating to yield estimates of argument strength in cases such as the examples given earlier: (a) the degree to which the premise categories resemble the conclusion categories, and (b) the degree to which the premise categories resemble members of the lowest-level category that includes both the premise and conclusion categories.

For a clearer idea of what these variables mean, consider argument [5] again. Variable (a) reflects the similarity between alsatians and rottweilers (the premise categories) on the one hand, and borzois (the conclusion category) on the other. The lowest-level category that includes alsatian, rottweiler, and borzoi is *dogs* (higher-level categories would be *mammals*, then *animals*, and so on). Variable (b) corresponds to your knowledge of the similarity between alsatians and rottweilers, and all dogs. So, you know that alsatians and rottweilers have a certain property, know that they are both dogs, think it therefore likely that all dogs may share this property, and so extend it to another member, borzois (Osherson et al., 1990).

Rips only used single-premise, specific arguments such as [1]–[3] above. A specific argument is defined by Osherson et al. as one where the premise and conclusion categories are at the same level. They point out that it is also possible to have arguments that traverse category boundaries, such as:

[6]
Alsatians have sesamoid bones
Rottweilers have sesamoid bones
Dogs have sesamoid bones

They call this a general argument: the conclusion category is more general (i.e. at a higher level) than the premise categories. There are also mixed arguments, which are neither specific or general, for instance in [7] where one of the premise categories is not included in the conclusion category:

[7]
Alsatians have sesamoid bones
Persian cats have sesamoid bones
Dogs have sesamoid bones

In extending Rips' analysis beyond specific arguments, Osherson et al. introduce another important variable: coverage (hence the name of the theory). They found that similarity was not sufficient to explain all the observed phenomena of category-based induction. An important aspect is the amount of total possible similarity accounted for by the category members named in the argument. You can see how coverage operates in examples [8] and [9]: you are likely to assess argument [ii] as being stronger than argument [i] in both cases:

[8i]
Alsatians have sesamoid bones
Dogs have sesamoid bones

[8ii]
Alsatians have sesamoid bones
Rottweilers have sesamoid bones
Dogs have sesamoid bones

— in [8ii] an additional premise increases coverage.

[9i]	[9ii]
Alsatians have sesamoid bones	Alsatians have sesamoid bones
Rottweilers have sesamoid bones	Chihuahuas have sesamoid bones
Dogs have sesamoid bones	Dogs have sesamoid bones

Here the second premise in [9ii] contains a less similar category than the second premise in [9i], hence increasing coverage.

These principles are used by Osherson et al. to develop a formal, symbolic theory from which they predict a range of phenomena of category-based induction. For example, premises containing typical members of a conclusion category lead to stronger arguments than premises with less typical members, as in:

[10i]	[10ii]
Alsatians have sesamoid bones	Borzois have sesamoid bones
Dogs have sesamoid bones	Dogs have sesamoid bones

Alsatians are more typical dogs than are borzois, and so will share more common attributes with the general category (that is what typicality means), hence [10i] seems stronger than [10ii]. A second phenomenon, premise diversity, was illustrated in arguments [9]. A third, premise monotonicity, shows how coverage works: such an example would be arguments [8], with "dogs" replaced by "borzois" (or another dog name). Introducing a new premise from the lowest-level category that includes the premise and conclusion categories increases coverage. There are 10 more such phenomena that are accounted for by the similarity-coverage theory. Empirical data confirmed the theory's predictions. The theory has also recently been extended to deal with non-blank properties (Smith, Shafir, & Osherson, 1994), mainly by including premise and conclusion plausibility alongside similarity as a determinant of argument strength: a kind of belief-bias factor (see Chapter 4).

Sloman (1993) offers a modification of the theory, based on features rather than categories. He argues that by basing induction on categories, Osherson et al. must propose that new categories are created, perhaps where none existed before, in order to explain the kinds of induction we have been considering. Argument [4] is an illustration: what is the lowest-level common category here? It cannot be just "dogs", more likely something like "big, fierce dogs". Sloman denies the need for this manoeuvre by proposing that "argument strength is, roughly, the proportion of features in the conclusion category that are also in the premise categories" (1993, p. 242). This proposal has the consequence that conclusion categories with relatively few features will lead to stronger arguments, everything else being equal, because they will tend to share more of their features with the premise categories (there are simply fewer to share). The Osherson theory has no grounds for this prediction.

We can venture beyond dogs to illustrate this, using Sloman's own example. He used existing similarity norms to construct the following pair of arguments:

[11i]	[11ii]
All collies produce phagocytes	All collies produce phagocytes
All Persian cats produce phagocytes	All horses produce phagocytes

[11i] should seem stronger than [11ii]. The premise is the same in each case but the conclusion categories are different; knowledge about horses was found to be richer than knowledge about Persian cats, and this factor is proposed to account for the difference in argument strength. Subjects' ratings were as predicted. Sloman further claims to account for all the phenomena accounted for by the Osherson theory. Sloman's own formal theory is based on connectionist mechanisms.

Sloman also offers an informal explanation of induction with non-blank properties (e.g. examples [1]–[5]). He suggests three ways in which non-blank properties may affect induction. The first arises from an assumption that non-blank properties consist of features that have some known connection to features of the premise and conclusion categories. Premises would then influence argument strength to the extent that they were surprising in relation to this knowledge. For instance, you think that guard-dogs need to be big. If you then found out that poodles also guard scrapyards, your belief that all dogs guard scrapyards would probably be strengthened.

Sloman also advances a version of the belief-bias principle. He argues that his model implies that arguments will be judged strong when there is a strong prior belief in the conclusion (see also Smith et al., 1994, mentioned earlier). However, this would, he argues, depend on some unspecified degree of overlap between premise and conclusion features, otherwise the following sorts of inductions would be judged as strong, when clearly they are not:

Alsatians have legs
Tables have legs

Sloman's third informal principle for non-blank properties is a principle of relevance (again, this has been referred to before in the context of deduction: see Chapter 5). The idea is that non-blank properties select category features that are relevant. For instance:

Alsatians make good guard-dogs
Rottweilers make good guard-dogs

You may know a lot about these breeds, but what is picked out here is size and fierceness; we say that alsatians and rottweilers are similar with respect to these features, and judge the strength of the argument on that basis and not, perhaps, on their colour, which is also similar.

Sloman (1994) provides evidence for another important influence on category-based induction: *explanatory coherence*. If a premise and a conclusion of the type we have been considering have the same plausible explanation, belief in the conclusion is raised. The arguments about guard dogs illustrate this: if you are given the statement that alsatians guard scrapyards and asked to evaluate the conclusion that, therefore, rottweilers guard scrapyards, your belief in the conclusion will be increased (relative to your belief in it without the initial premise) depending on the availability of a common explanation. In this case, it is that both are large, fierce dogs and that these properties come in handy for guarding. On the other hand, differing explanations may lead to the reverse effect: a decrease in belief in the conclusion. Consider this argument (from Sloman, 1997):

Many college students work nights
Many telephone operators work nights

Here the most likely explanations are different (largely because "work" means something different in these two categories). With arguments like this, belief in the conclusion falls, something that Sloman (1997) calls a *discounting effect*. Discounting effects tend to be weaker than coherence effects, and in some cases are observed even when the premise and conclusion are completely unrelated, as in:

Most baseball players own a bat
Most zoos own a bat

To account for the finding that discounting occurs with both these types of argument, and not just with those with inconsistent explanations between statements, Sloman (1997) proposes that it not only depends on the premise and conclusion having different explanations, but also that the argument as a whole is the worst possible argument in the set in question when a judgement is being formed. Both inconsistent and blatantly unrelated arguments satisfy these conditions.

Sloman's new work invites comparison with research on causal reasoning (see Chapter 4), but as yet the connection has not been worked out. The fact that we can point to notions such as relevance and causality having been discussed in the area of deduction as well as induction indicates that some theoretical integration may be possible in the future, which is itself a feature-based inductive inference.

Rational analysis and induction

Another case of similar approaches being adopted in different areas of reasoning is that of *rational analysis* (see Chapters 2 and 5). Recently, this technique has been applied to category-based induction by Heit (1998).

Heit takes a different tack from those we have considered so far. He takes induction to be not a process of making inferences about the conclusion category, but one of using the new information in the premises to make better estimates of the range of *properties*. So, going back to example [5], the inference is not about borzois, but about the range of the property "has sesamoid bones", i.e. that it may extend to borzois. People are assumed to have prior knowledge of the range of properties (this clearly allows Heit's scheme to deal more comfortably with non-blank properties), and this knowledge is revised in the light of the information contained in the premises. Construing category-based induction as a process of belief revision in the face of evidence enables a straightforward application of a Bayesian model, the heart of rational analysis.

This was introduced when reviewing the information-gain approach to reasoning in Chapter 5. To reiterate, the Bayesian model uses a formula which allows us to compute the change in belief in a set of hypotheses H_i as a result of new data D. Degree of belief in each hypothesis before getting the new data, called the prior degree of belief, is expressed as p(H), i.e. probability of H. Belief after the data, called the posterior degree of belief, is expressed as p(H|D), i.e. probability of H given D. This has to be compared against the probability of the data given the hypothesis, and the probability of competing hypotheses. The standard Bayesian formula is shown in Table 5.2 and again in Table 7.1.

Let us use example [2] to see how this analysis works. There are four possible ranges of the property "chases sticks" with respect to alsatians and borzois: that it is true of both, true of alsatians but not of borzois, not true of alsatians but true of borzois, and not true of either. These are the four possible hypotheses about a novel property, so any novel property must be one of these types. Now we assume some prior beliefs in each of the four hypotheses regarding any new property and how it may relate to alsatians and borzois. These are shown in Table 7.1 in the column headed $p(H_i)$; they are purely imaginary figures. Prior beliefs expressed as probabilities can vary between 0 (certainly false) and 1 (certainly true). Table 7.1 shows that you believe that what is true of alsatians will also be true of borzois with probability .70; that what is true of alsatians will not be true of borzois with probability .05; and so on. Combining these two probabilities (i.e. hypotheses 1 and 2) yields your overall belief that alsatians will have the new property: .75. Combining hypotheses 1 and 3 gives your belief that borzois will have it: .75 again.

Now we have the new evidence in the shape of the premise: alsatians chase sticks. This is the data D, and it can be used in the Bayesian formula to update your belief in the conclusion, that borzois chase

TABLE 7.1

Example of a Bayesian analysis of category-based induction. (After Heit, 1998)

Hypothesis		Range	Degree of Prior Belief $p(H_i)$	$p(D \mid H_i)$	Posterior Belief $p(H_i \mid D)$
1	A:	true	.70	1	.93
	B:	true			
2	A:	true	.05	1	.07
	B:	false			
3	A:	false	.05	0	0
	B:	true			
4	A:	false	.20	0	0
	B:	false			

Bayesian formula:

$$p(H_i \mid D) = \frac{p(D \mid H_i p(H_i)}{\sum_{j=1}^{n} p(D \mid Hj)p(Hj)}$$

A, Alsatians; B, Borzois.

Calculation of $p(H_i \mid D)$: begin by multiplying the prior belief, $p(H)$, by the probability of the data, D. Your data are that alsatians chase sticks: the probability of the data is therefore 1 for hypotheses 1 and 2, and 0 for hypotheses 3 and 4. So for hypothesis 1, $p(H_1 \mid D)$, the top line of the Bayesian formula multiplies .70 by 1, giving .70. For the bottom line, add together all the calculations for all the hypotheses. We already have the first: .70. For hypothesis 2, $p(H)$ was given as .05 and D is 1 again. We do not need to try to calculate the others, because D is given as 0, so these terms must result in zero too. The bottom line is therefore (.70)(1) + (.05)(1) + (0) + (0) = .75. Dividing .70 by .75 equals .93. For hypothesis 2, divide .05 by .75 = .07.

sticks. You are looking to compute the posterior degree of belief in each of the four hypotheses (so in the formula, $n = 4$). Table 7.1 gives details of how this is done: simply read off the values given for the prior beliefs and data and plug them into the formula. The outcomes are given in the column headed "Posterior belief" in the table. You can see that belief in hypotheses 1 and 2 has been strengthened, whereas belief in hypotheses 3 and 4 has vanished altogether. Given the information about stick-chasing and your prior beliefs about alsatians and borzois, you now think it is very likely that both alsatians and borzois chase sticks: [2] seems like a strong argument.

Heit uses the Bayesian analysis to predict the phenomena we looked at earlier. I shall use the case of the premise-diversity effect, illustrated in examples [9], and explained by Osherson et al. (1990) in terms of coverage. You will recall that a set of premises with relatively diverse (or dissimilar) categories, such as alsatian and chihuahua, leads to stronger arguments than a set of premises with relatively similar categories, such as alsatian and rottweiler. The data D in this case is a compound event: that two categories have a given property, such as sesamoid bones. To compare the two arguments [9i] and [9ii], we are dealing with four categories: alsatians, chihuahuas, rottweilers, and all dogs. This yields 16 possible hypotheses, but we can omit the ones that have a zero value for prior belief, and which could not affect our evaluation of the conclusion that all dogs have sesamoid bones. This leaves four hypotheses.

The sets of figures (again imaginary) necessary for the Bayesian calculations are given in Table 7.2. The $p(H_i)$ column shows the higher prior belief that alsatians and rottweilers are similar (.20) than that alsatians and chihuahuas are similar (.10). As before, just plug the figures into the formula and they will produce the values in the two critical columns headed "Posterior belief". The premise diversity effect is reflected in the row dealing with hypothesis 1: you can see that the figure for the posterior belief in the conclusion that all dogs have sesamoid bones is greater (.67) given that alsatians and chihuahuas have sesamoid bones, shown in the column headed $p(H_i \mid A\&C)$, than is the figure for belief in the conclusion given that alsatians and rottweilers have them (.57), shown in the column headed $p(H_i \mid A\&R)$.

Heit extends this analysis to the other phenomena as well. He also concedes some general problems with his approach. First, this analysis, like Oaksford and Chater's (1994a) analysis of the selection task (see Chapter 5), does not offer a truly cognitive account, in terms of mental processes supposed to underlie this form of thinking. Rather, it offers what is known as a computational-level account (see Chapter 10): an

TABLE 7.2
Bayesian analysis of the premise diversity effect. (After Heit, 1998)

Hypothesis Range		Prior Belief $p(H_i)$	$p(A\&R \mid Hi)$	Post. Belief $p(H_i \mid A\&R)$	$p(A\&C \mid H_i)$	Post. Belief $p(H_i \mid A\&C)$
1	A: true R: true C: true D: true	.40	1	.57	1	.67
2	A: true R: true C: true D: false	.10	1	.14	1	.17
3	A: true R: true C: false D: false	.20	1	.29	0	0
4	A: true R: false C: true D: false	.10	0	0	1	.17

A, alsatians; R, rottweilers; C, chihuahuas; D, all dogs.

account of what the mind is computing, rather than how it is doing it. Second, there is the question of where the knowledge assumed to drive this probabilistic form of reasoning comes from. Like many other theorists in this area, Heit has to fall back on some version of the availability construct (see also the earlier section on Johnson-Laird's approach to induction). We shall look more closely at this important idea in the next chapter, where we shall see that it has its problems as well as its strengths.

Induction and analogy

Sources, targets, and stages

Category-based induction is related to another aspect of thought common in everyday contexts: reasoning by analogy. Induction in analogical thinking also involves noticing similarities between one domain and another, but in this case with the explicit aim of solving a problem. This activity is called for when you have insufficient knowledge about one domain (the target domain) to solve a problem in it. You may then seek to recruit knowledge from another domain (the source or base domain) to suggest a solution. There are many documented cases of this process being used creatively in both art and science; for instance, early nuclear physicists used an analogy between the known properties of the solar system (the source domain) and the supposed structure of the atom (the target domain). See Johnson-Laird (1993) for an extended discussion of the relation between analogical thinking and creativity.

This simple description masks some complex psychology. We have to ask first, how source domains are selected: there is a potentially infinite range of them. Second, which features of the source domain will be useful in solving the problem in the target domain?

The second question was addressed first in the work of Gick and Holyoak (e.g. 1980). Their test-bed was a well-known problem from Gestalt psychology, the tumour problem. If you have never seen it before, you might like to attempt it and see if you are one of the few who solve it without help.

> Imagine you are a surgeon with a patient who has a stomach tumour. If the tumour is not destroyed, the patient will die. However, his condition is such that an operation is impossible: that would also kill him. All you have available are machines producing rays that can destroy tumours; however, rays at sufficient intensity to do this will also destroy surrounding healthy tissue, and that will kill the patient too. How can you save him?

As Holland et al. (1986) argue, this problem is relatively ill-defined: you need some information that may suggest more specific operators to get you from the initial state (a life-threatening tumour) to the solution state (the threat removed). Gick and Holyoak had subjects read a story before attempting the tumour problem; one concerned the efforts of a general to capture a fortress in the middle of a country. If you are stuck on the tumour problem, see if this will help suggest a solution.

> Many roads led out from the fortress. Each road was mined so that only small groups of people could travel over them safely. However, the general needed all his forces to capture the fortress. The general decided to split his army and send small groups down each of the roads so that they converged at the fortress.

The solution to the tumour problem is to use several weak rays that can pass through the healthy tissue without damaging it, but converge on the tumour and so destroy it. Gick and Holyoak found that about 10% of subjects solved the tumour problem without an analogical story; that about 40% did so when they read the fortress story beforehand; but that almost 80% did so when they were given the story with a hint that it might be useful in solving the tumour problem. Thus, there is an interesting contrast between people's *use* of analogical information once it has been seen as useful, and their ability to see it as *relevant* in the first place.

Several investigations into analogical thinking have been reported since Gick and Holyoak's pioneering work. It is possible to survey them (as several recent authors have done, e.g. Keane, Ledgeway, & Duff, 1994; Reeves & Weisberg, 1994; Spellman & Holyoak, 1996) and pull out what they say in common about the process. All posit a series of stages, and most are agreed on what those stages comprise.

First, you have to *represent* the target problem in some way, and you must also have some representation of the source domain. How this is done can affect the likelihood of finding a solution (Keane et al., 1994). Second, you have to *retrieve* a useful source analogue, such as the solar system when thinking about atomic structure. This stage can be separated into processes of activating a set of potential source analogues, then selecting one for relevance to the target problem (Reeves & Weisberg, 1994). Third, the source analogue is *applied* to the target problem. This is called analogical mapping, and is the process that is unique to analogical thinking. Keane et al. break this stage into two subprocesses: matching the corresponding concepts in the two domains, and transferring part of the structure of the source to the target. Fourth, there is increasing evidence for *schema induction* (a type of inductive generalisation; see earlier) as a result of the mapping process and that this in turn influences the chance of solution.

Successful analogical thinking involves going beyond the surface attributes of the two domains and recognising deeper, structural relations between them, as the tumour and fortress examples illustrate: they are utterly different in content, and yet you can recognise that in both cases the problem is solved by a general method of splitting and converging forces. Surface details, on the other hand, play a role in invoking potential source analogues, although surface-level similarities become less important the more you know about the target domain (Reeves & Weisberg, 1994).

Structure- and exemplar-based explanations

Two types of theory have been put forward to account for the transfer of information between domains in analogical thinking. First, there are what might be called "deep" theories, i.e. those that emphasise the role of mapping between higher level (i.e. below-surface) features of the source and target. The two dominant approaches are the "pragmatic" or constraint-based view developed by Holyoak and his associates (e.g. Holland et al., 1986; Spellman & Holyoak, 1996), and the structure-mapping theory of Gentner and colleagues (e.g. 1983). Holyoak's theory is based on the notions of constraint satisfaction and schema abstraction.

Constraint satisfaction is a principle that guides processing through the degree to which certain abstract elements in the problem are matched or not. Holyoak picks out three types of constraint; the degree to which each is satisfied determines mapping between source and target. First, there is the structural constraint: mapping will occur when target and source domains have either the same or a consistent structure. Second, there is the semantic similarity constraint: mappings will be favoured when source and target share elements that mean similar things. Keane (1987) found that the tumour problem was solved more often by subjects given a medical source story than by those given the structurally similar fortress story. Third, there is the pragmatic centrality constraint: mapping will be easier when, for instance, the goals expressed in the source and target are the same, as they are in the tumour and fortress example.

Schema induction occurs when a number of analogues have been encountered: you will then be able to abstract the principles common to each. When a new problem arises, it will share features with this schema which in turn will enable the schema to be retrieved and used to suggest a solution, so analogical thinking should be facilitated by either the induction or the provision of a schema. This view, not surprisingly, is very similar to Cheng and Holyoak's (1985) account of deductive reasoning, which was reviewed in Chapter 5.

Gentner's model also deals with the transfer of structural relations between the source and the target, but gives less of a role to pragmatic factors, after the retrieval stage, than does Holyoak's theory. For Gentner, surface elements are those such as individuals and objects (e.g. "general", "tumour") and their attributes (e.g. "famous", "lethal"). Structural elements are divided into first-order (e.g. "converge") and higher-order (e.g. "cause", as in converging of forces causes capture of fortress). Source and target can match at any level, but matches at the highest level will be favoured. Structural matches will therefore tend to emerge, as opposed to matches on the basis of surface elements. Thus, pragmatic and surface problem elements will fall away in terms of their influence on thinking as structure-mapping proceeds.

Reeves and Weisberg (1994) point out a problem with these "deep" approaches: in order for below-surface similarity relations to be induced, thinkers must already have some idea of what the deeper properties of the target are, and if they do, they are some way towards a solution already, and so have less need of a source analogue! One way around this is to put less emphasis on structure, which is what exemplar theories do.

Exemplar theories hold that analogical transfer is based on specific experiential knowledge. Ross (1987) put forward such a theory, based on the idea that target problems are solved to the extent that the solver is reminded of particular, similar episodes from experience. Similarity can be based on surface or structural features. Ross's view is that general knowledge about problems is always bound up with particular knowledge about problem content. However, schema abstraction is still possible, although Ross proposes that this occurs strategically, not automatically, i.e. you have to do it deliberately. A prediction of this view is that analogical thinking will be best promoted when a schema is given along with contextual information rather than by itself, and there is evidence that this does happen (Ross, 1987), which the Holyoak and Gentner theories cannot explain. There is a role for expertise in this process: people seem to rely on surface details less as their expertise increases (Gentner & Toupin, 1986).

As so often happens in highly active research areas, we have here a number of apparently different explanations all of which have some merit. It will not surprise you then to find out that Reeves and Weisberg have suggested a hybrid theory of analogical thinking, combining the strengths of all three approaches I have summarised. They point to the Ross theory's invocation of episodic memory and hence its ability to account for content and context effects; to the Holyoak theory and its detailed account of schema induction and the role of pragmatic factors such as goals; and to the Gentner theory's account of the forms of structure mapping and hence its central place for the influence of expertise.

Summary

1. Inductive thinking was generally defined as "any process of thought yielding a conclusion that increases the semantic information in its initial observations or premises". Semantic information was in turn defined as equivalent to the number of possible states of affairs a proposition rules out as false.
2. Basic forms of induction are general induction and specific induction, and each can be either descriptive or explanatory. General

induction can be classed as instance-based or condition-simplifying, with most psychological work concerned with the former.

3. Instance-based generalisation (going from observed items to general rules) depends critically on (i) available knowledge of the relative proportions of items that are consistent and inconsistent with a rule, and (ii) perceived variability of the reference class for the items. Specific induction has been relatively little explored by psychologists, with the most extensive treatment given by mental model theory.

4. General induction is related to categorisation. Research has concentrated on how categories are induced, how category membership is decided, and how categories are used to make inferences (category-based induction). Contemporary views of category formation reject the notion of common elements for members in favour of some form of prototype theory.

5. Category-based induction is where a judgement of confidence is made about an argument where premises typically concern information about properties of category members, and the conclusion concerns other members, or the category as a whole. Most of the research has used "blank" properties, those of which the person has minimal knowledge, although non-blank properties have been addressed more recently.

6. Three views of category-based induction have emerged: (i) the similarity-coverage model, based on perceived similarity between premise and conclusion categories and higher-level common categories; (ii) the featural model, based on the number of features shared by premise and conclusion categories; and (iii) the Bayesian optimal model, which construes category-based induction as an inference about the range of properties.

7. In analogical induction, information from a source domain is used to suggest a solution to a problem in a target domain. Major research questions are how source domains are selected, and how information is transferred from the source to the target (the mapping process). Explanations of the mapping process divide between structure-based and exemplar-based approaches, with one recent review proposing a hybrid theory containing elements of both.

Judging probability 8

Everyone judges probabilities, and does so every day. You may find yourself wondering how likely it is to rain tomorrow, whether the fact that you have sneezed twice in the last 10 minutes means you have got a cold coming, or if you will be likely to meet a friend if you go to Murphy's Bar on Friday evening. This kind of thinking is an aspect of inductive reasoning: you are going further than the information given to produce a conclusion that, although plausible, is not guaranteed to be true. The preceding chapter showed how some inductive tasks indeed ask explicitly for judgements of probability, e.g. of argument strength. Sometimes our judgements of probability are not so explicit.

As with the study of deductive reasoning, it is possible to link the judgements people make with those which a formal system tells them they should make. The scientific problems associated with this research strategy are just the same: we shall see shortly that there have been some deep arguments concerning how we should characterise supposed deviations from normative conclusions, and whether the right norms have been assumed in the first place.

The particular branch of probability theory that is most commonly invoked in this area is Bayesian theory. We have already seen how Bayes' rule has been applied in other areas (see Chapters 5 and 7), and we shall return to it here. The specific formula set out in this chapter looks slightly different, but is in principle the same as the one used before.

Research on judgement has been dominated by the work of Kahneman, Tversky, and their associates (see Kahneman et al., 1982, for a survey of their early work). They have introduced a series of classic experiments that, like Wason's tasks in other fields, have largely determined how the research has been done. They have also raised important issues for investigation, and provided a theory to explain the findings. The theory has come in for sustained attack in recent years.

We shall begin with a brief account of how, in principle, probabilities can be worked out, focusing on the Bayesian formula for doing so. We shall then look at the research issues, and see how the various psychological theories account for their associated findings.

Probability and Bayes' rule

Probability means different things to different people—it even means different things to different probability theorists. There are three theoretical ways to express the idea of probability: as logical possibility, as frequency, or as degree of belief (Baron, 1994a).

Possibilities, frequencies, and beliefs

The logical theory really only applies to objectively unbiased situations such as true games of chance. For instance, the probability of there being an ace at the top of a properly shuffled deck of cards is 4 (the number of aces) in 52 (the number of cards in total), or 1 in 13. That has to be the case given the nature of the situation and the numbers of the various possibilities. As you may know, probabilities are usually expressed as numbers in the range 0 (for an event that is certain not to happen) to 1 (for an event that is certain to happen). So the probability of an ace would be written as .077: 1 divided by 13.

It is possible to work out more complex probabilities from this principle. What is the probability that the card will be an ace or a king? Because the two categories are exclusive (the card cannot be both an ace and a king), you have exactly twice the chance, so you add the two probabilities together: the answer is 2 in 13, or .154. What about the chances of drawing an ace and then a king? For this, you have to take into account both the chance of drawing an ace, written p(A), which is .077, and the chance of drawing a king given that you have drawn an ace, written p(K | A), which is also .077, as there are also four kings in the pack. You do this by multiplying the two numbers together, and this gives a probability of .006: a very slim chance.

This is how you can work out your chances of winning a lottery. The British National Lottery, for instance, asks you to select six numbers from the set 1–49, with no repetitions. The chance of your first one being drawn is therefore 1 in 49. The chance of your second one is 1 in 48, as the first is no longer available, and so on. Multiplying all these probabilities gives the combined probability of your six numbers coming up in that order, but of course, order does not matter, so you have to divide this number by the number of possible orders in which your six may be selected: this is 6 x 5 x 4 x 3 x 2 x 1. The odds calculation can therefore be expressed like this:

$$\frac{1/49 \times 48 \times 47 \times 46 \times 45 \times 44}{6 \times 5 \times 4 \times 3 \times 2 \times 1}$$

The result yields odds of 1 in just under 14 million (use cancelling if you want to work it out yourself, otherwise the top line will probably defeat your calculator): you can therefore expect all 6 winning numbers to come up, if you play once a week, i.e. 52 times a year, about every quarter of a million years. In fact you can win smaller amounts for picking 3, 4, or 5 correct numbers, and there is a "bonus" number as well; see if you can work out the odds for these combinations. And of course I am omitting the expected value of the gamble, where the size of the win as well as its likelihood must be taken into account in deciding whether to play; see the next chapter.

The lottery example gives some hints as to the other formal ways of viewing probability: as frequency or as degree of belief. Probability for frequency theorists simply means how often something has happened as a proportion of how often it could have happened. For instance, when it is said that your chances of dying in a plane crash are far lower than your chances of dying on the journey to the airport, the claim is based on the relative numbers of deaths per mile travelled in aircraft compared to other forms of transport. So the frequentist's way of telling you your chance of winning next week's lottery jackpot would depend on counting how often it has been won before, compared to the total number of bets.

The idea of probability as degree of belief allows, obviously, a role for individual judgement. Horse-race odds are a common example: here, bookmakers assign numerical odds based on a variety of information. Obviously, logical possibility is not one of them: a horse race is not a truly random, unbiased event—you cannot even be sure that any of the horses will finish (I once watched a race in which all the horses fell). The bookies will take into account the horses' form, i.e. their performance in past races—that is frequency information; they will also look at their breeding, the conditions of the racecourse, the form of the jockeys and trainers, and so on. They will also quote you odds on events such as the capture of the Loch Ness monster, or Elvis Presley being found alive. Clearly, these odds cannot be based on logical possibilities or frequencies.

Bayes' rule

Assigning a number to a degree of belief can be done purely formally: the technique for combining information in order to do this is Bayes' rule. This rule enables both frequency and judgemental information to be included in a computation of probability. It therefore provides a ready normative system for probability judgement, i.e. a system that tells you what judgements you should ideally make. In this respect, it is comparable to the role of logic in deductive reasoning, and from that comparison one psychological research strategy suggests itself straight away: we can explore the extent to which people conform to Bayesian norms in their judgements.

First, an account of how Bayes' rule can be used formally to deliver a probability number. You have already seen a version of the rule in Chapters 5 and 7, so you may recall that the essential computation is of the probability that a hypothesis is correct, given some evidence. We have some *prior knowledge* about the chance of the hypothesis being true, and this can be combined with information about the *likelihood* of the evidence, or data, given this hypothesis and the alternative hypotheses. In the present context, there is only one alternative: that our hypothesis is not true.

In Table 8.1 you will see how this rule can be worked through to yield a number expressing how probable the hypothesis is, in the face of some new data, using an example adapted from Baron (1994a). Suppose you would like to meet a particular person, Sharon, and you think she may be in Murphy's Bar on Friday night: that is your hypothesis, H. From previous experience, you know she is there most Fridays: about 80%. This is your prior probability that she will be there, written p(H). You walk to Murphy's and look through the window. From where you are standing, you can see exactly half of the bar. She is not in that half. That is the data, D. What is the probability that Sharon is in Murphy's bar?

If your hypothesis is true, i.e. that she is in the bar somewhere, the probability that you will not see her, written p(D|H), is, of course, .5: only half the bar is visible. The probability of the data given the alternative hypothesis, that she is not there at all, is p(D|¬H). This must be 1: if she is simply not there, she certainly will not be in the visible half. We combine the first of these probabilities with the prior probability, and compare this with the likelihood of the data (that you cannot see her)

TABLE 8.1

Bayes' rule for calculating probability judgements, and a worked example

$$p(H|D)= \frac{p(D|H) \times p(H)}{[p(D|H) \times p(H)] + [p(D|\neg H) \times p(\neg H)]}$$

Sharon goes to Murphy's bar on Fridays about 80% of the time: $p(H)$ is .8, and $p(\neg H)$ is .2.

You look through a window which shows half the bar and she's not there; $p(D|H)$ is therefore .5, whereas $p(D|\neg H)$ is 1.

$$p(H|D) = \frac{.5 \times .8}{[.5 \times .8] + [1 \times .2]} = \frac{.4}{.4 + .2} = .67$$

given the two alternative hypotheses. The resulting computation, which you can follow in Table 8.1, yields a *posterior* probability, p(H|D), of .67. Thus, the posterior probability is lower than the prior, which was .8: seeing she is not in the visible half has made you revise your estimate downwards. However, Sharon is still more likely than not (i.e. the probability is greater than .5) to be in the bar. As to whether you go in, that is up to you. We shall deal with decision making in the next chapter.

Bayes' rule is a powerful instrument in providing a formal way of deciding the probability of events, because it can take into account information from a number of sources. All you need are some numbers to represent the probabilities of H, ¬H and D. In this example, the prior estimate of H is based on a frequency, but it could just as well have come from an estimate of the probability of a single event: a mutual friend could have said that there is an 80% chance that Sharon will be in the newly opened Murphy's on Friday. This particular issue, of how people may cope with information about frequencies and single events, has become a live one recently, and we shall look at it later. For now, we shall address the more general psychological question: that of the extent to which people's actual judgements conform to the Bayesian norms.

We shall begin with a topic that goes right to the heart of the question of the extent to which people can, and should, be considered natural Bayesians: the use of base-rate information.

The base-rate fallacy

Base-rate information is generally the kind of information you should take account of in estimating a prior probability, p(H). As the name implies, it usually takes the form of frequency information, as when you estimate the prior probability that Sharon will be in Murphy's Bar on previous experience of her Friday night social habits. The idea that people may have a problem with this kind of information was raised by Kahneman and Tversky (1972, 1973). These authors have been responsible for an enormous research programme devoted to questions of human judgement, and this is one of their best-known cases. As with many of their ideas, it is linked to a famous problem that has been given to hundreds of experimental subjects around the world. It is called the taxicab problem.

> A taxi is involved in a hit-and-run accident at night. In the city, there are two taxi firms, the Green Cab Company and the Blue Cab Company. Of the taxis in the city 85% are Green and the rest are Blue.

A witness identifies the offending cab as Blue. In tests under
similar conditions to those on the night of the accident, this
witness correctly identified each of the two colours 80% of
the time, and was wrong 20% of the time.
What is the probability that the taxi involved in the accident
was in fact Blue?

As with most of the problems in this book, it will help greatly if you
have a go at it before reading on.

Here is the answer, using Bayes' rule. We want to work out the
probability that the cab was Blue, given that the witness said it was Blue,
i.e. p(H|D). The prior probability that it was Blue is .15, because only
15% of the city's cabs are Blue. The witness's testimony constitutes the
data, D. This person was 80% accurate. So we need to compare the
probability that when he says Blue it really is, taking into account that
only 15% of the city's cabs actually are Blue, and that when the cab is
Green he will say it was Blue on 20% of occasions as he is only 80%
accurate, and the great majority of the city's cabs are Green. In Table
8.2 you can see how these numbers are put into Bayes' rule. The outcome
is that p(H|D), the probability that the cab was Blue given that the
witness said it was, is .41. Note that this is less than .5, so it is actually
more likely that the cab was in fact Green!

Do not console yourself that this kind of thinking is just a
preoccupation of experimental psychologists: it underlies some vital
real-world judgements, such as medical diagnosis and jury verdicts.
Here is an imaginary case of medical diagnosis, adapted from Eddy
(1982). Your old friend Clyde has been listening to news stories about
skin cancer caused by sunburn, and has noticed a large new mole on
his arm. He goes to the doctor, who decides to test him for skin cancer.
She tells him that in people who have cancer, the test shows positive in

TABLE 8.2

Bayesian solution to the taxicab problem

What is the probability that a taxi involved in an accident was Blue?
85% of the city's cabs are Green and the rest, 15%, are Blue: p(H) is .15 and p(¬H)
is .85.

The witness is accurate 80% of the time and mistaken 20% of the time:
$p(D|H)$, that the witness says Blue when the cab was Blue, is therefore .8, and
$p(D|¬H)$, that he says Blue when the cab was Green, is .2.

Using Bayes' rule from Table 8.1:

$$p(H|D) = \frac{.8 \times .15}{[.8 \times .15] + [.2 \times .85]} = \frac{.12}{.12 + .17} = \frac{.12}{.29} = .41$$

90% of cases; in people who do not have cancer, the test shows positive, falsely, in 20% of cases. People with new moles like Clyde's are found actually to have cancer 1% of the time, and to be clear 99% of the time. His test comes out positive. What is the probability that Clyde has skin cancer? Give your intuitive answer before reading on.

The prior probability—the base rate—that he has the disease, p(H), is .01; the probability of the data (a positive test) given that he has cancer, p(D|H), is .9, and the probability that the test will be positive although he is clear, p(D|¬H), is .2. You should now be able to apply Bayes' rule, just as in the cab problem. If you work through it (which will be a very useful exercise), you will find that the chance that Clyde has cancer, given his positive test result, is .043, i.e. a chance of just over 4%. In other words, it is highly likely that he does not have skin cancer at all, even though his test was positive.

If you found these calculations hard to follow, and the conclusions hard to believe, don't worry, because in the section on frequency formats later, I shall show you a method for working out p(H|D) that most people find much easier. You had better hope that your doctors have a clear understanding of how to use probabilistic information when they make their diagnoses.

When Tversky and Kahneman (1982a) ran the taxi problem in an experiment, they found that their subjects also seemed to find it hard to follow, that is, few of them came up with the right answer, or anything like it. Most of them said that the probability that the cab was Blue was .8. This is simply the figure for the witness's reliability, i.e. p(D|H), and so it seems from this and similar studies that people ignore base-rates, hence the name, the base-rate fallacy. Eddy (1982) uses real medical data in his examples, and provides some rather troubling evidence that doctors fall prey to the same sorts of error in making their estimates that subjects do in psychological experiments: doctors also tended to give a figure close to p(D|H) when asked to estimate p(H|D).

Not surprisingly, such results have generated a lot of interest. First, we shall look at Kahneman and Tversky's explanation for the apparently non-Bayesian performance of their subjects, and then at some recent literature raising further questions about the base-rate fallacy and its interpretation. After that, we shall review some related aspects of judgement research.

Heuristics and the base-rate fallacy

Tversky and Kahneman (1982a) found that subjects were less likely to ignore the base-rate information in the taxicab problem (and similar problems) when the task was modified in one of two ways. If the information about the witness's reliability was *left out*, then most subjects gave a figure of .15 for the probability that the cab was Blue: this, of course, is just the base rate information. Thus, when base rate was the only information available, the subjects used it and it became "diagnostic" (cf. Chapter 6). More interestingly, Tversky and Kahneman also found that judgements were influenced by base-rate when the relevance of this information was enhanced by making it *causal*. This was done by stating that "85% of cab *accidents* in the city involve Green cabs and 15% involve Blue cabs" (1982, p. 157; emphasis added). With this information, subjects' average $p(H|D)$ estimate was .60, still some way above the Bayesian answer, but below the typical "fallacy" response, showing that base rates had had some influence on estimates.

Tversky and Kahneman distinguish between causal and *incidental* (non-causal) base rates, and go on to suggest that base rates that are seen as incidental are ignored. This is a form of relevance hypothesis, which we saw applied to deduction in Chapters 4 and 5. The other side of this explanation is that people will base their judgemental estimates not on an attempt to integrate all the information, as Bayes' rule dictates, but on a simpler assessment: of the degree to which the sample in question is representative of the class to which it has been compared. In the taxicab problem, people would therefore be using the witness's reliability as the sole index of how representative the case (a Blue cab) was of the cabs involved in accidents.

Rather disturbingly, this aspect of representativeness has been shown to reflect prejudiced thinking. Hewstone, Benn, and Wilson (1988) translated the taxicab problem, using exactly the same numbers, into a problem about burglary said by a witness to have been committed by a white or black youth, with the base rates of white and black youths given either for living in the area (i.e. incidental base rates) or for committing burglaries (causal base rates). Base-rate information was completely ignored by the (white) subjects in the incidental condition, and used in the causal condition, but used differentially between judgements concerning whether the burglar was likely to be white or black: $p(H|D)$ was given as .21 and .60 respectively. Note that the first figure is some way below the Bayesian result, which is .41, of course. Base-rate information seems, as Hewstone et al. put it, to have been used (indeed modified) to "exonerate" the white suspect but not the black suspect.

Representativeness is known as a *heuristic*: a useful but inexact method of forming judgements. In certain circumstances, such as the taxicab and diagnosis problems, such heuristics can lead to *biases*, in this case, the under-weighting of base-rate information. Thus, the approach to judgement associated with Tversky and Kahneman is often tagged the "heuristics and biases" approach. Representativeness is said to be in operation when you evaluate the probability of an uncertain event or a sample by assessing either (i) the degree to which it is essentially similar to its parent population, or (ii) the degree to which it reflects salient features of the process by which it was generated (Tversky & Kahneman, 1982b). The taxicab problem thus seems to rest on the second of these kinds of judgement: people expect a generally reliable process, eyewitness testimony, to lead to a specifically likely outcome.

The first kind of representativeness, based on similarity, has also been explored, and again has been linked to other supposed fallacies in judgement. We shall go into these after we have considered some alternative perspectives on the base-rate fallacy.

Base rates reconsidered

Koehler (1996) gives a wide-ranging review and critique of research on the base-rate fallacy, and his paper is accompanied by nearly 30 commentaries from other scientists. His overall conclusion is that "We have been oversold on the base-rate fallacy ... from an empirical, normative, and methodological standpoint" (p. 1). Let us look briefly at each of these areas.

Koehler makes a point that has often been made about how research is summarised by reviewers: that secondary sources sometimes over-simplify the outcomes of large research programmes. He gives several examples of where reviewers claim that base rates are generally ignored, and calls such claims "dreadfully misleading" (p. 3). He presents data from several studies showing that results from base-rate studies are not consistent: some show a greater degree of base-rate neglect than others, even using the same problem. Although it is hard to say why there is this variation, Koehler points to some factors which do reliably seem to induce subjects to take account of base rates.

As with the use of a causal context (see earlier), the general effect of these factors seems to have been to increase the perceived relevance of the base-rate information. For instance, if subjects are given several forms of a problem in which the base-rate information is varied, they tend to take more account of it: its variability seems to act as a cue to its relevance. Similarly, people take more account of the base rate when they have to learn it for themselves, rather than when they are simply given it, as they are in the earlier examples. Reassuringly, in view of Eddy's work, Christensen-Szalanski and Beach (1982) reported that doctors who learned the relationship between base rates of disease and test results from their clinical experience were strongly influenced by base rates when making diagnoses. A third way of inducing base-rate influence, frequency presentation (which may be similar to what is happening with learning base rates by experience), will be dealt with later in a separate section.

There are several aspects to the normative issue. In general, the question is whether human performance is being compared with the right kind of norms: are the prescriptions of Bayes' rule really the standard to which we should aspire? One problem is deciding just what the appropriate base rate actually is. This is a version of the *reference-class* question, which was mentioned in Chapters 4 and 7. Consider the taxicab problem. What is the appropriate reference class from which to take the base rate: cabs in the city, cabs in the city at night, cabs in accidents, cabs in accidents at night? Or the skin cancer diagnosis: is the reference class people in general, people around Clyde's age, males, 25-year-old males with light skin who had severe sunburn within the last year? There is in principle an infinite range of reference classes: you could end up with one just called Clyde. Cohen (1981) argued that base rates ought to be ignored in cases where the reference class was not clearly relevant, but it is difficult, if not impossible, to decide on which is the most relevant reference class; the best that can be said is that some are more relevant than others, e.g. those that preserve a causal relation to the case in hand, such as "cabs in accidents" versus just "cabs".

More fundamentally, there are problems over whether Bayes' rule can, or should, really be applied to human judgement. For instance, base rates and prior probabilities are often treated as if they are the same, but they may not be. People may not encode base-rate information accurately in memory, as when they typically over-estimate the probability of rare causes of death and under-estimate common causes (Slovic, Fischhoff, & Lichtenstein, 1980). They may take other information into account when assigning priors, as in the case of bookmakers with horse-race odds (see earlier), or parents choosing a school for their child: the number of exam passes is a base rate, but a lower rate may be due to the school's having to work with a more challenging intake, and may indicate that this school provides more "added value" to its pupils than the apparently more successful one.

As a result of these and other observations, Koehler (1996), besides arguing that evidence for the base-rate fallacy should be treated cautiously, makes a positive case for a more "ecological" approach to studying human judgement, using methods that depend less on laboratory tasks and more on real-world situations, so that patterns of base-rate use and neglect can be detected. It is hard to argue with this conclusion, although it returns us to the oldest dilemma in psychology: the trade-off between the rigour of the laboratory and the realism of the outside world.

Representativeness and other biases

One of the strengths of Kahneman and Tversky's heuristic theory is that it can predict results in a wide range of tasks. We saw earlier that the representativeness heuristic can be invoked not only by the extent to which a sample reflects the process that produced it, but also by the extent to which a sample seems similar to a class. Resulting biases are not only reflected in the base-rate fallacy. Another famous case can be illustrated by the Linda problem, which was set out in Chapter 1.

A brief personality description was given of Linda, as follows:

> Linda is 31 years old, single, outspoken, and very bright. She majored in philosophy. As a student, she was deeply concerned with issues of discrimination and social justice, and also participated in anti-nuclear demonstrations.

You are asked to choose from a number of possible alternative additional properties of her. Among these is that she is a feminist, a bank clerk, and a bank clerk who is a feminist. If you think that Linda is more likely to be a feminist bank clerk than just a bank clerk, then you have committed a logical error known as the *conjunction fallacy*. It simply cannot be the case that a conjunction of two properties is more probable that either one alone; the most that can happen is that the conjunction is equally likely. Thus there will almost certainly be more bank clerks than feminist bank clerks, because there are bank clerks who are not feminists (probably). There cannot be more guard dogs than just dogs.

Tversky and Kahneman (1983) present a series of investigations of the conjunction fallacy. With the Linda problem, she was seen as most likely to be just a feminist. However, some 89% of subjects reckoned that she was more likely to be a feminist bank clerk than a bank clerk. The error persisted even when Tversky and Kahneman resorted to what they describe as "increasingly desperate manipulations" aimed at reducing it, such as giving only the two critical alternatives, bank clerk and feminist bank clerk, for subjects to evaluate. The fallacy was committed in a variety of domains, not just those involving imaginary Linda-type characters. For instance, doctors given a brief description of a patient's condition thought it more likely that the patient would have a rare and common symptom together than that she would have just the rare symptom; students thought it more likely that Bjorn Borg would lose the first set and win the 1981 Wimbledon final than that he would lose the first set; and so on.

As with the base-rate research, several theorists have questioned whether a fallacy is truly being committed in these studies. For instance, Politzer and Noveck (1991) point to a possible linguistic interpretation of subjects' behaviour on the Linda problem. Using the Gricean maxim of quantity (that people aim to give not too much or too little information when they communicate, and will be assumed to do so; cf. Chapter 2), they argue that there is a hidden *implicature,* that has been ignored by Tversky and Kahneman in the item "Linda is a bank clerk", when it is set alongside the item "Linda is a bank clerk who is active in the feminist movement". Politzer and Noveck argue that the first item will imply to subjects that "Linda is a bank clerk and not a feminist", which, given the "radical" personality description, will be seen with some justice as less likely than that she is a feminist bank clerk; and there will also be no conjunction fallacy, because the implicit sentence also introduces a conjunction.

To test this, they used a modified Borg-type problem in which the conjunction of two aspects of a person could be stated implicitly or explicitly, as in the following example:

> In high school, Daniel was always good at maths and science. He likes human contact, he has a strong sense of helping others, and he is very determined. Here are some statements regarding Daniel's studies:
>
> (Implicit condition)
> He entered Medical School
> He dropped out of Medical School for lack of interest
> He graduated from Medical School
>
> (Explicit version)
> He entered Medical School
> He entered Medical School and dropped out for lack of interest
> He entered Medical School and graduated

Obviously, you have to enter Medical School before you can drop out or graduate from it, and so sentence 1 should be seen as most likely. Politzer and Noveck argue that the Gricean implicature will be blocked in the implicit version because subjects will *not* see one sentence ("He entered Medical School") with a qualifier (e.g. "and graduated") and one without. However, in the explicit version the implicature will be reinstated, i.e. sentence 1 would be likely to be seen as implying "... and did not drop out/graduate". So there should be more instances of the conjunction fallacy, with sentence 1 being ranked less likely than sentence 2 or 3, in the explicit condition than in the implicit condition.

That was what they found: 31% of subjects committed the fallacy in the implicit condition compared with 53% in the explicit condition. Note that the latter figure is some way below that found with Linda-type problems: Politzer and Noveck argue that this is because their material made the inclusion relation more salient (i.e. relevant). Dropping out of college clearly implies having entered in the first place, more than the possibility of being a feminist follows from being a bank clerk. Note also that this Gricean explanation does not explain why subjects only commit the fallacy in one direction: remember, most think that it is more likely that Linda is just a feminist than a feminist and a bank clerk. The conjunction fallacy only seems to operate with the non-representative value: Linda's job, or the rare symptom, or Borg (who had won Wimbledon five times in succession before 1981) losing a set.

More heuristics and biases

The theory that people use heuristic methods in judging probabilities is not, of course, restricted to one heuristic, representativeness. Kahneman and Tversky, and other researchers since, have set out other heuristics to explain further aspects of judgement, and the apparent biases that result from their use. We shall briefly look at three, in descending order of the research interest that they have attracted: availability, anchoring and adjustment, and numerosity. I shall not spend as much time on critiques of them, because the general idea of the kind of criticism the heuristics-and-biases school tends to attract should be fairly clear now. However, after this, we shall review the most sustained critique of the whole programme, which will involve some more detail about particular ideas and experiments.

Availability

Almost simultaneously with the representativeness heuristic, Tversky and Kahneman (1973, p.164) introduced the other for which they are best known, the availability heuristic. Their definition is as follows: "A person is said to employ the availability heuristic whenever he estimates frequency or probability by the ease with which instances or associations could be brought to mind." They go on to say that you do not actually have to perform this bringing-to-mind, just estimate how easy it would be to do so.

Strength of association can obviously come from frequency, as in rote memory tasks. The availability heuristic throws this relation into reverse: it uses strength of association as a cue to frequency, and thereby to probability. The subtlety in the theory comes from the fact that strength of association can derive from processes other than frequency; thus, our estimates of probability will be open to non-probabilistic influences, and hence bias.

Characteristically, Tversky and Kahneman give some striking and ingenious demonstrations of the effects of availability. Here is a selection. For each one, you should give your immediate, intuitive answer, not spend time with paper and pencil working the answer out.

(a) For the following five letters, say for each one whether they occur most often as the initial letter or as the third letter in English words: K, L, N, R, V.

(b) Quickly (within 5 seconds) write down your estimate, to the nearest 100, of the results of the following calculations:

8 x 7 x 6 x 5 x 4 x 3 x 2 x 1
1 x 2 x 3 x 4 x 5 x 6 x 7 x 8

(c) Consider these two structures:

A	B
x x x x x x x x	x x
x x x x x x x x	x x
x x x x x x x x	x x
	x x
	x x
	x x
	x x
	x x

A path is a line that connects an x in the top row to an x in the bottom row, passing through exactly one x in each row in between. In which of the two structures are there more paths?

Here are the formally correct answers.

(a) According to statistics, all of the five letters given are more common as third letters than as initial letters. If you thought any of them were more common as initial letters, you have done what availability says. Here, it is assumed that it is easier to "bring to mind" words in terms of their initial letters than their third letters (Scrabble players will agree), and so there is a tendency to over-estimate the frequencies in those terms.

(b) You may have already spotted the trick: both calculations result in the same answer. Tversky and Kahneman's subjects were in separate groups, each of which saw just one. For the first, their average estimate was 2250; for the second, it was 512. The real answer is 40,230! The availability effect here is due to the problem presentation: you read the numbers in left-to-right order, so in the first case the larger numbers are more available, whereas in the second case the smaller numbers are.

(c) Most people think there are more possible paths through structure A than structure B. In fact, there are equally many: 512. In A, there are eight columns and three rows. So each x in the top row can connect with 8 in the next row and 8 in the bottom row, i.e. 8 x 8 x 8, or 8^3. In B, each x in the top row can connect with 2 in the next row, and so on down to the bottom row, which is the ninth. Hence there are 2^9 possible paths. 8^3 and 2^9 both equal 512. The availability effect here is that the greater number of columns in A makes more possible paths apparent; similarly, paths are less likely to overlap in A than they are in B, hence they will be more distinctive.

You do not have to stay with such examples to demonstrate possible effects of availability: there are real-world cases too. For instance, Ross and Sicoly (1979) asked a group of husbands and wives to estimate, independently, each other's share of 20 household chores. Both the husbands and the wives thought that they had the greater share of 16 of the 20 chores; they cannot both be right. Ross and Sicoly give an availability explanation: one's own actions are easier to bring to mind than are those of others, even of a partner. You are always there when you do something, so you are bound to observe more of your own than another's actions, and in addition, you are likely to attach more significance to your own actions. Students conducting group assignments should be aware of this bias. There is a relation here with the Fundamental Attribution Error in social psychology: "the tendency to attribute behavior exclusively to the actor's dispositions, and to ignore powerful situational determinants" (Nisbett & Ross, 1980, p. 31). The "actor" here refers to other people; when explaining the causes of your own behaviour, however, you are more likely to invoke situational factors ("it wasn't my fault"). Clearly, such factors are more available to you yourself; you may not even be aware of your own dispositions.

Nisbett and Ross also draw a parallel with vividness of information. Information can be more or less vivid depending on a number of factors, such as concreteness, emotional interest, or proximity. Concreteness refers to the degree to which the information can be elaborated in memory, for instance by imagery. Thus "85-year-old Albert Hall's house was ransacked" is more concrete than "A house was burgled". Emotional interest is clearly related to this factor: Nisbett and Ross give degree of personal involvement as an important aspect of this. Imagine if Albert was your neighbour, or your grandfather. Proximity can be spatial (Albert lives in your street, or on the other side of town), temporal (Albert was burgled an hour ago, or last year), and sensory (you heard it happen, or you read it in the papers). Vividness may be one reason for the over-estimation of the frequency of rare events (Slovic et al., 1980; see earlier). By their nature, rare events are newsworthy, and so they tend to be over-represented by the news media. Air crashes always make the news, car crashes rarely, in proportion to the number that occur, so people over-estimate their likelihood of death by the former, and under-estimate the latter. Vividness may thus actually affect the frequency with which you encounter stories of such events, in addition to making them memorable for the above reasons.

Anchoring and adjustment

This is a heuristic tutors marking assessments should be aware of. When people are given a point along a scoring scale and asked to estimate another score on the same scale, they tend to under-adjust. That is, they give a lower score when their "anchor" point is low than they do when it is high. This happens even when the anchor is known to have been chosen completely by chance.

For example, Tversky and Kahneman (1974) report assigning a number between 0 and 100 by spinning a wheel of fortune. Subjects then had to estimate the number of African countries in the United Nations first by saying whether the number was higher or lower than the assigned random number, then by moving from that number to produce the estimate. Subjects whose assigned number was 10 gave an average estimate of 25; subjects whose assigned number was 65 gave an average estimate of 45. Similarly, Lichtenstein et al. (1978) found that people's judged probabilities of dying by various causes depended on the anchor they were given: e.g. 50,000 annual deaths by motor accidents, or 1000 deaths by electrocution. These were accurate figures for the United States at the time. Estimates by subjects given the smaller number were smaller for most other frequencies, e.g. for murder or heart disease, than they were for subjects given the larger number—sometimes by a factor of 5.

Whether anchoring is a distinct heuristic is debatable. Tversky and Kahneman (1974) give the multiplication problem (b in the section or Availability, p.178) as an instance of anchoring, but earlier gave it as an instance of availability, as we saw. Clearly the provision of an anchor makes a value available, but availability does not by itself predict the resulting under-adjustment. The base-rate fallacy could also be seen in this light: perhaps people "anchor" on the data and under-adjust for the base-rate (see Gigerenzer, 1996a, and later for more on ambiguity between heuristics). Anchoring is also related to the "framing" effect in decision making, which we shall review in the next chapter.

Numerosity

For once, this is a heuristic not introduced by Kahneman and Tversky. It was recently explored by Pelham, Sumarta, and Myaskovsky (1994). They point to evidence from some unlikely sources, such as the animal behaviour literature, for a tendency to over-infer quantity, i.e. the amount of something, from numerosity, i.e. the number of units into which that something is divided. Many animals have been found to work harder for food that has been divided into small pieces than for food that has not: the small pieces are more reinforcing. So if you want your fat cat to lose weight, chop up its food more finely: it will eat less of it. Clearly, numerosity is strongly correlated with quantity in the real world, but equally clearly, equating numerosity with quantity can lead to bias.

Do people also tend to think in this way? Do you think you have more chocolate in a bag of "fun-size" bars than in a single block of the same weight, or that dicing food is a useful slimming technique, or that you have more money in a bag of small coins than in one coin of equal value? It seems doubtful, because unlike animals, people have some high-level cognition at their disposal that can lead them to look beyond the surface properties of stimuli. However, Pelham et al. (1994) found that people indeed do seem to succumb to this bias under certain circumstances.

The main circumstance is when the task is made difficult. As an example, subjects were asked to estimate the area of a circle when it was whole, and when it was cut into slices, like a pizza. Estimates were higher for the pieces, and this bias was greater when the pieces were arranged in a straight line rather than in a circular pattern. The straight line makes it harder to see that the pieces actually comprise a circle.

Similarly, quick estimates of the results of calculations were higher when the sums contained many small elements than when they contained fewer large ones—the real results were, as in example (b) in the section Availability, the same in both cases. This finding only occurred in the difficult condition, when subjects had a simultaneous second task to perform. Interestingly, the anchoring and adjustment heuristic predicts that sums with larger units should lead to higher estimates. And yes, people asked to estimate the value of sets of coins did give higher estimates when there were many coins compared with fewer, even though the values of each set averaged the same; this effect was more pronounced with shorter inspection times.

In seems then as if difficult problems make it hard for us to use our higher-order processes, and we fall back on a crude numerosity = quantity heuristic, along with chickens and rats. It should be emphasised that, as with Kahneman and Tversky's heuristics, you should not conclude that use of heuristics such as numerosity inevitably leads to bias. In many, perhaps most, natural circumstances, their use will lead to usefully accurate estimates; in other words, such heuristics can be seen to be *adaptive*, in an evolutionary sense. Alternatively, as Pelham et al. (1994) remark, one can view their results in the easier conditions as showing how higher-level cognition can correct for bias. In the next section, we look at arguments against the whole idea that probability is estimated using heuristics.

Frequencies and a critique of heuristics and biases

At the start of this chapter, it was mentioned that probability can be considered in three ways: as logical possibility, degree of belief, or frequency. For a frequency theorist, probability is the number of times in which an event has occurred as a proportion of the number of times in which it could have occurred. Asking for a probability of a unique event, on this view, is simply nonsense, as by definition it has not occurred before.

That may be the formal situation, but we can also ask for the evidence that people in their ordinary lives, and in the versions of them explored in psychology experiments, adopt one or other conception of probability, Recently, there has been an upsurge of interest in research using frequency formats. The interest largely stems from the different view of human performance that has emerged (different from the heuristics and biases programme, that is), and what this different view implies for theories of human judgement.

Making biases disappear

I promised earlier in this chapter that I would show you an easy way to arrive at estimates of probability in tasks such as the taxicab and diagnosis problems. Here it is: turn the elements of the problems from proportions to frequencies. You should find the explanations of the answers much easier to follow, perhaps even obvious.

In the taxicab problem, imagine that there are 100 taxis in the city. You know that 85 are Green company cabs and 15 are Blue. The witness to the accident correctly identifies cab colour 80% of the time, and is wrong on the other 20%. Thus, out of the 15 Blue cabs, the witness will correctly say "blue" 12 times (80% of 15); but also, of the 85 Green cabs, the witness will wrongly call them "blue" 17 times (20% of 85). So he says "blue" 29 times but is right on only 12 of them: 12/29 is .41.

Now for Clyde's diagnosis. Imagine 1000 patients like Clyde. They are found to have cancer 1% of the time, but in 99% of cases they are clear. Thus, out of these 1000 patients, 10 will have cancer. The doctor's test gives a positive result 90% of time in patients who have cancer, but also gives a false positive result in 20% of patients who are clear. So out of the 10 patients who have cancer, 9 will show positive on the test, and out of the 990 patients who are clear, 198 will also show positive (20% of 990). So out of these 207 patients who show positive, how many actually have cancer? Nine; 9/207 is .043.

Why do frequency formats make judging probabilities so much easier? We shall look at the research on this question in the next section. Much of it has been conducted by Gigerenzer and his colleagues. Gigerenzer (1996b) sums up the information you need to derive the answers to problems such as these two examples: (i) number of cases where the report is correct, e.g. that have both the symptom and the disease, (ii) number of cases where the report is incorrect, e.g. that have the symptom but not the disease. The calculation thus reduces to:

$$p(H \mid D) = \frac{a}{a + b}$$

Experiments with frequency formats

We shall consider how frequency formats have led to some surprising findings with three well-known judgemental biases: the base-rate and conjunction fallacies, which you have met before, and overconfidence bias.

Base-rate problems

Cosmides and Tooby (1996) used various frequentist versions of diagnosis problems, similar to the one used earlier as an example. Previous research with the "standard" format, with information expressed as percentages or proportions, had found that people, even those with expertise in the field, tended to give $p(D|H)$ as the answer, i.e. just the reliability of the test, uninfluenced by base-rate information, with very few giving a "Bayesian" answer. When the problem was presented in frequency form, this pattern was reversed: now, most subjects (up to 92% when a graphical display was used) gave a "Bayesian" answer, and few gave just the reliability information. Some even over-weighted base rate and gave just the base-rate score as the answer. Frequentist presentation even helped when answers were required in single-event probability form, although to a lesser degree than when a frequency format was also allowed for the answer.

Gigerenzer and Hoffrage (1995) consider why frequency formats should produce higher levels of Bayesian reasoning in base-rate problems. One overall factor, which should be obvious from what we have seen earlier, is that these formats are computationally simpler: one only needs to compare a and a + b, instead of the complicated series of parts in the standard Bayesian formulae. A consequence of this view is that base rates can be rationally ignored: all you need to know in, for instance, the diagnosis problem are the absolute frequencies of a (patients with the disease who test positive) and b (patients without the disease who test positive). Gigerenzer and Hoffrage, along with Cosmides and Tooby, contend that frequency counting of this kind is natural, in an evolutionary sense: they call it *natural sampling*.

Revisiting the conjunction fallacy

Evidence that frequency formats can also lower, or even remove, the conjunction fallacy was first reported, surprisingly, by Tversky and Kahneman (1983), but they made little of it. The observation was first explored in detail by Fiedler (1988) and then Gigerenzer (1991). A conjunction task such as the Linda problem (see earlier and Chapter 1) can be turned into frequency form by asking subjects to assess how many of 100 people like Linda would be bank clerks or feminist bank clerks. Fiedler found that the number of subjects committing the conjunction fallacy fell to around 20% when this was done, compared to over 80% in Kahneman and Tversky's original report; the latter had found a similar effect, using a medical content.

Hertwig and Gigerenzer (in press) explain this finding by arguing that the standard format of the problem leaves open several possible interpretations of the term "probability", some of which are non-mathematical, such as "credible". Such interpretations will lead to the fallacy, because avoiding the fallacy depends on adopting a mathematical interpretation. Frequency formats, on the other hand, allow far less scope for such paraphrases, and more or less force people to adopt a mathematical interpretation. Hertwig and Gigerenzer present experimental evidence that backs up their case.

Overconfidence

Here are two questions (from Gigerenzer, 1993):

(i) Which city has more inhabitants: Hyderabad or Islamabad?

(ii) How confident are you that your answer is correct: 50%, 60%, 70%, 80%, 90%, 100%?

A 50% rating means that you are guessing; 100% means you are absolutely sure. Lichtenstein, Fischhoff, and Phillips (1982) found in a survey of the literature that there was a systematic *overconfidence* effect: on questions where subjects reported 100% confidence, they were actually correct about 80% of the time; when they reported 90% confidence, they were actually correct about 75% of the time; and so on. Pulford and Colman (1997) found that men tended to be more overconfident than women, thus confirming one popular stereotype.

Gigerenzer (1993; Gigerenzer, Hoffrage, & Kleinbölting, 1991), consistent with his reinterpretation of the base-rate and conjunction fallacies, argues that there is no bias in such results at all. This is because two kinds of information are being confused and compared: *single-event confidence* and *relative frequency*. Frequency theorists would argue that probability refers only to frequencies, and therefore has nothing to say about single events; hence it makes no sense to point to a difference between assessments of the two as indicating a bias.

Following this argument, Gigerenzer et al. (1991) presented subjects with 50 questions about city size, and asked subjects to give their confidence in each answer and to assess how many of their answers had been correct. If there were a bias due to some confidence heuristic, then there should have been evidence for overconfidence in both estimations, but frequentist theory predicts that the effect should disappear in the question about frequency of correct answers. That was exactly what they found; if anything, subjects under-estimated the number of correct answers.

The theory of Probabilistic Mental Models

To explain how it is that people make inductive inferences such as those about city sizes, Gigerenzer and colleagues introduced the theory of Probabilistic Mental Models, or PMMs (Gigerenzer, 1993; Gigerenzer et al., 1991; Gigerenzer & Goldstein, 1996). A PMM is a "frame of inference" that relates items to a reference class that contains the items. The target variable, i.e. the basis on which the items are being compared, is related to a set of cues that covary with it. Another city-size question, adapted from Gigerenzer and Goldstein, will show how this explanation works:

> Which city has more inhabitants: Duisburg or Mönchengladbach?

Suppose your answer is Mönchengladbach, and that you are fairly confident you are right: how did you come up with that answer? One of the possible cues you could use is whether a city has a team in the Bundesliga, the top German football (soccer) league. You may even be able to name the relevant team: Borussia Mönchengladbach; however, you cannot retrieve any knowledge of a team for Duisburg—there is none. In fact, whether a city has a team in the Bundesliga turns out to be a good predictor of its size: Gigerenzer and Goldstein found that, for all possible pairings of all German cities with more than 100,000 people, the city with a team in the Bundesliga was the biggest 87% of times, or .87. This value is known in PMM theory as the ecological validity. Each person has a corresponding mental representation of this called the cue validity; this may or may not, of course, accurately reflect the ecological validity.

However, what if there are two cities that do not have major football teams, or you simply do not know anything about football? Obviously, you will have to use another cue. Here is an example: which has the most people, Heidelberg or Herne? Neither has a Bundesliga team. If you said Heidelberg, you may well have used the same cue I did: you have heard of Heidelberg but not of Herne. This is known as the *recognition principle.* Assuming, as a frequentist would, that people's cue validities are reasonably well adapted, i.e. fairly close to the ecological validities, such cues can be fairly reliable. Availability could thus be seen as a cue in the PMM sense.

PMM theory can therefore explain not only why a frequency format makes overconfidence bias disappear, but also why there is a difference between confidence and frequency in the standard overconfidence experiments: different PMMs have to be constructed in each case. In the confidence task, the reference class is German cities, the target variable is city size, and the cues are ones such as football team or name recognition. If your cue validity matched the ecological validity for the football team cue, then you would expect confidence ratings of around 87%. In the frequency task, the reference class is "sets of similar questions in tests like this", the target variable is "number I have got right before", and the cue would be something like "base rate of previous performance". There will be a difference between this score and confidence scores when questions have been selected to be difficult, i.e. they are not a representative sample from the domain of knowledge in question. Of course, this is exactly what quiz-type questions are like: deliberately difficult.

PMM theory also makes several novel predictions, but I shall refer to just one, as it is the most surprising. It is called the *less-is-more effect*. Gigerenzer (1993) reports an experiment in which city-size questions about German cities were given to German subjects. The 75 largest German cities were used as materials. The subjects' accuracy on these questions was 75.6%. What would you predict would be the accuracy of the same subjects when asked the same questions about pairs of the 75 largest American cities? German subjects will know less about American cities, so you would probably expect that their accuracy would be lower. In fact, their accuracy was almost exactly the same: 76%. How is this possible? PMM theory does not say that you will use all the possible information in such a task, only that you will find the best cue and, if it seems to work, use it and no other. This is known as the *take-the-best* principle (Gigerenzer & Goldstein, 1996). We may assume that the only cue available to these subjects in the American condition was whether they had heard of a city or not. This cue is of high validity (about .90 in independent ratings): it predicts city size very well. Using it gives the same sort of score in this condition as does using another cue, such as the Bundesliga cue, in conditions in which the subjects have more knowledge. The point is that not all this knowledge is used.

By the way, Islamabad is smaller that both the Hyderabads, the one in Pakistan and the one in India. If you thought it was larger, you were probably using the "capital" cue—Islamabad is the capital of Pakistan. Duisburg is larger than Mönchengladbach, and Herne is larger than Heidelberg.

An intense debate

Gigerenzer's work has serious implications in two areas: ideas about human rationality, and the heuristics and biases research programme of Kahneman, Tversky, and their followers. We shall consider rationality in detail in the last chapter; to conclude this one, will shall take a brief look at the debate between the two rival theories we have focused on here.

Kahneman and Tversky have rarely responded to critics. They broke with this custom in 1996, just before Tversky's death, in a direct address to Gigerenzer's critique. Their paper is followed by a reply from Gigerenzer (1996a), and each has postscripts addressing the other's comments: it is a highly-charged exchange, as you might expect.

Kahneman and Tversky's (1996) main points of disagreement with Gigerenzer are on what they say are his misrepresentations of the heuristics and biases programme, and on the philosophical question of the norms against which people's judgements are compared. They point out, for instance, that they were first with a demonstration of a frequency effect in reducing the conjunction fallacy (see earlier, but, as we have seen and as Gigerenzer notes, little was made of this finding in the paper in which it was reported). Gigerenzer in turn accuses them of over-playing the idea that frequency formats always abolish the biases observed in heuristics and biases experiments: his work has specified conditions under which, say, overconfidence effects will be demonstrated, removed, or even inverted. There is a lot more in this vein, and it is clear that these crucial issues are far from settled.

More fundamentally, each party points to a separate difference of principle. For Kahneman and Tversky, it is the question of norms: they believe that there are norms for single-event judgements, whereas Gigerenzer allies himself to the frequentist position, and denies this. Gigerenzer is uncomfortable with appealing to the fact that ordinary people do assign probabilities to single events, e.g. in saying that there is a 30% chance of rain today: untutored intuitions do not constitute a normative theory of probability. He also argues that Kahneman and Tversky's norms are too narrow and neglect the ways in which people represent the information they are given.

Gigerenzer's central dispute is over research strategy. He condemns constructs such as availability and representativeness as "one-word explanations" that "lack theoretical specification" (1996a, p. 594). He argues on this basis that they can explain everything, and therefore nothing; we saw earlier how even supporters of heuristics can be unsure about which is said to be operating. His preferred research strategy is to set out a cognitive process theory (PMM theory is an example) which can be used to predict when and why probability judgements will be valid, and when "biases" will appear and disappear.

When debates become as intense as this, it is tempting to dismiss them as so much academic ping-pong, but you must not do so. There can be few more important questions about human mentality in the world at large, as well as in psychological theory, than whether judgement is or is not generally biased, and the conditions that may raise or lower such biases. Bear that in mind next time you see your doctor.

Summary

1. Judging probabilities can be considered in three ways: as logical possibility, as frequency, or as degree of belief. Bayes' rule enables both frequency and judgemental information to be included in a computation of probability.
2. Experiments on the base-rate fallacy have been used to illustrate how people can deviate from Bayes' rule by ignoring the prior probability of an event in favour of current evidence. However, there are several studies showing that Bayesian answers can be increased if base-rate information is made relevant.
3. Kahneman and Tversky have proposed that effects such as base-rate neglect arise because people use heuristics to derive their answers. The three main heuristics they propose are representativeness, availability, and anchoring and adjustment; others, such as numerosity, have also been proposed.
4. Several studies have challenged the heuristics and biases explanations. In particular, Gigerenzer and his colleagues have focused on the frequency interpretation of probability, and have argued that frequency formats can lead to the disappearance of apparent biases.
5. There is an intense and continuing debate between the schools of thought associated with Kahneman and Tversky and Gigerenzer, concentrating on the questions of theoretical norms and research strategies.

Decision making 9

In the preceding chapter, we examined some of the evidence regarding the ways in which people judge probabilities, and the sometimes intense debate this evidence has provoked. Judging probabilities may be interesting in itself, but it attracts extra interest because it has for a long time been acknowledged as central to a central human activity: making decisions. Thus, it may be interesting to see how people figure out whether someone will be in a certain place, or whether it will rain today, or what the odds are in a lottery, but it is even more interesting to see how they decide whether to go into the bar, cancel a picnic, or buy a ticket. Decision making thus fundamentally concerns combining information about probability with information about desires and interests: how much do you want to meet her, how important is the picnic, how much is the prize worth?

As with the other areas of thinking reviewed in this book, we can compare the kinds of decisions people actually make with those a normative system says they should make. When we find, as we usually do, that the two do not always coincide, a debate ensues as to how we may characterise the difference. The debate is just as vigorous in this area as in any other. We begin with the foundational normative theory of decision making, Subjective Expected Utility theory.

Subjective Expected Utility (SEU) theory

It is easy to confuse the idea of *utility* with similar ideas such as pleasure or value. Sometimes these terms do mean similar things, but sometimes they do not: utility refers to decision outcomes that are desirable, in the sense of being in your best interests. Something thus has utility for you if it helps you attain some goal you have. If you are ill and your goal is to get better, then having a certain treatment will have utility, but it might not be pleasant; and it might cost you money, but you would probably prefer having the treatment to keeping the money.

"Value" refers to money value (or some equivalent), and this idea is relevant because much of the initial work in the area came from economics. Since the 18th century, economic theorists have tried to explain the behaviour of buyers and sellers in terms of utility: the standard "economic man" is one who is assumed to be perpetually seeking to maximise utility. In the modern era, the major theoretical influences on the psychology of decision making have been von Neumann and Morgenstern (1944), who began the strategy of analysing decisions as if they were bets or gambles, and Savage (1954), who set out mathematically how to combine subjective utilities and subjective probabilities by analysing the *preferences* that people express. What is now standard SEU theory derives from the basic ideas of these theorists, and others, bundled together.

Principles of SEU theory

Treating decisions as if they were gambles is the basis of SEU theory. It means that we have to trade off the *utility* of a certain outcome (positive or negative) against its *probability*. It is easy to see how this can be done if you consider simple gambles such as betting on rolls of the dice, where money value and utility can be treated as the same. Imagine I have a pair of dice, and you place a bet of $1 on each throw (I use the $ sign to indicate "units of money"; it does not denote any particular currency.) If a pair of 2s, 3s, 4s, or 5s comes up, I will pay you $2; if you get a pair of 6s, I will pay you $5; and if you get "snake eyes"—a pair of 1s—I will pay you $10. If any other combination comes up, I keep the $1 stake.

We can work out the expected utility of each outcome from these figures. Take snake eyes: the utility of this outcome, in money value terms, is 10. The probability is 1/36, or .028 (there are six faces to each die, so there is a 1 in 6 chance of any one face showing; with two dice, the chance of the same two faces showing is 1/6 x 1/6, i.e. 1 in 36). The expected utility of this gamble is obtained by multiplying these two figures: 10 x .028 = .28. That is, for every $1 bet on snake eyes, you can expect to win $0.28 (in the long run). We can do the same for the other winning pairs: the expected utility of two 6s is 5 x .028 = .14; and for each other pair it is 2 x .028 = .056. The expected utility for this whole set of possible outcomes is computed simply by adding all these figures up. The general formula for doing this is:

$$SEU = \Sigma p_i U_i$$

The symbols have the following meanings: SEU; subjective expected utility; p, probability; U, utility; i, each outcome, and Σ, add. In words, the formula means that to calculate subjective expected utility, take each outcome, multiply its utility by its probability, then add all these results together.

So will you accept this bet? If you calculate total SEU, you will see that it comes to about .63: that is, for every $1 you stake, you can expect $0.63 back (another way of looking at it is to see that there are only 6 out of 36 possible dice rolls where I will pay you money—the six pairs; the total amount I will pay in the long run is $10 + $5 + (4 x $2) = $23 for every $36 stake money I receive). SEU theory thus tells you that this is a bad decision: you stand to lose more than you gain. Of course, that is true of all real-world gambles such as horse racing and lotteries, and yet people play them and their organisers make lots of money. This is one piece of evidence that tells us that, even in this simple situation, there is more to utility than money value. We will return to this point.

Using SEU as a means of telling you what you should do is to use it as a normative theory, in the same way that logic has been used in deduction. Some authors make a finer distinction between normative and prescriptive theories (see e.g. Baron, 1994a), although there have been questions about just what a prescriptive theory might consist of (Beyth-Marom, 1996). A normative theory tells us what we should do under ideal conditions. These ideal conditions must include the ability to perform the sorts of calculations outlined earlier. Clearly, this is unrealistic, especially when one considers that most of our everyday decisions are likely to be far more complex than rolling two dice.

Axioms of SEU theory

Certain underlying assumptions about decision making are made in proposing that people either do or should act according to SEU theory. These can be expressed as a set of axioms, all of which make intuitive sense. If a person keeps to these axioms, he or she will end up following the dictates of SEU theory, as von Neumann and Morgenstern (1944) showed.

The two most important axioms, for our purposes, are those known as *weak ordering* and *independence*. Weak ordering assumes that there is some relation between, say, the two outcomes you are trying to decide on. Call these O1 and O2: you must prefer O1 to O2, prefer O2 to O1, or be indifferent (i.e. have no preference); you cannot decide not to decide. This in turn means that preferences are transitive, hence ordered: if you prefer O1 to O2, and O2 to O3, then you must prefer O1 to O3. Given these conditions, we can then say that O1 is the option that has the highest utility for you.

The independence axiom states that if there is an outcome that occurs under all options, then your decision should not be affected by that outcome. So, for instance, if you are deciding which of two clubs to go to, and both close at the same time, then closing time should not be a factor in your decision. This principle leads to a further one, which Savage (1954) called the *sure thing principle*: that if you prefer O1 to O2 in every possible situation, then you should prefer O1 to O2 when you do not know what situation you are in. So, if you would rather go to Murphy's Bar than the Red Lion when Sharon is in Murphy's and also when she is not, you should prefer Murphy's when you do not know where she is.

These axioms and principles may well strike you as quite reasonable—obvious, even. However, you will not be surprised to learn that there are exceptions to them, both theoretical and empirical. In the next section, we shall therefore consider some problems SEU theory and its associated ideas have encountered. Later in the chapter, we shall consider how we may interpret these deviations.

Limits, deviations, and problems with SEU

I have already hinted at one of the problems with SEU theory, at least in using it as a descriptive theory of the kinds of decision making that people actually do: the theory asks too much of human cognitive capacities. To operate according to the canons of SEU requires us to undertake exhaustive computations of utilities and probabilities (and hence of the consequences of our choices, another issue we shall return to later). We saw in the preceding chapter that people may not always compute probabilities along the exact lines of the formal calculus of probability, so there is a problem straight away.

There are also problems concerning people's calculations of utility. Some of these take the form of "thought experiments", where the argument depends on your intuitions (as the founding principles of normative theories generally do), and some depend on experimental work. We shall look at three classic *paradoxes* of preference and choice, then at preference reversals and framing effects. They are all phenomena that should not happen under a strict application of SEU principles.

Three paradoxes

The oldest paradox was reported by the 18th-century mathematician Bernoulli, and is known as the St. Petersburg paradox, after the journal in which it appeared. It concerns the relation between value and utility, which we have already touched on. Suppose I toss a coin and tell you that if it comes down heads on the first throw, I will give you \$1; if it comes down heads on the second throw, I will give you \$2; \$4 if it comes down heads on the third throw; \$8 on the fourth; \$16 on the fifth; and so on. How much will you pay me for the chance to play this game? Bernoulli thought that a "fairly reasonable man" would sell his chance for $20, whereas Baron (1994a; p. 325) reports that most people he asked would pay no more than $3–4.

The paradox occurs because the expected value of this gamble is infinite. The expected value on the first throw is 1 (the value) x .5 (the probability of heads) = .5; on the second, it is 2 x .25 (the probability of a tails followed by heads is .5 x .5) = .5, and so on indefinitely— there is no telling when heads will show up. Why then are people reluctant to pay very much to play? Bernoulli appealed to the economic principle of diminishing marginal utility for the explanation: each unit of money you acquire is worth less and less to you. If your current salary is $10,000 per year and you are offered another job worth $20,000 per year, you are likely to be more impressed than if you are offered an income of $110,000 per year when you already earn $100,000 per year. In each case, you are $10,000 better off. Thus, utility is not the same as money value.

The second paradox is due to Allais (1953), who developed alternative gambles in which people's choices violate the independence axiom (see earlier). Here are two choices: which would you prefer?

> (1a) $1000 with probability 1 (i.e. certain)
>
> or
>
> (1b) $1000 with probability .90
> $5000 with probability .09
> $0 with probability .01

Thus, you are being asked to choose between a certain gain in 1a and a lesser probability of a greater gain, plus a small risk of no gain at all, in 1b. Most people choose 1a. Now, which of the following two choices you would prefer?

> (2a) $1000 with probability .10
> $0 with probability .90
>
> or
>
> (2b) $5000 with probability .09
> $0 with probability .91

If you are like most of the people presented with this second choice, you will prefer 2b to 2a. The paradox arises because the choices between the (a) and (b) items are in principle the same in situations 1 and 2, so your choices should, on SEU grounds, be the same: you should prefer

(a) to (b) in both or (b) to (a) in both (the direction depends on your utility for certainty versus risk).

To make this clear, look at Table 9.1. Imagine, along the lines of the frequentist judgement presentations in the preceding chapter, that we are dealing with 100 lottery tickets rather than numerical probabilities—both are shown in the table for comparison. The tickets in each situation deliver the outcomes shown: in situation 1a, all tickets show $1000, whereas in 1b, ticket number 1 shows $0, tickets numbered 2–10 show $5000, and tickets numbered 11–100 show $1000; in situation 2a, tickets numbered 1 and 2–10 show $1000 and tickets numbered 11–100 show $0; in situation 2b, tickets numbered 1 and 11–100 show $0, and tickets numbered 2–10 show $5000.

You have effectively been asked, in each situation, to choose whether to play the (a) lottery or the (b) lottery. Now recall the independence axiom: that outcomes that are the same for each option should not affect the decision. You can see that the (a) and (b) options are the same in the two situations, except that in option 1 you get $1000 for a ticket numbered 11–100 whereas in option 2 you get nothing. However, this particular outcome is the same for (a) and (b), so overall, your preference between (a) and (b) should be the same. But it was not. We shall consider how to explain this deviation from SEU later, in the section on prospect theory.

The third paradox was introduced by Ellsberg (1961) and concerns a different kind of violation of independence: Ellsberg called it the *ambiguity effect*. It crystallises two quite different ways of thinking about probability in decision making: the distinction between risk and uncertainty. First, here are some more choices for you to consider. Imagine you are again contemplating playing a lottery, this time involving a lucky dip for coloured balls. There are 90 balls from which you can draw one. Thirty of these balls are red, and the other 60 are either black or yellow—you do not know the exact numbers. In situation

TABLE 9.1

The Allais paradox expressed as a set of lotteries

	Probabilities		
	.01	.09	.90
	Ticket Numbers		
Options	1	2–10	11–100
1a	$1000	$1000	$1000
1b	$0	$5000	$1000
2a	$1000	$1000	$0
2b	$0	$5000	$0

1, which would you prefer: (a) to win \$10 if a red ball is drawn, or (b) to win \$10 if you draw a black ball? Most people go for (a). Now think of situation 2, where a yellow ball also wins you \$10, but in all other respects the gamble is the same: there are 30 red balls and 60 balls that are either black or yellow, and in (a) you get \$10 for drawing a red ball (and this time \$10 for a yellow ball too), whereas in (b) you get \$10 for a black ball or a yellow ball. Which do you prefer, option (a) or option (b)? Most people now go for (b).

SEU theory tells us that we should be indifferent as to options (a) and (b) in both cases, because the expected value of each outcome is the same: although we do not know how many yellow or black balls there are, if this was decided at random, in the long run the proportions would be about half and half, i.e. 30 each. That would be your best estimate. Second, the independence axiom tells us, once again, that our choices should not reverse between situations 1 and 2, because the status of the yellow balls is the same in either case: they give you nothing under either option in the first case, or \$10 under either option in the second. Table 9.2 shows this.

What seems to be happening is that people prefer options in which probabilities are known to those where they are unknown. The former is decision under risk, the latter is decision under uncertainty. In situation 1, people know for sure how many red balls there are, but the number of blacks and yellows could vary between 0 and 60; they can be more confident, they feel, about their chances of winning with option (a). In situation 2, they know for sure that there are 60 winning balls with option (b), but are not so sure this time with option (a), because the number of yellows to be added to the 30 reds is uncertain. Note that what is "known" here is questionable: it is possible to make well-grounded probability estimates even when you are not given the information explicitly. Baron (1994a) gives instances of where the ambiguity effect seems to be reflected in real life, as in the case of insurance premiums, which seem to be lower for known risks, such as in motor accidents, than for uncertain events, such as in times of war.

TABLE 9.2
The Ellsberg paradox and the ambiguity effect

	Options	Red 30 Balls	Black 0–60 Balls	Yellow 0–60 Balls
1a	\$10	\$0	\$0	
	1b	\$0	\$10	\$0
	2a	\$10	\$0	\$10
	2b	\$0	\$10	\$10

Framing and preference reversals

We have seen from these classic paradoxes that people's expressed preferences can deviate systematically from the requirements of SEU theory and its related axioms and principles. These are not the only such observations, though, and in this section we deal with some more modern results that also pose problems for the status of SEU as a descriptive or prescriptive theory.

The violations of independence set out earlier show how preferences can *reverse* when they should not. One of the most striking examples of preference reversal was reported by Tversky (1969). It had the additional effect of violating the principle of transitivity of preferences (see earlier). Tversky gave subjects pairs of college applicants to assess, and decide which to admit. The applicants were graded according to intelligence, emotional stability, and social facility. Subjects were given these details for sets of applicants in all possible pairs, and the ordering that typically emerged is shown in Table 9.3, i.e. A was preferred to B, B to C, and so on. However, when comparing A to E, subjects typically preferred E: The ratings for intelligence, fairly narrowly different between the ordered pairs, are now large enough to make the preference reverse, in a clear violation of transitivity. Given that subjects preferred A to B, B to C, C to D, and D to E, they should have preferred A to E. Intelligence clearly seems to be considered the most important attribute for college applicants here, so as to overrule the quite large differences on the others. Baron (1994a) proposes that small differences, such as those in intelligence on the A–B etc. comparisons, are excessively underweighed, perhaps even ignored altogether, as a means of simplifying the decision task.

Tversky is also responsible for one of the best-known demonstrations of preference reversal, and one of the most troublesome for SEU theory, the *framing effect* (see Tversky & Kahneman, 1981). Here

TABLE 9.3

Example of information in Tversky's (1969) intransitivity experiment. (After Baron, 1994a)

Applicants	Dimensions		
	Intelligence	Emotional Stability	Social Facility
A	69	84	75
B	72	78	65
C	75	72	55
D	78	66	45
E	81	60	35

are some more choices for you. In Chapter 1, the following problem was set out. You are a health service official making plans for dealing with a new disease that is about to break out. It is expected to kill 600 people. Your expert scientific advisers tell you about the consequences of two possible treatment programmes: Programme A will definitely save 200 lives, whereas Programme B will have a one-third (.33) chance of saving 600. Which programme will you approve? Most subjects in Tversky and Kahneman's study chose A. Now consider the situation faced by your colleague: her choice is between Programme C, which will certainly result in 400 deaths, and Programme D, which has a two-thirds chance (.67) that 600 people will die. Which does she approve? Most subjects chose D from this perspective.

The problems are of course identical: from either perspective, you are considering whether to opt for 200 certainly alive and 400 certainly dead, versus either 600 x .33 alive or 600 x .67 dead; the expected values are the same. What has happened here is a demonstration that people tend to be averse to risk when gains are in prospect, but liable to take a risk to avoid a possible loss. From the point of view of SEU theory, a decision should not depend on how it is framed, because the figures are not changed.

Reasons, decisions, and the sure thing principle

Savage (1954) was convinced that the sure thing principle was almost uniquely compelling: it states that, if you prefer A to B in situation X, and prefer A to B when not in situation X, you should prefer A to B when you do not know which situation you are actually in. Baldly stated in this way, it is hard to see how anyone could go against it. However, Tversky and Shafir (1992; see also Shafir, 1993a; Shafir & Tversky, 1992) have recently shown that people can violate it: whether they do or not seems to depend on the *reasons* people have for their choices, a factor we have not considered so far.

Tversky and Shafir presented subjects with the following problem:

> Imagine that you have just taken a tough qualifying examination. It is the end of the fall quarter, you feel tired and run-down, and you are not sure that you passed the exam. In case you failed you have to take the exam in a couple of months—after the Christmas holidays. You now have the opportunity to buy a very attractive 5-day Christmas vacation package to Hawaii at an exceptionally low price. The special offer expires tomorrow, but the exam grade will not be available until the following day.

The subjects had to choose whether to buy the holiday, not buy it, or pay a $5 fee for the rights to buy the holiday at the discount price after finding out the exam result. The majority (61%) chose this third option; only 32% chose to buy the holiday. We can tell that this is a violation of the sure thing principle, rather than merely suspecting that it is (on the assumption that people would generally prefer going to Hawaii to not going) because Tversky and Shafir used a second condition in this experiment in which some subjects were told they had passed, and others were told that they had failed. In this case, the majority (54% in the pass group, 57% in the fail group) chose to buy the holiday; 30% who passed and 31% who failed opted for the deposit.

Tversky and Shafir call this the *disjunction effect*: when people do not know what situation they are in, i.e. they are in a state of uncertainty, they tend to withhold making a choice, even though the choice would go the same way whatever situation they were in. The effect has been observed in a number of decision-making contexts as well as the kind outlined here (see Shafir & Tversky, 1992). It appears that having a reason for making a choice—for instance, to celebrate passing, or cheer yourself up after failing—enables people to "think through" (as the authors put it) the consequences of choices more clearly than when they do not have a particular stance (we shall look more closely at the relation between choices and consequences at the end of the chapter). Tversky and Shafir interpret "over-testing" by doctors in this light: doctors sometimes ask for tests that will not affect their treatment decisions. These apparently redundant tests provide the doctors with more reasons to justify the treatments they have already prescribed.

The influence of reasons on choices, and the way in which they can lead to violations of normative principles, was further illustrated by Shafir (1993b). In one experiment, subjects had to imagine they were involved in deciding child custody in a divorce case. They were given the following attributes of the warring couple:

Parent A	Parent B
Average income	Above-average income
Average health	Very close relationship with the child
Average working hours	Extremely active social life
Reasonable rapport with the child	Lots of work-related travel
Relatively stable social life	Minor health problems

Half the subjects were given this information and asked to decide which parent to award custody to; the other half were asked which they would deny custody. The results were as follows:

	Award	Deny
Parent A	36%	45%
Parent B	64%	55%

Note that Parent B is the majority choice both for awarding and denial, and also that these figures sum to more than 100. Neither of these things should have happened if choosing and rejecting were simple complements of each other, which strictly speaking they should be. Shafir explains the effect by pointing out that A is "the impoverished option … with no striking positive or negative features". B, however, "the enriched option", does have striking positive and negative features, and subjects focus on one or the other kind when looking for reasons to choose or reject.

Prospect theory: An alternative to SEU

Kahneman and Tversky (1979; see also Tversky & Kahneman, 1986, 1992) introduced a theory that was intended to account for the main patterns and paradoxes in decision making, in other words, to be a descriptive theory of what people actually do. It is called *prospect theory*, and although it has its foundations in the principles of SEU theory, it includes some fundamental properties of its own that account for deviations from SEU's norms.

Prospect theory shares SEU's basis of treating decisions as if they were gambles, and hence of regarding the process of decision making as the combination of an assessment of utility with a judgement of probability. As we have seen, people deviate systematically from the abstract norms in both of these cases, leading to non-normative choices such as the ones reviewed earlier.

Let us take prospect theory's treatment of utility first. Its two components are the idea of a *reference point*, and the notion that subjective utility and objective value are not linearly related, as they should be in SEU terms. The reference point is usually assumed to be the current state you are in. Decisions can thus result in a gain or a loss relative to this point. This opens up the possibility of framing effects, as what counts as a reference point is clearly a psychological matter, and can therefore be affected by the way in which the current state is described, i.e. framed (is your glass half full or half empty?). The notion of the reference point also makes decision making a two-stage process: framing and valuation (Tversky & Kahneman, 1992).

The *non-linear relation* between value and utility is described using the S-shaped Value Function, and is derived from the observed choices people make. For instance, we have seen Bernoulli's use of the principle of diminishing marginal utility to explain the St. Petersburg paradox. It has also been observed that people will generally not accept fair bets, i.e. those with an equal chance of winning and losing. Thus, people will not pay $1 for an equal chance of winning $10 or losing $10: the negative utility of the $10 loss is greater than the positive utility of the $10 gain.

A generalised value function is shown in Fig. 9.1. The two axes show money value on the horizontal axis and utility, which Kahneman and Tversky also call value, on the vertical axis. Figure 9.1 shows the three essential properties of this function: (i) that value is defined with respect to a reference point—the place where the axes cross, (ii) the curve is concave for gains (the top right-hand sector) and convex for losses (the bottom left-hand sector), and (iii) the function is steeper for losses than for gains. The function is therefore steepest around the reference point: the first part of any difference from that point will be the most significant for you. Thus, prospect theory claims that value (in the theory's sense) is a matter of gain or loss, not of the final utility of a particular outcome.

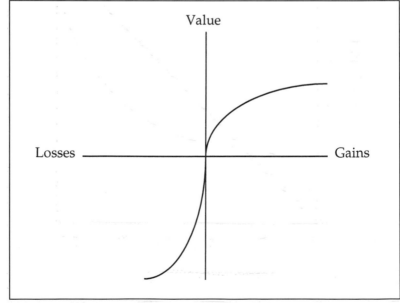

FIG. 9.1.
The generalised value function in prospect theory. From Kahneman and Tversky (1979). Reprinted with permission of the publisher.

The classic framing effect set out earlier can be explained using this function, as can other apparent decision biases. In the first situation, the reference point is 600 people dead, and the action regarding treatments is framed in terms of gains: people saved. However, in the second situation, the reference point is the current state, before the disease has struck: no one has yet died, and the programme is now framed in terms of possible losses, i.e. people dead. Because people are averse to risks when gains are in prospect, they choose the certain gain of 200 saved in the first situation; because they tend to seek risk when losses are in prospect, they choose the uncertain outcome of 600 saved in the second situation.

Playing off certainty against uncertainty is of course related to the account that prospect theory gives of probability in decision making. In general, prospect theory proposes that small probabilities are over-weighted in decisions, whereas larger probabilities are under-weighted (relative to what the calculus of probability dictates), with zero and 1 (the certainties) treated properly. This function is shown in Fig. 9.2, and is called the weighing function; it is expressed using the Greek letter π.

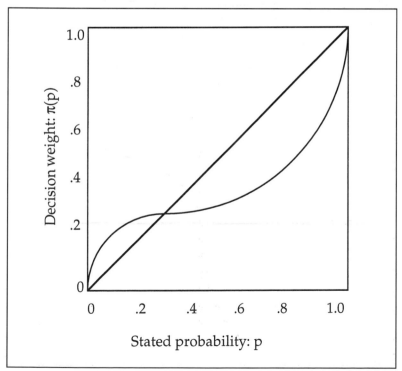

FIG. 9.2.
The weighing function in prospect theory, based on Tversky and Kahneman (1992). Reprinted with kind permission from Kluwer Academic Publishers.

Kahneman and Tversky use a vivid example to illustrate the effect: suppose you were playing Russian roulette. Would you pay more to reduce the number of bullets from 3 to 4, or from 1 to 0? The second, obviously, although there is no formal reason for this. Rather less dramatically, the weighing function explains effects such as the *certainty effect* that contributes both to the Allais paradox and the medical framing effect: that people prefer, where gains are concerned, a certain gain to an uncertain gain of the same, or even a greater, value. We also saw in the preceding chapter that people tend to judge the probabilities of rare events, such as air crashes, as being higher than they really are, in frequency terms.

Prospect theory explains a number of findings: in addition to the ones already pointed out, Tversky and Shafir (1992) use it to explain the disjunction effect. It has recently been extended by Tversky and Kahneman (1992) to cover cases such as the ambiguity effect, and decision under uncertainty as well as risk. It is probably the most influential contemporary descriptive theory of decision making. However, its success is not unrestricted. For instance, it is not clear how it would deal with the demonstrated influences of the anticipated emotions that will occur when people consider the range of possible decision outcomes: utility of one outcome should be independent of utility of other outcomes that could have occurred but did not. For example, if the anticipated regret if you lose a certain gamble outweighs the anticipated rejoicing if you win (as distinct from the utility of the outcome), you will not play, particularly when the difference is large (Bell, 1982). This approach to decision making was termed *regret theory* by Loomes and Sugden (1982): they propose that anticipated emotion is over-weighted, especially with large differences. Think of the case of shyness: if you ask someone out, will you feel terrible or just mildly put out if you are turned down, compared to the elation you will feel if you are accepted? If it is the former, you may not ask in the first place— another decision you may come to regret!

Payne, Bettman, and Johnson (1992, 1993) have concentrated on such considerations in proposing an alternative approach to decision making, which they call the adaptive or constructive processing approach. They argue that there are numerous psychological cross-currents involved in any decision, all of which may be responsible for systematic deviations from normative standards. We have seen, for instance, that decisions that should be the same can vary due to, for instance, they way the problem is described (e.g. the framing effect).

Payne et al. attribute such effects to three general factors. These are conflicting values, decision complexity, and uncertain values. The first refers to the fact that in many complex decisions, one option may be superior in some respects whereas the other is superior in others. Second, many decisions are complex: they involve a host of options, values, probabilities, and possible outcomes. Third, people may be uncertain about the values of possible outcomes. For instance, in a study by Kahneman and Snell (1992), subjects were asked to predict how their tastes would change given daily exposure for one week to, for instance, plain yogurt. Most predicted that they would like it less, but in fact there were wide variations in preferences at the end of the week, and in general, liking for plain yogurt actually increased. Predicted values in this and other conditions bore little relation to those that were actually expressed.

Note that from this point of view, it is artificial to separate probability from utility, as the classic theories do: there is uncertainty inherent in utility itself. People will thus have to develop strategies to simplify the decision problem, and will have to trade off the costs and possible benefits in deploying them: "people often adapt their behavior in ways that seem reasonable given a concern for both decision effort and decision accuracy" (Payne et al., 1992, p. 112). We shall consider further aspects of the ways in which people deal with complex decisions in the next section; the general question of dealing with complexity will be addressed in the next chapter.

More complex decisions

The forms of decision making we have considered so far may seem complicated enough, but they are highly simplified versions of the kinds we are faced with all the time, as the remarks about the approach of Payne et al. indicate. We shall now go on to look at two broad classes of more complex cases: multi-attribute decisions, and decisions involving people and time.

Multi-attribute utility theory (MAUT)

MAUT is an extension of utility theory, introduced by Keeney and Raiffa (1976), and is applied to decisions involving outcomes that vary along a number of dimensions, or aspects. Take the example of buying a car. You have to take a number of factors into account, and consider the values of them and your preferences between them, in combination. You might be concerned about, for instance, price, performance, and styling, and unconcerned about economy, reliability, or colour.

Clearly, not only do you need to assess which aspects are relevant, but also how important they are: that is, you need to assess the relative weights of the utilities associated with each aspect. MAUT provides a formal method for doing this. It is based on a mathematical technique used in the economic field of decision analysis called conjoint measurement. To find the utilities for a range of attributes (where "attribute" is defined as a point on some dimension), you can take two points on a dimension such as price. Then take another dimension, say performance; assume that you prefer faster cars. The cars you are considering vary in performance terms between 1 (slow) and 5 (very fast): these numbers mark steps in your utility for performance. You are prepared to pay between $5000 and $10,000 for a car. Given a car with performance rating 4 (fast) at a price of, say $7000, which you are prepared to pay, how much would you be prepared to pay for a car rated 2 (quite slow) such that you are indifferent as to the two cars—i.e. you are not bothered which you buy?

The answer is entirely yours, of course, but you can establish a price scale to go alongside the performance scale, and having done so, you can use it to establish scales for other aspects. MAUT requires that these aspects should be independent, i.e. your scaling between two dimensions should not depend on any other. In the real world, this condition may be hard to meet: performance, for instance, is related to economy, styling, and price. This is one of the problems with applying this approach psychologically, as a descriptive theory. MAUT can in fact use techniques other than conjoint measurement, but the essence of the method is the same: collate the relevant aspects (these will depend on your personal goals—if you want to look cool, you will include styling and perhaps make of car as well as performance), find their ranges of values, and scale each in terms of the other. If the decision you are faced with can be realistically subjected to a MAUT analysis, MAUT will tell you what the utility-maximising choice would be.

It might strike you that using MAUT, even if you were familiar with its techniques, would be a lot of bother. The adaptive approach of Payne et al. (see earlier) recognises this, and Baron (1994a) gives cases where people seem to avoid the cognitive work involved in difficult personal and political decisions by using simplifying strategies such as *lexical rules*. These are personal codes such as "honesty is the best policy", or "human life is paramount". The trouble with such rules is that they can lead to intractable dilemmas: if you held to them rigidly, you would end up, for instance, by hurting the feelings of a loved one when a little lie would have spared that person, or spending huge sums of money on a single operation when the money could have saved more lives by being used to fund, say, a health promotion programme. More on the positive use of lexical rules later.

Trade-offs

The kinds of decision addressed by MAUT, and simplified by devices such as lexical rules, largely concern *trade-offs* between aspects. MAUT is a way of arriving at a normative solution to this difficult real-world problem but, as we have seen, you have to take a lot of trouble if you are going to apply it: businesses and governments might have the resources to do so, but you and I generally do not. One proposal as to how we may make complex multi-attribute decisions in real life was put forward by Tversky (1972): the heuristic (cf. Chapter 8) of *elimination by aspects*.

Let us go back to the car problem. You are in the happy position of being able to afford a nice used car, and you are considering a choice between two options: a VW and a BMW. It is a hard choice: the VW has a reputation for reliability, it is economical, cheaper to buy and insure; but you think the BMW is faster, better looking, and altogether cooler. How are you going to make your choice? According to Tversky, people tend to focus on one aspect and find the options that score worst on that: they can be eliminated. You can go down the list of aspects in this way until you are left with one remaining option, and the decision is made. So, if your highest priority is performance, and the VW does not satisfy your criteria for this aspect, it is eliminated and you choose the BMW.

It is not hard to see that this must be a purely descriptive account (for which Tversky, and others since, have provided empirical evidence), as elimination by aspects is a heuristic for avoiding trade-off considerations: it could therefore, in principle, give rise to decisions that violate the norms set by utility theory. Thus, what would, objectively, have been the best overall option could find itself eliminated at an early stage—perhaps the VW really outscored the BMW on all aspects except performance, but you eliminated it because you focused on performance above the others.

Time and people: Dilemmas and traps in decision making

There are other factors that involve trade-offs and that add further layers of complexity to real-life decision making: ultimately, they can produce genuine *dilemmas*, where there is no clear objective criterion for saying which decision is best; and *traps*, where decisions from one angle appear quite sensible, but from another may have fearsome consequences. The two factors we shall consider here are time and other people. The time factor involves trading off the short-term and long-term consequences of decisions, whereas the people factor involves trading off the consequences for yourself against those for the people around you.

There are large literatures on both these factors, especially the people factor, so I shall give a few illustrative cases here.

Decisions and time

The two cases we shall consider are the sunk-cost effect, and short-term/long-term dilemmas. The sunk-cost effect will be familiar to anyone: it is captured in the phrase "throwing good money after bad", and there are plenty of imaginary and real examples available to illustrate it. Here is an imaginary one (from Arkes & Blumer, 1985). You win a ticket to a football game and, because you do not want to go alone, you persuade a friend to fork out $12 to go with you. On match day, it starts to snow, and you decide not to go. However, your friend is outraged and insists on going, otherwise he considers he has wasted his $12. This is a bad decision, because the $12 has gone in any case: why put up with hours in the freezing cold as well? And here is a real example: in the 1960s, the British and French governments continued funding the supersonic airliner Concorde long after it became clear that the plane would never recover anything like its development costs; in fact, only two airlines (British and French) ever bought any. This led to the sunk-cost effect being called the Concorde Fallacy by the evolutionary biologist Richard Dawkins (see Over & Manktelow, 1993). Arkes and Blumer also provide experimental evidence. So the existence of the sunk-cost effect seems beyond dispute.

Sunk costs do not have to refer just to money: in the Concorde example, for instance, there were undoubtedly considerations of national prestige as well, and more mundanely, one can think of, for instance, unhappy couples who do not split up because of prior long-term emotional commitment. In other words, the more general construct of utility applies.

How can we explain the sunk-cost effect? First, consider why further commitment to a dead loss is a bad decision: normative theories have it that you should decide on an option in view of the *consequences* of the decision, i.e. what will result; what is done is done and should not affect this assessment. The sunk-cost effect is thus a clear violation of a norm, in this case, the norm of *consequentialism* (about which I shall say a little more in a later section). Arkes and Blumer (acknowledging Thaler, 1980) argue that the effect is partly interpretable using prospect theory. When you start investing, you are at the reference point, the point where the axes for value and objective loss/gain intersect (see Fig. 9.1). As you continue making investments, you incur costs, and wind up at the bottom of the loss curve (in the lower left sector). You will recall that this value function for losses is convex. What this entails is that further losses will not hurt quite as much as the earlier ones did. Recall also the certainty effect: people will choose to take a risk to avoid loss, and to curtail investment is to incur a certain loss. So you continue to invest.

However, Arkes and Blumer, along with Brockner and Rubin (1985), argue that there is more to the sunk-cost effect than can be explained by prospect theory. In particular, there are factors concerning perceived waste, and self-presentation: the only possibility of avoiding a huge loss, and losing face into the bargain, is to carry on risking further costs. Thus different, non-economic utilities come into play.

Short-term/long-term dilemmas share certain features with the sunk-cost effect, but distinct varieties can be identified. A dilemma exists when there is a clash of utilities between outcomes in the present, or the immediate future, and outcomes in the longer term. There are clearly two broad situations in which utilities can clash in this way: (i) where the short-term utility is positive but the long-term utility is negative, i.e. short-term gains lead to long-term losses; (ii) where the short-term utility is negative but the long-term utility is positive, i.e. short-term losses lead to long-term gains. What counts as a gain or loss obviously depends on one's goals and values (on goals, values, and plans see Baron, 1994a).

Several examples of these two types of utility-clash dilemmas are provided in a classic paper by Platt (1973). For instance, in the case of type (i), Platt refers to drug-taking: here, the tension between the short-term gain of getting high and the long-term loss of addiction and ill health are probably clearer than in any other aspect of life, so much so, of course, that some drugs have been banned. Curiously, from a psychological point of view, not all of them have: alcohol and tobacco, for instance, have not. Other everyday instances of this category of dilemma include credit cards (immediate acquisition versus future debt) and unprotected sex (immediate pleasure versus unwanted pregnancy or disease, perhaps even death).

People also seem prey to the type (ii) dilemma, in failing to accept an immediate loss that will lead to a longer-term gain. Drug addiction is again a good example, as when a smoker finds it hard to give up (while admitting that it would be best to do so: there is no dilemma for a person who does not want to stop in the first place). Other examples include saving money rather than spending it right now, or taking out a pension plan.

There is a third type of related dilemma as well: that of whether to forego an immediate benefit in favour of a delayed but larger benefit. You see this kind of dilemma in the winnings in the kinds of competitions that appear on the back of cornflake packets: would you rather win $1 million now, or $50,000 a year for life? People generally take the first option. This phenomenon is known as discounting, and has been observed in children as well as adults, even in animals. It is well known in economics, as its name implies.

There are many explanations for these dilemmas, and many difficulties in deciding what is normative, i.e. whether there is anything wrong in favouring the present over the future. Platt (1973) gives a Skinnerian explanation, in terms of *sliding reinforcers*: immediate reinforcement is well known to be more effective than delayed reinforcement, and there are good evolutionary reasons why it should be. It is a kind of biological certainty effect: eat now, for you may not find any food later. It is possible to go back even further: these dilemmas were originally discussed by Plato and Aristotle (see Over & Manktelow, 1993). They introduced the concept of weakness of the will (e.g. you know you should not have that extra drink, but you give in), and Plato argued that the effect is a kind of cognitive illusion, where long-term consequences, good and bad, seem "smaller" than immediate consequences, just as distant objects seem smaller than near ones.

More modern explanations are based on the economic theory of discounting, where the analogy is drawn between this behaviour and the "discount rate" in banking: this is the amount of interest that has to be offered on the money you currently hold to induce you not to spend it (see Thaler & Shefrin, 1981). Alternatively, taking the lower immediate benefit could be seen, as mentioned, as a kind of certainty effect, or a fee for not waiting, as when we pay more to have our photos developed today rather than next week. The value function for gains in prospect theory would lead us to expect these effects. A prescriptive argument for resisting the temptation to have everything now is that statistically you are more likely than not to live a good many years if you are young at present, so it is in your interests, in the long term, to safeguard your future. The point about these dilemmas is not that people always take immediate pleasure: clearly sometimes they do forego this, or incur costs for future benefit. Rather, it is that there is a theoretical as well as personal dilemma in determining what people *should* do in these circumstances: there is no formal calculus for this, only arguments that you may or may not accept (see also the next chapter).

Decisions and people

The dilemmas and traps associated with the trade-offs between our own losses and gains and those of other people are related to the short-term/long-term dilemmas just reviewed: Parfit (1984), for instance, argues that the person you are in the future, compared to today, can be seen, for decision purposes, as being equivalent to another person. It can be difficult to argue why you should care more about the future you, who is not you, than about someone else, who also is not you. I shall give three examples of the kinds of dilemmas that result from taking into account the interests of others: bystander apathy, the prisoner's dilemma, and commons problems. You might already be familiar with these from courses in social psychology.

The most famous instance of bystander apathy was the Kitty Genovese case, reported in the 1960s. Kitty was a woman who was attacked and murdered outside an apartment block in New York, in full view of dozens of onlookers, none of whom went to her aid, or even called the police. Similar cases appear in the press from time to time, the reports nearly always missing the point that it is *because* there were so many people present that no one helped. Platt (1973) calls this a "missing-hero" trap, and points to other less dramatic instances, such as when a traffic jam builds up owing to an obstruction in the road, which any individual could remove. What is required here is for someone to incur a cost, or the risk of a cost, for the benefit of others. In the bystander apathy case, the risks are real, e.g. retaliation on the part of the assailant, having to appear as a witness in court, or looking silly should it turn out that the situation was not what it seemed. It is easier, and less risky, to leave it to some other hero, and this is easier when there are others present.

The prisoner's dilemma became enormously popular from the 1950s onwards, and has been used not just by psychologists, but also economists, political scientists, mathematicians, and historians. According to Colman (1995), who provides a highly detailed and fascinating review of problems of this kind, over 1000 papers have been written about the prisoner's dilemma and related "games" (Colman's book is concerned with a normative system called game theory, an alternative approach to decision theory, to which, because of lack of space, we cannot do justice).

A schematic prisoner's dilemma is shown in Table 9.4. The dynamics of the situation it portrays are as follows. A pair of suspects, Lefty and Scarface, have been arrested for a robbery. They are kept in separate cells, and offered the following choice. They can admit they both did it, or deny it. Denial is an act of cooperation—with each other, not the

TABLE 9.4
Pay-off matrix for the Prisoner's Dilemma

Scarface	Lefty			
	Cooperates *deny*		Defects *Admit*	
Cooperates *deny*	S: 2	L: 2	S: 10	L: 0
Defects *Admit*	S: 0	L: 10	S: 5	L: 5

The cells show the years served by Scarface (S) and Lefty (L) given the choices of the two parties.

police. Admitting is an act of defection, again with respect to each other. If both confess, they will be sent to prison for 5 years. If both deny, then the police will only be able to nail them on a lesser charge, and they will serve only 2 years. But if Lefty confesses and implicates both (defects) but Scarface denies, Lefty goes free and Scarface goes down for 10 years; and vice versa. If you were one of these characters, what would you do?

The dilemma occurs because there is a genuine clash between what is best from an individual or from a collective viewpoint. Each party gets a larger payoff from defecting, irrespective of what the other does, so the rational choice from an individual standpoint is to defect, and confess. However, if both parties defect, their payoff is worse than if they both co-operate. Thus, if they act in concert, or simply trust each other, they will be better off than if they act as single agents—which is why the police keep them in separate cells.

This basic form of the prisoner's dilemma is just one instance of a number of "games" whose strategic characteristics, i.e. the choices that deliver certain patterns of payoffs, vary according to the payoff matrix. It can also be adapted for situations where there are more than two parties, and for situations in which there are repeated plays at the game. Both of these factors, of course, are common features of real-life social exchanges. As a frightening example of the latter, Colman (1995) quotes game-theoretic analyses of the nuclear arms race, under which several generations have had to grow up. Table 9.5 shows the US–Soviet arms race represented as a prisoner's dilemma, with the payoffs given in words. Here, cooperation means limiting arms production and defection means increasing production. The dominant individual strategy is the same as before: to defect, irrespective of the actions of the other party. But this leads to an unending arms race and the threat of Armageddon: it would be better for both parties, and the world, if they cooperated and limited their arms production. The real arms race ended only when one party, the Soviet Union, was forced to quit the "game" owing to, among other things, economic collapse—contributed to by the arms race. This

TABLE 9.5

The nuclear arms race as a prisoner's dilemma. (From Colman, 1995)

	USSR	
	Limit arms Production	*Increase arms Production*
US		
Limit arms production	Status quo	Advantage to USSR
Increase arms production	Advantage to US	Arms race

Reprinted with permission of the copyright holder.

left the game in the state represented by the lower left cell; whether this is a good outcome is for your own values to decide.

Commons problems are also easily related to real life; in fact, their inspiration came from analyses of real-life dilemmas, as their name implies. In the abstract, commons problems can be viewed as an example of a prisoner's dilemma game: in both cases, the clash between individual and collective utility is thrown into sharp relief.

The essential problem was set out in a famous paper by Hardin (1968) as follows. Imagine that there are six farmers who each own a cow weighing 1000lb. Each has access to a common pasture on which they can freely graze their animals. However, each additional cow over the existing six leads to a depletion of the common grazing, such that each animal will decrease in weight by 100lb. Now, if only Farmer Palmer buys an extra cow, he will be left with two 900lb cows instead of one 1000lb cow, so he will come out ahead. But if all his neighbours do the same, each will find themselves with two scrawny 400lb beasts, totalling 800lb, instead of the fine 1000lb specimen they began with. Ultimately, of course, the common resource may collapse completely.

This particular dilemma is a clear instance of the kind of problem associated with the exploitation and conservation of natural resources: it may be in the interest of you, or your country, as individuals to consume as if there is no tomorrow—but if everyone does so, there won't be. When there is a resource crisis, there is a complementary problem: that any action you take will be of no overall benefit. Take fuel crises: should you give up your car, or at least buy a more economical model? Any effects of this action on the rate of depletion of the world's oil resources will be barely detectable; but if everyone exercises their continuing preference for gas-guzzling motors, we will all pay. Colman (1995, Ch. 9) gives a list of other everyday "defections" of this type, including ordering an expensive meal when your party has agreed to split the bill equally, carrying a gun, refusing to join a union while benefitting from its work, rushing for an exit in a fire, and even standing on tiptoe to watch a parade! You can probably add to this list from your own experience.

Escaping from dilemmas and traps

Whether it is possible to escape from dilemmas and traps depends partly on the view of *rationality* that one adopts, an issue that will be gone into in greater detail in the next chapter. Simple appeals to greater altruism are of limited use. Take the commons problem: Farmer Palmer may become altruistic and prefer that his neighbours graze their cows instead, but if they all take this course, the commons will be depleted just the same as if they were all selfish (Over & Manktelow, 1993).

In the case of individual dilemmas, such as the short-term/long-term ones reviewed earlier, a role has been urged for "self-control" methods such as *lexical rules* (see e.g. Ainslie, 1986). You can simply tell yourself and your friends, for instance, that you do not drink and drive, or have given up smoking (and then hope that they will not have fun by trying to deflect you). Alternatively, you can just remove the object of your desires—throw your cigarettes away, use the no-smoking train carriage—or engage in attention-distracting behaviours, such as talking about anything other than smoking, or finding something else to do with your hands.

Social traps are rather harder to escape from, because, as hinted already, it can be difficult to decide whether a real dilemma exists at all, as there are no uncontroversial normative criteria for deciding whether you should, absolutely, act as an individual or as a group member. However, the likelihood of cooperative choices has been found to be influenced by a number of factors. One such factor is group size: in general, the larger the group, the less the amount of cooperative choices (as in the classic case of bystander apathy). We have already encountered a possible reason for this: people in large groups may be aware of the fact that their choice will have less influence on the whole situation than when they are in small groups. This is known as the personal efficacy hypothesis, and there is some evidence for it. A related phenomenon, for which there is also evidence, is deindividuation: when people in prisoner's dilemma-type situations are allowed to remain anonymous, they tend to cooperate less than when their identities are known to the other players. Simply communicating with other players raises the levels of cooperation, partly because these communications contain a lot of discussions of rules and promises, which in turn lead to an increase in group solidarity and identity. Colman (1995) reviews these factors in detail.

Consequentialism and non-consequentialism

Consequentialism is a principle underlying any normative theory of decision making: it states that we should make a decision according to the expected outcomes, or consequences, of our choices. We have come across instances of this idea earlier: for example, it is the principle that enables the sunk-cost effect to be classed as a fallacy of thought. It is a basic component not just of standard SEU theory, but also of normative approaches that are critical of SEU (see e.g. Frisch & Clemen, 1994).

However, it is one thing to acknowledge that consequentialism has this basic status, and another to ask whether people adhere to it in practice. Baron (1994b) has recently compiled a general review of *non-consequentialist* decisions, which shows that this fundamental tenet can be readily, and knowingly, violated. Some of these violations have been mentioned earlier in this chapter. Besides the sunk-cost effect, we have seen that the sure thing principle is violated under conditions of uncertainty (Tversky & Shafir, 1992). A similar effect was observed by the same researchers using a prisoner's dilemma game: subjects were more likely to cooperate when they did not know whether the other player had cooperated or not than when they knew he or she had actually cooperated, again in clear violation of the sure thing principle and hence of consequentialism (Shafir & Tversky, 1992).

Baron (1994b) reports a striking case of non-consequentialist thinking from his own research: *omission bias*. Ritov and Baron (1990) presented subjects with a decision over which all parents agonise: whether to have a baby vaccinated. If you do not immunise the child, there is a risk that the child will die from the disease, say 10 in 10,000. But vaccinations also carry risk: some babies are damaged directly by the vaccine and may die. What level of risk would you be prepared to accept before you immunise your child? Most subjects reported a risk level of about 5 in 10,000 before they would immunise, when any figure below 10 should clinch it. It is as if people regard themselves as being more responsible for a death from their positive action than a death from their inaction. Such a bias results overall in decisions that fail to have the best consequences.

Baron attributes many of the apparent violations of consequentialism to the over-application of rules, which may themselves have had consequentialist origins, but which can be extended beyond their useful limits. Examples would include the lexical rules that have already been mentioned. In the vaccination case, perhaps the subjects were bearing in mind a "mother's knee" rule such as "don't do things which might harm others" or "if it ain't broke, don't fix it". Ritov and Baron found that omission bias could be counteracted by presenting the subjects with an alternative "golden rule", one that states that you should offer people the outcomes that are in their best interests. Given the figures in the vaccination experiment, that would be to immunise where the risk of vaccine damage is below the risk from the disease.

Examples of non-consequentialist thinking are important and interesting, because not only do they show that there are other influences on our decisions beside those we have looked at in this chapter, but they also lead us to think carefully about what we mean by a rule and a consequence. The commentaries that follow Baron's paper go into great detail on these issues, and show clearly that there is still much to discuss and discover about human decision making.

Summary

1. The classic theory of decision making is derived from economics, and is called Subjective Expected Utility (SEU) theory. It proposes that decisions are made by computing the utility and probability of ranges of options, and lays down norms for good decision making.
2. SEU theory demands that preferences be connected and transitive: i.e. that if you prefer option 1 to option 2 and option 2 to option 3, you must prefer option 1 to option 3. Other principles, such as independence and the sure thing principle, flow from these features.
3. SEU theory does not describe what people actually do: there are problems with their computations of probability and utility, and several well-known paradoxes. Decisions can also be affected by people's reasons, and by the way in which a problem is described.
4. Kahneman and Tversky (1979) put forward prospect theory as a descriptive theory to account for deviations from SEU. It has a value function and a weighing function that explain why people tend to avoid risk when gains are in prospect, and seek risk when losses are in prospect.
5. More complex decisions include those involving options with many attributes, those where short-term and long-term consequences may clash, and those where there may be a difference between individual and collective utility.
6. Several dilemmas and traps can be identified that result from these trade-offs, not all of which can be avoided, easily or in principle.

Reasoning, thinking, and rationality 10

In this concluding chapter, we examine a theoretical issue that has been the subject of increasing attention in recent years: the question of human rationality. Most people think they know what they mean when they say that someone's thoughts or actions are rational or irrational, and official versions of this intuition can be found, for instance, in the law or in medical practice. People have been debating rationality ever since Aristotle, who first claimed the capacity for reason as a distinguishing mark of humanity: the human species thus became the "rational animal" (see Wetherick, 1993). The rationality debate was a philosophical matter until quite recently; only in the last couple of decades or so have the findings of psychological research, and the theoretical ideas they have led to, had much of a bearing on the case. I shall concentrate on the psychological aspect of the debate, since this is a psychology book, and leave it up to you to go further into the philosophical (and political and economic) areas, should you choose to.

Several psychological topics are relevant to our consideration of rationality. We will look at the notion of bounded rationality and "satisficing"; the related question of computational theories and the kinds of theoretical questions they throw up; evolutionary arguments and other kinds of optimality arguments; and recent directly psychological approaches to rationality.

Bounded rationality

Several times in the preceding chapters a similar point has been made about the relation between normative systems, such as formal logic, the Bayesian probability calculus, or utility theory, and descriptive theories of human thought, i.e. systematic accounts of what people actually do when presented with reasoning, judgement, or decision problems. That point is that the formal systems ask too much of ordinary human minds. Furthermore, it is not just that human thinking does not meet the normative standards: there are powerful arguments that it *could not*, in principle. Thus, if one defines rational thinking as thinking fully in accord with an abstract normative system, then we are condemned as irrational before the trial even begins.

Computational tractability

The main element in the argument about the futility of setting abstract standards for human rational thinking concerns the sorts of operation the mind would have to perform if it were to function as some kind of computer, implementing logic or decision theory. Take utility theory. We saw in the preceding chapter that the foundation of utility theory rests on a base called consequentialism: that is, decisions should be taken with regard to the consequences of the choices among the available options. To be fully in accord with abstract norms, then, you would need to know a number of things, and know them with perfect accuracy. You would need to know what all the available options were. You would then need to know what all the possible consequences were of each action you might take, and what value, or utility, you would assign to each. Not only that, you would need to know how likely each one was, i.e. its probability.

Even decision theorists who are not psychologists concede that this is an impossible standard to expect people to live up to (e.g. Savage, 1954). The fact that people have been observed to deviate from normative standards when tested in experiments, as the preceding chapters of this book have shown, is not really the essential point. It is an impossible task in the first place. For a start, there is what is known as a *combinatorial explosion* once you get past a very small number of possibilities from which you are having to choose: the number of options simply goes out of control. This can be shown fairly straightforwardly with games—which in themselves are far simpler than the messier real-world situations we find ourselves in from day to day.

Colman (1995) gives the example of chess, a well-known test-bed for trying to get computers to out-perform people. Chess-playing computers engage in a form of utility maximisation: they compute the possible moves available from each position and select the "best". However, they, like us, run into the problem of the combinatorial explosion, as this is a property of the information being dealt with, not the kind of processor involved. There are about 30 moves available from each chess position, and on average a game of chess takes about 80 moves, 40 from each player. The number of possible chess games therefore is around 30^{80}. This figure exceeds the total number of particles in the universe (upper estimate of 10^{80}). As Colman says, even if you were playing a computer that could compute options at a rate of 1 billion (10^8) per second, it would still be considering its first move after billions of years. Even chess-playing computers thus have to have their processes *bounded*, and of course thousands of people, none able to perform billions of calculations per second, play chess to a decent standard every day. We simply cannot do it by "brute-force" computation. (Psychological accounts of how we do do it are interesting, but off the point of this discussion.)

Now consider the imaginary everyday situation given by Evans and Over (1996a), that of deciding whether to turn left or right when on a car journey. We need to make assumptions such as that we prefer to arrive at our destination in the shortest possible time, then compute the degree to which turning left or right gets us closer to this goal, then assess the probabilities of complicating factors such as the likelihood of rain if we take the right-hand or left-hand road (perhaps the latter takes us through the mountains). We decide to turn left; but then at the junction we see that this would result in our being hit by a bus, which we would prefer not to be, so we have to re-compute the expected utilities on the spot … and so on. If we had to perform these computations for every decision we took, small or large, we would find, like the chess-playing computer, that the world would end before anything got done.

Human rationality, the kind used by ordinary people untrained in logic or decision theory, must therefore also be bounded. The term *bounded rationality* was introduced as long ago as 1957 by the Nobel Prize-winning economist and cognitive scientist Herbert Simon. Much of the work of people studying reasoning and thinking since then has been concerned with mapping these bounds, as well as making proposals for what goes on within them.

Oaksford and Chater (1993, 1995c) follow the implications of arguments for bounded rationality for the task of explaining thinking; they focus on reasoning rather than decision making, although bear in mind that the division between these two areas has begun to crumble recently (see, for instance, the discussion of deontic reasoning in Chapter 4, and later). The question of *computational tractability*, i.e. proposing cognitive processes that could actually run in real time and would avoid the sorts of problems just mentioned, has, in their view, profound consequences for the sorts of descriptive theory that could be written.

Oaksford and Chater focus on another aspect of computational tractability: the problem of how to access relevant knowledge from memory. This problem has bedevilled artificial intelligence for some time, but has not had nearly so obvious an impact on psychological theory compared, say, to the widely acknowledged (e.g. by mental model theorists; see Chapter 5 and later) constraints on the capacity of working memory. In artificial intelligence, this is known as the *frame problem*: given a task that requires the use of stored knowledge, how does the computer, or the mind, select from all the available knowledge only that which is relevant? For the human mind, we also need to know how this can be done quickly enough to be useful.

This is a problem for reasoning theory only if one expects such theories to "scale up" from their role in explaining the results of laboratory problems to a role in explaining reasoning in general, outside the laboratory. Presumably that is the aim of researchers otherwise, as Oaksford and Chater observe, the psychology of thinking becomes self-contained and trivial, rather as would a psychology of Monopoly or crossword puzzles that did not look beyond them. Scaling up to the real world raises the issue of *defeasibility* of inferences: most of the statements we make about the world, including those that find their way into psychology labs, can be defeated by new information. All birds can fly? What about ostriches and penguins?

Logic, of course, deals in statements that are taken as certain, so if our everyday statements are all to some degree uncertain, theories based on logic (a category into which Oaksford and Chater place mental models theory too) appear to have a problem. However, there are logical systems for dealing with uncertainty (e.g. the systems known as non-monotonic logics), so this problem is not in itself decisive. It can be argued, though, that in real life we use statements as *default rules*. A default rule is one that can be assumed to be true until we learn otherwise. And this is where the frame problem arises, because every time you want to find out whether you can draw a conclusion from a default rule, i.e. whether its truth (its certainty) can be assumed, you have to search your knowledge for possible exceptions to it. This, Oaksford and Chater argue, means searching your entire knowledge base.

Using a mathematical analysis known as computational complexity theory, they show that even for constrained problems, the search process becomes intractable: it would for practical purposes take an infinite amount of time and resources to run. They give the example of Bayesian decision making in the medical domain, which we looked at in Chapter 8. Taking a patient with only two symptoms, and some reasonable assumptions about what doctors know about the numbers of possible symptoms and diseases, it can be shown that over 10^9 (10 billion) numbers representing these relations would need to be stored in memory. However, doctors may in practice consider 30 or more symptoms, and the numbers of possibilities to search through in this instance, were the doctors to attempt a Bayesian decision process, would exceed the numbers of all the connections between all of the cells in the brain (Oaksford & Chater, 1993). Not surprisingly, as we saw, there is evidence that doctors do not perform well at Bayesian diagnostic tasks.

Oaksford and Chater's analysis is much more detailed than I can convey here. They go on to assess classes of reasoning theory in terms of their ability to supply legitimate, computationally tractable processes, and find most of them lacking. However, they do suggest some positive solutions to the tractability problem. In the next section, we shall briefly look at some psychological proposals for bounded rationality, and refer back to this issue along the way.

Psychological proposals for bounded rationality

Expecting people to live up to the standards of logic, decision theory, or the calculus of probability is unrealistic, as we have seen, and violates, Evans and Over (1996a) argue, the ethical principle that "ought" implies "can": I should only tell you you ought to run the marathon, or fix the car, if I know that you can. Thus, we should not condemn people as irrational for not conforming to abstract normative standards because they cannot. Rationality must be bounded in some way. The earliest proposal along these lines came from Simon (e.g. 1957, 1978, 1983), who invokes the notion of satisficing. This is a handy blended word combining "satisfy" with "suffice": it means that instead of searching for the best possible decision outcome, for instance—which, as we have seen, might literally take forever—you take one that will satisfy some criterion, one that is good enough. Simon called this criterion an aspiration level.

Satisficing algorithms

In the preceding chapter, we saw a systematic account of satisficing in decision making in the shape of Tversky's principle of elimination by aspects. You may recall the case of choosing which of two cars to buy: take an important aspect such as performance, and eliminate any car that does not meet your criterion. The snag is that the item you eliminate might have been a superior all-round choice, leading to a paradox of rationality: you came to a sub-optimal, hence irrational, conclusion by a rational, satisficing, process.

A more recent approach based on the satisficing principle has been developed by Gigerenzer and his colleagues; it was mentioned in

Chapter 8. It is based on the theory of Probabilistic Mental Models or PMMs (see Gigerenzer, 1993; Gigerenzer et al., 1991), and has been recently updated by Gigerenzer and Goldstein (1996). Gigerenzer acknowledges, along with Oaksford and Chater and Simon, two essential a priori arguments for bounded rationality: that human computational resources are limited and some problems are computationally intractable; and that human inference must be adapted to the environment in which it operates. He is concerned mainly with probabilistic judgements, and with inductive inference more generally (see Chapters 7 and 8).

I shall not go into great detail about PMM theory here, as it can be found elsewhere in the book. The core of Gigerenzer's account is that people making probabilistic judgements use a "fast and frugal" algorithm (decision rule), which he calls the *Take the Best* rule. "Fast and frugal" is a phrase that captures the advantages of such an algorithm over the mental implementation of a formal system: it is quick, and inexpensive on computational resources. Take Gigerenzer's standard case of judging which of two cities is the biggest. You simply search your memory for cities for a cue that discriminates between them, and if you find one, use that. The first cue will be whether you have heard of them or not. If you have heard of one but not the other, then you opt for the familiar one; if you have heard of both, then you search for another cue, such as whether one has a premier league football club; if you cannot find a cue, then you choose at random.

Take the Best, like elimination by aspects in decision making, does not do most of the things a normative system would: it does not search among all cues and consequences, and integrate this information before making its decision; it can therefore produce judgements that sometimes violate abstract norms. However, when lined up against more complex algorithms that do have these features in computer simulation tests, Take the Best produced as many formally correct decisions as did the more complex algorithms, and did so more quickly. In fact, a "minimalist" algorithm that simply chose cues at random was slightly quicker and almost as accurate (Gigerenzer & Goldstein, 1996). PMM theory also accounts for an impressive array of empirical results with real people, as we saw in Chapter 8.

PMM theory does what Oaksford and Chater applaud: it discards formal systems completely, and offers a cognitive process account that makes minimal contact with abstract rules, thereby escaping the frame problem and the risk of computational intractability. In that respect, it bears certain similarities to Kahneman and Tversky's heuristics: they also propose "fast and frugal" means of arriving at judgements and decisions (such as the availability heuristic, to which Gigerenzer's recognition cue bears some resemblance). This is slightly ironic, given Gigerenzer's vehement opposition to the heuristics and biases research programme.

Mental logic and mental models

Mental logic theories propose that the mind contains mental equivalents of the sorts of principles found in formal logical systems; in other words, that it contains inference rules (see Chapters 2 and 5). The issue of rationality as far as contemporary mental logic theorists are concerned largely centres on the relation between the norms provided by the logic and observed human performance. We are therefore back with the issue of rationality as adherence to norms. However, as we have seen in the chapters on deduction in this book, there is a mass of evidence showing that people deviate from logical norms when given deductive problems. Does this then amount to an empirical case for human irrationality?

Some philosophers have come to just this conclusion (e.g. Stich, 1985, 1990), but mental logic theorists themselves avoid it. O'Brien (1993) confronts the issue directly: as he asks in his title, if we can put a man on the moon, why can't we solve logical reasoning problems? How can we be so apparently rational and yet irrational? The answer is that mental logic theory does not propose that all problems with a logical structure will infallibly be solved if people have a mental logic. As Rips (1994) puts it, people "have a certain pool of inference rules at their disposal but sometimes fail to apply them correctly" (p. 382). Both Rips and O'Brien deny that mental logic includes formally illogical rules or that people simply make random slips, so mental logic has to embrace a form of bounded rationality to account for observed reasoning errors.

The answer is to point to processing capacity limits: modern mental logic theorists acknowledge that a straightforward mental implementation of formal logic is not feasible, and instead allow for "extra-logical" processes. We saw what these are said to consist of in Chapters 2 and 5 and I shall not repeat that material now. What follows from the inclusion of extra-logical processes, including capacity restrictions, is that some problems will just overwhelm the resources of the system, and error will result. O'Brien (1993) and Rips (1994) explain the low levels of logical performance with the abstract selection task, and the particular patterns of choices that people tend to give (see Chapters 3 and 4) in this way.

However, a bounded mental logic does not escape the tractability arguments of Oaksford and Chater. They contend that logical proof is in any case an intractable process, so any mental logic theory must make one of two manoeuvres. Given the defeasibility of ordinary statements about the world, the components of reasoning problems must either be assumed to be exceptionless generalisations, a possibility that Oaksford and Chater dismiss out of hand, or reasoning problems are closed and self-contained: they do not "scale up" to the world outside the lab. If they are supposed to scale up, then logical premises must be treated as default rules, and intractability gets back in that way (see earlier).

Mental models theory appears to offer a way out of both the theoretical and the empirical problems posed by mental logic theory: it was designed in the first place to be a bounded system that explicitly recognises limited human processing capacity. For instance, in Chapters 2 and 5 we saw that a fundamental psychological element of the theory of mental models was its proposal that reasoners operate on what is explicitly represented in a model. Models make explicit the objects, relations, and properties in a situation and serve them up for inference and decision (Johnson-Laird & Byrne, 1993b). When a problem cannot be solved using that information alone, the set of models must be "fleshed out" so that a new search for a possible counterexample can be undertaken. This process embodies what Johnson-Laird and Byrne call the semantic principle of validity: reasoners test whether a conclusion is valid by searching for alternative models of the argument's premises in which that conclusion is false. If there is no such model, the conclusion is taken to be valid; if too many alternative models are required, then processing capacity is exceeded and performance crashes.

Rationality from the perspective of mental models theory is explored further by Johnson-Laird and Byrne (1993b). They take a view of rationality as including goals: people use their beliefs in the attainment of their goals. Thus, they need both to *believe* what is true (the authors refer to this as the precept of rational belief) and to *infer* what is true (the precept of rational thinking): these are the two central precepts of rationality for Johnson-Laird and Byrne's theory.

Both of these precepts throw up psychological questions: *rational belief* concerns processes of induction (Johnson-Laird has more recently applied the model theory to induction, as we saw in Chapter 7), whereas *rational thinking* is the point at issue for us here. Rational thinking is said to yield three essential questions: (i) whether a person can ever be said to have committed an error in reasoning; (ii) whether some deductive problems are beyond the capacity of reasoners untrained in logic; and (iii) whether rationality is relative to culture.

Johnson-Laird and Byrne answer these questions by showing how the theory of mental models can deliver valid deductions using the semantic procedure outlined earlier, and in Chapter 5. This procedure uses no inference rules. However, within the constraints of untutored mentality, it does appear, they claim, that people grasp the essential point about an inference being valid when there are no models of the premises in which the conclusion is false. What people lack are systematic procedures to guide the search for counterexamples. Thus, as the authors say (p. 205), people are rational in principle, but err in practice: because they do not know how to search exhaustively for alternative models, they will sometimes accept an invalid conclusion as valid, not having formulated an alternative in which the conclusion does not hold. Clearly, more systematic search techniques can be learned, and hence it is possible to devise extended deduction systems such as formal logic, or mental models. The semantic principle of validity is held to be present in all cultures, because all cultures need to be able to maintain truth in their beliefs and thinking; what is not culturally universal is a set of inference rules.

The theory of mental models, being by design a bounded system, might seem to evade the tractability problems of mental logic. Indeed, there exist computer implementations of it (see Johnson-Laird & Byrne, 1991), but then there are computer implementations of mental logic as well (Rips, 1994). However, Oaksford and Chater (1993, 1995c) are not impressed. First, they contend that the theory is an alternative attempt at a mental representation of logic: mental models rely on what is technically known as a model-theoretic method rather than the proof-theoretic methods of syntactic (i.e. rule-based) systems. Model-theoretic methods are just as logical. These methods are therefore open to the tractability problems of all logics.

The response of model theorists is to specify first that reasoners do not draw all the logically justified inferences available to them: they restrict their conclusions to those that preserve semantic information, and hence are not trivial or repetitive of information already given; and second, that the contents of models consist of tokens, or exemplars, of what they represent, along with their properties and relations. However, the problem with these tokens is that the theory gives no set procedure for guaranteeing that the right tokens, relations, and properties have been represented. To reply that the tokens are actually default assumptions is, once again, to reintroduce intractability through the frame problem. The tractability problem for mental models then largely centres on how the elements of the models come to be represented in the mind (both in the initial explicit model and by fleshing out); in the computer versions of the theory, these are provided by the person running the program, which for Oaksford and Chater just finesses the problem.

Information gain and rational analysis

As I remarked earlier in reviewing satisficing algorithms, the broad approach Oaksford and Chater advocate so as to avoid the problems associated with computational explanation involves getting away from logical or logic-based systems entirely, into purely cognitive accounts that embody bounded knowledge and processes directly. That is why they approve of the approach, if not the substance, of Kahneman and Tversky's heuristics and Gigerenzer's satisficing theory too. They also put forward their own possible solutions. One is to adopt a connectionist stance; however, this is not worked out in detail and so I shall say no more about it. Another is their own information-gain account of reasoning, which has been worked out in great detail, as we saw with respect to syllogisms in Chapter 2 and the selection task in Chapter 5.

The information-gain approach is a radical reformulation of what people are actually doing in reasoning experiments. Oaksford and Chater appeal to a hugely influential theoretical distinction made originally by a vision scientist, the late David Marr (e.g. 1982). Marr set out the distinction between different levels of theory. Among these levels are what he called the *computational* level and the *algorithmic* level (do not confuse these terms with their meanings in earlier different contexts). Broadly, a computational-level theory states what it is that the mind is computing; an algorithmic-level theory states how the mind is doing it. The information-gain theory is a theory at the computational level: it states that what people are really doing in reasoning and thinking experiments is not, say, trying to test whether an inference is valid or a rule is true or false, but rather, searching for the most useful information to update their beliefs. What counts as useful information is worked out using Anderson's (e.g. 1990) strategy of "rational analysis" (Chapters 2 and 5 give details on this), which contains the assumption that cognition will be optimally adapted to the structure of the environment. Comparing the predictions of such an analysis with the results of a large number of reasoning experiments, there is evidence, as we saw, that the observed results are consistent with the rational analysis.

The introduction of the idea of rationality as adaptability is related to a basic distinction between two forms of rationality that has recently been put forward by Evans and his colleagues. We shall therefore round off our consideration of rationality in the final section of this chapter by concentrating on this recent idea.

Dual rationality

We are all familiar with the notion of ideas whose time has come, and the idea of dual forms of rationality is one of them. It has been implicit in much of the earlier discussion, and appears in the writings of several contemporary theorists. Anderson (e.g. 1990, 1991), for instance, distinguishes between adaptive and normative rationality: behaviour is adaptively rational if it is optimised to an organism's environment, i.e. best helps achieve its goals, and normatively rational if it is consistent with logical rules. Similarly, Gigerenzer and Hug (1992, p. 127) open the abstract of their paper with this question: "What counts as human rationality, reasoning processes that embody content-independent formal theories ... or reasoning processes that are well designed for solving important adaptive problems?" We have seen earlier how the idea of reasoning as a means to attain one's goals also informed the consideration of rationality by mental models theorists, and a similar concern can be found in Baron's perspective on thinking. For Baron (1994a, p. 3), rational thinking is "the kind of thinking we would all do, if we were aware of our own best interests, in order to achieve our goals".

The distinction between goal-directed and rule-congruent rationality has been addressed in detail by Evans and his colleagues (see Evans, 1993b; Evans & Over, 1996a; Evans, Over, & Manktelow, 1993/94). It was motivated by the paradox that has been noted throughout this book and addressed directly in this chapter: that humans have a demonstrated capacity for highly intelligent action in achieving goals and thereby promoting the species' survival and, for some, prosperity, while at the same time embarrassing themselves when having their reasoning and decision processes tested. So, we seem rational from one angle, and irrational from another.

Evans' solution is to argue that the term "rational" can be used to mean two fundamentally different things, and that arguments over human rationality have often come about because these two meanings have been glossed over or confused. You will already have some idea of this distinction from the earlier quotations. Evans distinguishes between *personal* rationality, which he terms "rationality$_1$", and *impersonal* rationality, termed "rationality$_2$". Rationality$_1$ is the goal-directed kind; its term in Evans (1993b) was *rationality of purpose*, and it has been recently defined by Evans and Over (1996a) as:

Rationality$_1$: Thinking, speaking, reasoning, making a decision, or acting in a way that is generally reliable and efficient for achieving one's goals. (p. 8)

The second form of rationality was termed *rationality of process*, and here is Evans and Over's current definition:

Rationality$_2$: Thinking, speaking, reasoning, making a decision, or acting when one has a reason for what one does sanctioned by a normative theory. (p. 8)

Evans and Over give an informal example of how these two forms of rationality can be detached. Consider an argument where a sexist man, Sid, tries to discredit a woman's views on a subject by saying that women just do not understand it. From the rationality$_2$ standpoint, we can slap him down as irrational: Sid has no good reason for his statement, and indeed is engaging in a logically disreputable form of argument known as *ad hominem* (literally "to the man"): attacking the messenger, not the message. But is Sid irrational$_1$? Not necessarily. Sid might be well aware that if he destroys his opponent, by whatever means, he will win his case, at least in front of the audience he is currently facing; that may be his goal, and he might be going about it in an efficient, hence rational$_1$, way. Such strategies are well known in parliament and the courtroom.

Evans' case is that not only has the distinction between the two rationalities remained largely implicit, but that the standards for ascribing rationality in the psychological and philosophical literature have referred overwhelmingly to logicality; hence people have been judged mostly against rationality$_2$, and that is where they have been found wanting. Evans and his colleagues point to two areas of research where not only can the distinction between rationalities be sharply lit, but where it is possible to give some clear indications of sound rational$_1$ thinking.

The first of these areas is the belief-bias effect in syllogistic reasoning. This was dealt with in detail in Chapter 4, so I shall only summarise the evidence here. You may recall that logically valid arguments tend to be accepted more than invalid arguments, and that believable arguments are accepted more than unbelievable arguments, but the effect of believability is much stronger on the invalid arguments than on valid ones: belief and logic interact. Thus, although there is evidence that people are sensitive to the logic of these problems (as shown by the higher acceptance rate for valid forms), there is equally clear evidence that their reasoning is affected by an extra-logical factor, believability.

This is a clear violation of rationality$_2$: structure, not content, is what normatively determines an argument's validity. However, if we adopt a rational$_1$ perspective, things look different. The experiments show that we are far more critical of arguments that go against our beliefs than those with which we agree. This is rational$_1$, say Evans and colleagues, for two reasons: first, because it is not useful to revise our beliefs unless we have a good reason to, and second, because to examine all our beliefs against all of the evidence that comes at them in our daily lives would place an impossible processing burden on our minds: we would be forever stuck in a state of doubt, cognitively paralysed.

The second research area Evans examines in this context is that of deontic reasoning. This was also reviewed in Chapter 4. Deontic reasoning is about the kinds of thinking involved in working out what we should or must do or not do, and it is interesting for an additional reason: it has been subjected to a decision-making analysis, as well as an analysis from the point of view of deductive reasoning. In Chapter 4, we saw that there was a sharp distinction to be drawn between deontic and indicative forms of the Wason selection task in terms of what should count as a "correct" response. The usual normative answer for the indicative task is that a conditional sentence of the form "If p then q" can be falsified by finding a combination of p and ¬q (not-q) values, hence the p and ¬q cards should be selected (we leave aside for the moment the critique of this "normative" solution that has come from information-gain theory; see Chapter 5).

However, there are numerous solutions possible in the deontic task: p ¬q, ¬p q, and ¬p ¬q, from two perspectives. It is hard even on intuitive grounds to see these solutions as anything but rational, although the second and third do not satisfy logical norms. They can though be justified on decision-theoretic grounds, and this justification contains the rational$_1$ argument that, in their appropriate contexts, these solutions will be the ones that are in the solver's best interests to look for; and they are the ones that people do look for. Note that this analysis does not let in rationality$_2$ through the back door: the decision-theoretic approach to deontic reasoning does not entail an acceptance of SEU theory as normative (see Chapter 4 and Over & Manktelow, 1993). Note also that the information-gain analysis of the indicative selection task offers a rational$_1$ justification for the patterns of performance it predicts: these patterns are optimal in terms of the information they supply for the reasoner's epistemic (i.e. belief-revising) goals.

Thus, there is ample evidence that, in experiments on both reasoning and decision making (there are more details about the latter in Evans & Over, 1996a, and Evans et al., 1993/94), people's tested performance is consistent with a rational$_1$ analysis, even when it is inconsistent with a rational$_2$ analysis. Evans goes further than this empirical generalisation and accepts rationality$_1$ as axiomatic: it can be assumed that people will generally think and act in ways that enable them to satisfy their goals. Rationality$_2$ will sometimes serve rationality$_1$, for instance when novel situations have to be dealt with, but sometimes it will not, for instance when there would be unrealistic demands on processing time and resources. In those cases, we should look for a satisficing process. The status of rationality$_1$ in this approach does not mean that people will never be irrational$_1$: Evans and colleagues are careful to specify a bounded rationality$_1$.

So are people rational or irrational?

Yes and no seems to be the answer. As so often in science, it depends on how you define the term. Faced with the sheer weight of evidence from psychological experiments showing that people systematically violate the norms of logic, probability theory, and decision theory (and from outside these areas: see Sutherland, 1992, for an entertaining account), researchers were faced with an apparent two-way choice. They could deny human rationality; such a position can be found in the philosophical literature (e.g. Stich, 1985, 1990). Alternatively, they could deny that the experiments tell us anything interesting about human thought, either on conceptual (e.g. Cohen, 1981) or evolutionary (e.g. Dennett, 1978) grounds. We can now see that there is a third way, which offers a resolution of this theoretical problem: to unpack the construct of rationality and be clearer about just what we mean when we use the word. Humans clearly have some deductive competence— they could hardly cope with novel problems or develop logic or mathematics without it. However, this competence is equally clearly highly restricted and, in ordinary affairs, or dubious usefulness. What humans come extensively equipped with, however, are batteries of fallible but useful strategies that have served, and still serve, their goal-attaining interests.

Let us not get carried away though: not all questions concerning human reason have been settled, either empirically or theoretically. For instance, the decision dilemmas reviewed in Chapter 9 give just as much trouble to dual rationality theory as they do to classical decision theory. Should you spend that money now or save it for Christmas, have that extra beer or switch to fruit juice? What is in your best interests, what is your goal? It is difficult to give an account in these terms which will tell you what is the rational action, in any sense, and just saying that it depends on your values seems equally weak. We need to know a lot more about human psychology before we can settle such thorny issues.

Summary

1. Most contemporary theorists adhere to the concept of bounded rationality. The main reasons are formal arguments that the computational processes required by logic and decision theories are intractable when applied to real-world problems.

2. Computational intractability means that specified processes could not run completely in real time on available cognitive resources. It has several aspects, including a combinatorial explosion when arguments or decisions have more than very few elements, and the frame problem that results from having to search memory when real-world default rules form the elements of arguments.

3. Several psychological proposals for bounded rationality have been put forward, including Simon's satisficing principle, Tversky's elimination-by-aspects strategy, and Gigerenzer's take-the-best algorithm.

4. Mental logic and mental models theorists have both proposed bounded systems, but both have been criticised for not avoiding tractability problems.

5. Evans and his colleagues have developed a psychological account of rationality in which the construct is split into two: rationality$_1$, or rationality of purpose, and rationality$_2$, or rationality of process. Under rationality$_1$, people are said to think or act to approach a goal effectively; under rationality$_2$, they are said to think or act in accord with a normative system. Failure to distinguish between definitions can lead to empty or misleading arguments about human rationality.

References

References

Adams, M.J. (1984). Aristotle's logic. In G.H. Bower (Ed.), *The Psychology of learning and motivation* (Vol. 18). New York: Academic Press.

Ainslie, G. (1986). Beyond microeconomics: Conflict among interests in a multiple self as a determinant of value. In J. Elster (Ed.), *The multiple self*. Cambridge, UK: Cambridge University Press.

Allais, M. (1953). Le comportement de l'homme rationnel devant le risque: critique des postulates et axioms de l'école américaine. *Econometrica, 21*, 503–546.

Almor, A., & Sloman, S.A. (1996). Is deontic reasoning special? *Psychological Review, 103*, 374–380.

Anderson, J.R. (1990). *The adaptive character of thought*. Hillsdale, NJ: Lawrence Erlbaum Associates Inc.

Anderson, J.R. (1991). Is human cognition adaptive? *Behavioral and Brain Sciences, 14*, 471–485.

Arkes, H.L., & Blumer, C. (1985). The psychology of sunk cost. *Organizational Behavior and Human Decision Processes, 35*, 124–140.

Armstrong, S.L., Gleitman, L.R., & Gleitman, H. (1983). What some concepts might not be. *Cognition, 13*, 263–308.

Baars, B.J. (1996). *The cognitive revolution in psychology*. New York: Guilford Press.

Bara, B.G., Bucciarelli, M., & Johnson-Laird, P.N. (1995). Development of syllogistic reasoning. *American Journal of Psychology, 108*, 157–193.

Baron, J. (1994a). *Thinking and deciding* (2nd ed.). Cambridge, UK: Cambridge University Press.

Baron, J. (1994b). Nonconsequentialist decisions. *Behavioral and Brain Sciences, 17*, 1–42.

Barsalou, L.W. (1983). Ad hoc categories. *Memory and Cognition, 11*, 211–227.

Begg, I., & Denny, J.P. (1969). Empirical reconciliation of atmosphere and conversion interpretations of syllogistic reasoning errors. *Journal of Experimental Psychology, 81*, 351–354.

Bell, D.E. (1982). Regret in decision making under uncertainty. *Operations Research, 30*, 961–981.

Berlin, B., & Kay, P. (1969). *Basic color terms: Their universality and evolution*. Berkeley and Los Angeles, CA: University of California Press.

Beyth-Marom, R. (1996). On the description of the prescription. *Behavioral and Brain Sciences, 19*, 321.

Bonatti, L. (1994). Propositional reasoning by model? *Psychological Review, 101*, 725–733.

Braine, M.D.S. (1990). The "natural logic" approach to reasoning. In W.F. Overton (Ed.), *Reasoning, necessity, and logic: Developmental perspectives*. Hillsdale, NJ: Lawrence Erlbaum Associates Inc.

Braine, M.D.S., & O'Brien, D.P. (1991). A theory of If: A lexical entry, reasoning program, and pragmatic principles. *Psychological Review, 98*, 182–203.

Braine, M.D.S., Reiser, B.J., & Rumain, B. (1984). Some empirical justification for a theory of mental propositional logic. In G. Bower (Ed.), *The psychology of learning and motivation: Advances in research and theory* (Vol. 18). New York: Academic Press.

Brockner, J., & Rubin, J.Z. (1985). *Entrapment in escalating conflicts*. New York: Springer-Verlag.

Bruner, J.S., Goodnow, J.J., & Austin, G.A. (1956). *A study of thinking*. New York: Wiley.

Byrne, R.M.J. (1989). Suppressing valid inferences with conditionals. *Cognition, 31*, 61–83.

Byrne, R.M.J. (1996). The core of cognition. *American Journal of Psychology, 109*, 318–325.

Byrne, R.M.J., & Johnson-Laird, P.N. (1992). The spontaneous use of propositional connectives. *Quarterly Journal of Experimental Psychology, 44A*, 89–110.

Carlson, W.B., & Gorman, M.E. (1990). Understanding invention as a cognitive process: The case of Thomas Edison and early motion pictures, 1888–1891. *Social Studies of Science, 20*, 387–430.

Ceraso, J., & Provitera, A. (1971). Sources of error in syllogistic reasoning. *Cognitive Psychology, 2*, 400–410.

Chapman, L.J., & Chapman, J.P. (1959). Atmosphere effect re-examined. *Journal of Experimental Psychology, 58*, 220–226.

Chater, N., & Oaksford, M. (in press). The probability heuristics model of syllogistic reasoning. *Cognitive Psychology*.

Cheng, P.W., & Holyoak, K.J. (1985). Pragmatic reasoning schemas. *Cognitive Psychology, 17*, 391–416.

Cheng, P.W., & Holyoak, K.J. (1989). On the natural selection of reasoning theories. *Cognition, 33*, 285–313.

Cheng, P.W., Holyoak, K.J., Nisbett, R.E., & Oliver, L.M. (1986). Pragmatic versus syntactic approaches to training deductive reasoning. *Cognitive Psychology, 18*, 293–328.

Cheng, P.W., & Nisbett, R.E. (1993). Pragmatic constraints on causal deduction. In R.E. Nisbett (Ed.), *Rules for reasoning*. Hillsdale, NJ: Lawrence Erlbaum Associates Inc.

Cheng, P.W., & Novick, L.R. (1991). Causes versus enabling conditions. *Cognition, 40*, 83–120.

Christensen-Szalanski, J.J.J., & Beach, L.R. (1982). Experience and the base-rate fallacy. *Organizational Behavior and Human Performance, 29*, 270–278.

Cohen, L.J. (1981). Can human irrationality be experimentally demonstrated? *Behavioral and Brain Sciences, 4*, 317–370 (including commentaries).

Collins, A., & Michalski, R. (1989). The logic of plausible reasoning: A core theory. *Cognitive Science, 13*, 1–49.

Colman, A. (1995). *Game theory and its applications*. Oxford, UK: Butterworth-Heinemann.

Cosmides, L. (1989). The logic of social exchange: Has natural selection shaped how humans reason? Studies with the Wason selection task. *Cognition, 31*, 187–316.

Cosmides, L., & Tooby, J. (1992). Cognitive daptations for social exchange. In J.H. Barkow, L. Cosmides, & J. Tooby (Eds.), *The adapted mind*. Oxford, UK: Oxford University Press.

Cosmides, L., & Tooby, J. (1996). Are humans good intuitive statisticians after all? Rethinking some conclusions from the literature on judgment under uncertainty. *Cognition, 58*, 1–73.

Cummins, D.D. (1995). Naive theories and causal deduction. *Memory and Cognition, 23*, 646–658.

Cummins, D.D. (1996a). Evidence of deontic reasoning in 3- and 4-year-old children. *Memory and Cognition, 24*, 823–829.

Cummins, D.D. (1996b). Evidence for the innateness of deontic reasoning. *Mind and Language, 11*, 160–190.

Cummins, D.D., Lubart, T., Alksnis, O., & Rist, R. (1991). Conditional reasoning and causation. *Memory and Cognition, 19*, 274–282.

Dennett, D. (1978). *Brainstorms*. Cambridge, MA: MIT Press.

Doherty, M.E., Mynatt, C.R., Tweney, R.D., & Schiavo, M.D. (1979). Pseudodiagnosticity. *Acta Psychologica, 43*, 111–121.

Dominowski, R.L. (1995). Content effects in Wason's selection task. In S.E. Newstead & J.St.B.T. Evans (Eds.), *Perspectives on thinking and reasoning. Essays in honour of Peter Wason*. Hove, UK: Lawrence Erlbaum Associates Ltd.

Dunbar, K. (1995). How scientists really reason: Scientific reasoning in real-world laboratories. In R.J. Sternberg & J.E. Davidson (Eds.), *The nature of insight*. Cambridge, MA: MIT Press.

Eddy, D.M. (1982). Probabilistic reasoning in clinical medicine: Problems and opportunities. In D. Kahneman, P. Slovic, & A. Tversky (Eds.), *Judgment under uncertainty: Heuristics and biases*. Cambridge, UK: Cambridge University Press.

Ellsberg, D. (1961). Risk, uncertainty, and the Savage axioms. *Quarterly Journal of Economics, 75*, 643–669.

Erickson, J.R. (1974). A set analysis theory of behaviour in formal syllogistic reasoning tasks. In R. Solso (Ed.), *Loyola symposium on cognition* (Vol. 2). Hillsdale, NJ: Lawrence Erlbaum Associates Inc.

Evans, J.St.B.T. (1972). Interpretation and matching bias in a reasoning task. *Quarterly Journal of Experimental Psychology, 24*, 193–199.

Evans, J.St.B.T. (1977). Linguistic factors in reasoning. *Quarterly Journal of Experimental Psychology, 29*, 297–306.

Evans, J.St.B.T. (1982). *The psychology of deductive reasoning*. London: Routledge & Kegan Paul.

Evans, J.St.B.T. (1983). Linguistic determinants of bias in conditional reasoning. *Quarterly Journal of Experimental Psychology, 35A*, 635–644.

Evans, J.St.B.T. (1989). *Bias in human reasoning: Causes and consequences*. Hove, UK: Lawrence Erlbaum Associates Ltd.

Evans, J.St.B.T. (1991). Theories of human reasoning: The fragmented state of the art. *Theory and Psychology, 1*, 83–105.

Evans, J.St.B.T. (1993a). The mental model theory of conditional reasoning: Critical appraisal and revision. *Cognition, 48*, 1–20.

Evans, J.St.B.T. (1993b). Bias and rationality. In K.I. Manktelow & D.E. Over (Eds.), *Rationality: Psychological and philosophical perspectives*. London: Routledge.

Evans, J.St.B.T. (1995). Relevance and reasoning. In S.E. Newstead & J.St.B.T. Evans (Eds.), *Perspectives on thinking and reasoning. Essays in honour of Peter Wason*. Hove, UK: Lawrence Erlbaum Associates Ltd.

Evans, J.St.B.T. (1996). Deciding before you think: Relevance and reasoning in the selection task. *British Journal of Psychology, 87*, 223–240.

Evans, J.St.B.T. (1998). Matching bias in conditional reasoning: Do we understand it after 25 years? *Thinking and Reasoning, 4*, 45–82.

Evans, J.St.B.T., Barston, J.L., & Pollard, P. (1983b). On the conflict between logic and belief in syllogistic reasoning. *Memory and Cognition, 11*, 295–306.

Evans, J.St.B.T., Clibbens, J., & Rood, B. (1995). Bias in conditional inference: Implications for mental models and mental logic. *Quarterly Journal of Experimental Psychology, 48A,* 644–670.

Evans, J.St.B.T., Clibbens, J., & Rood, B. (1996). The role of implicit and explicit negation in conditional reasoning bias. *Journal of Memory and Language, 35,* 392–409.

Evans , J.St.B.T., & Lynch, J.S. (1973). Matching bias in the selection task. *British Journal of Psychology, 64,* 391–397.

Evans, J.St.B.T., Newstead, S.E., & Byrne, R.M.J. (1993a). *Human reasoning: The psychology of deduction.* Hove, UK: Lawrence Erlbaum Associates Ltd.

Evans, J.St.B.T., & Over, D.E. (1996a). *Rationality and reasoning.* Hove, UK: Psychology Press.

Evans, J.St.B.T., & Over, D.E. (1996b). Rationality in the selection task: Epistemic utility versus uncertainty reduction. *Psychological Review, 103,* 356–363.

Evans, J.St.B.T., Over, D.E., & Manktelow, K.I. (1993/94). Reasoning, decision making, and rationality. *Cognition, 49,* 165–187. Reprinted in P.N. Johnson-Laird & E. Shafir (Eds.), *Reasoning and decision making.* Oxford, UK: Blackwell.

Eysenck, M.W., & Keane, M.T. (1995). *Cognitive psychology: A student's handbook* (3rd ed.). Hove, UK: Lawrence Erlbaum Associates Ltd.

Fairley, N., Manktelow, K.I., & Over, D.E. (in press). Necessity, sufficiency, and perspective effects in causal conditional reasoning. *Quarterly Journal of Experimental Psychology.*

Farris, H., & Revlin, R. (1989). The discovery process: A counterfactual study. *Social Studies of Science, 19,* 497–513.

Fiedler, K. (1988). The dependence of the conjunction fallacy on subtle linguistic factors. *Psychological Research, 50,* 123–129.

Fillenbaum, S. (1974) OR: Some uses. *Journal of Experimental Psychology, 103,* 913–921.

Fischhoff, B. (1996). The real world: What good is it? *Organizational Behavior and Human Decision Processes, 65,* 232–248.

Ford, M. (1995). Two modes of representation and problem solution in syllogistic reasoning. *Cognition,* 54, 1–71.

Frisch, D., & Clemen, R.T. (1994). Beyond expected utility: Rethinking behavioral decision research. *Psychological Bulletin, 116,* 46–64.

Garnham, A., & Oakhill, J. (1994). *Thinking and reasoning.* Oxford, UK: Blackwell.

Geis, M.C., & Zwicky, A.M. (1971). On invited inferences. *Linguistic Inquiry, 2,* 561–566.

Gentner, D. (1983). Structure-mapping: A theoretical framework. *Cognitive Science, 7,* 155–170.

Gentner, D., & Toupin, C. (1986). Systematicity and surface similarity in the development of analogy. *Cognitive Science, 10,* 277–300.

Gick, M.L., & Holyoak, K.J. (1980). Analogical problem solving. *Cognitive Psychology, 12,* 306–355.

Gigerenzer, G. (1991). How to make cognitive illusions disappear: Beyond "heuristics and biases". In W. Stroebe & M. Hewstone (Eds.), *European review of social psychology* (Vol. 4). Chichester, UK: Wiley.

Gigerenzer, G. (1993). The bounded rationality of probabilistic mental models. In K.I. Manktelow & D.E. Over (Eds.), *Rationality: Psychological and philosophical perspectives.* London: Routledge.

Gigerenzer, G. (1996a). On narrow norms and vague heuristics: A reply to Kahneman and Tversky (1996). *Psychological Review, 103,* 592–596.

Gigerenzer, G. (1996b). Why do frequency formats improve Bayesian reasoning? Cognitive algorithms work on information, which needs representation. *Behavioral and Brain Sciences, 19*, 23–24.

Gigerenzer, G., & Goldstein, D. (1996). Reasoning the fast and frugal way: Models of bounded rationality. *Psychological Review, 103*, 650–669.

Gigerenzer, G., & Hoffrage, U. (1995). How to improve Bayesian reasoning without instruction: Frequency formats. *Psychological Review, 102*, 684–704.

Gigerenzer, G., Hoffrage, U., & Kleinbölting, H. (1991). Probabilsitic mental models: A Brunswikian theory of confidence. *Psychological Review, 98*, 506–528.

Gigerenzer, G., & Hug, K. (1992). Domain-specific reasoning: Social contracts, cheating and perspective change. *Cognition, 43*, 127–171.

Girotto, V., Blaye, A., & Farioli, F. (1989). A reason to reason: Pragmatic bases of children's search for counterexamples. *European Bulletin of Cognitive Psychology, 9*, 227–231.

Girotto, V., & Legrenzi, P. (1989) Mental representation and hypothetico-deductive reasoning: The case of the THOG problem. *Psychological Research, 51*, 129–135.

Girotto, V., & Legrenzi, P. (1993). Naming the parents of THOG: Mental representation and reasoning. *Quarterly Journal of Experimental Psychology, 46A*, 701–713.

Girotto, V., & Light, P. (1991). The pragmatic bases of children's reasoning. In P. Light & G. Butterworth (Eds.), *Context and cognition: Ways of learning and knowing*. Hemel Hempstead, UK: Harvester Wheatsheaf.

Girotto, V., Light, P., & Colbourn, C. (1988). Pragmatic schemas and conditional reasoning in children. *Quarterly Journal of Experimental Psychology, 40A*, 469–482.

Gorman, M.E. (1992). *Simulating science: Heuristics, mental models and technoscientific thinking*. Bloomington, IN: Indiana University Press.

Gorman, M.E. (1995a). Hypothesis testing. In S.E. Newstead & J.St.B.T. Evans (Eds.), *Perspectives on thinking and reasoning. Essays in honour of Peter Wason*. Hove, UK: Lawrence Erlbaum Associates Ltd.

Gorman, M.E. (1995b). Confirmation, disconfirmation, and invention: The case of Alexander Graham Bell and the telephone. *Thinking and Reasoning, 1*, 31–53.

Gorman, M.E., Stafford, A., & Gorman, M.E. (1987). Disconfirmation and dual hypotheses on a more difficult version of Wason's 2–4–6 task. *Quarterly Journal of Experimental Psychology, 39A*, 1–28.

Grice, H.P. (1975). Logic and conversation. In P. Cole & J.P. Morgan (Eds.), *Syntax and semantics, Vol. 3: Speech acts*. New York: Seminar Press.

Griggs, R.A. (1995). The effects of rule clarification, decision justification, and selection instruction on Wason's abstract selection task. In S.E. Newstead & J.St.B.T. Evans (Eds.), *Perspectives on thinking and reasoning. Essays in honour of Peter Wason*. Hove, UK: Lawrence Erlbaum Associates Ltd.

Griggs, R.A., & Cox, J.R. (1982). The elusive thematic-materials effect in Wason's selection task. *British Journal of Psychology, 73*, 407–420.

Hardin, G. (1968). The tragedy of the commons. *Science, 162*, 1243–1248.

Hardman, D.K., & Payne, S.J. (1995). Problem difficulty and response format in syllogistic reasoning. *Quarterly Journal of Experimental Psychology, 48A*, 945–975.

Harris, P., & Nuñez, M. (1996). Understanding of permission rules by preschool children. *Child Development, 67*, 1572–1591.

Heit, E. (1998). A Bayesian analysis of some forms of inductive reasoning. In M.R. Oaksford & N. Chater (Eds.),

Rational models of cognition. Oxford, UK: Oxford University Press.

Hertwig, R., & Gigerenzer, G. (in press). *The "conjunction fallacy" revisited: How intelligent inferences look like reasoning errors.*

Hewstone, M., Benn, W., & Wilson, A. (1988). Bias in the use of base rates: Racial prejudice in decision-making. *Cognition, 18,* 161–176.

Holland, J.H., Holyoak, K.J., Nisbett, R.E., & Thagard, P. (1986). *Induction.* Cambridge, MA: MIT Press.

Holyoak, K.J., & Cheng, P.W. (1995). Pragmatic reasoning about human voluntary action: Evidence from Wason's selection task. In S.E. Newstead & J.St.B.T. Evans (Eds.), *Perspectives on thinking and reasoning. Essays in honour of Peter Wason.* Hove, UK: Lawrence Erlbaum Associates Ltd.

Inhelder, B., & Piaget, J. (1958). *The growth of logical thinking.* New York: Basic Books.

Johnson-Laird, P.N. (1983). *Mental models.* Cambridge, UK: Cambridge University Press.

Johnson-Laird, P.N. (1993). *Human and machine thinking.* Hove, UK: Lawrence Erlbaum Associates Ltd.

Johnson-Laird, P.N. (1994a). A model theory of induction. *International Studies in the Philosophy of Science, 8,* 5–29.

Johnson-Laird, P.N. (1994b). Mental models and probabilistic thinking. *Cognition, 50,* 189–209.

Johnson-Laird, P.N. (1995). Inference and mental models. In S.E. Newstead & J.St.B.T. Evans (Eds.), *Perspectives on thinking and reasoning. Essays in honour of Peter Wason.* Hove, UK: Lawrence Erlbaum Associates Ltd.

Johnson-Laird, P.N., & Byrne, R.M.J. (1991). *Deduction.* Hove, UK: Lawrence Erlbaum Associates Ltd.

Johnson-Laird, P.N., & Byrne, R.M.J. (1993a). Précis of "Deduction".

Behavioral and Brain Sciences, 16, 323–333.

Johnson-Laird, P.N., & Byrne, R.M.J. (1993b). Models and deductive rationality. In K.I. Manktelow & D.E. Over (Eds.), *Rationality: Psychological and philosophical perspectives.* London: Routledge.

Johnson-Laird, P.N., & Byrne, R.M.J. (1996). Mental models and syllogisms. *Behavioural and Brain Sciences, 19,* 543–546.

Johnson-Laird, P.N., Byrne, R.M.J., & Schaeken, W. (1994). Why models rather than rules give a better account of propositional reasoning: A reply to Bonatti and to O'Brien, Braine and Yang. *Psychological Review, 101,* 734–739.

Johnson-Laird, P.N., Legrenzi, P., & Legrenzi, M.S. (1972) Reasoning and a sense of reality. *British Journal of Psychology, 63,* 395–400.

Johnson-Laird, P.N., & Steedman, M.J. (1978). The psychology of syllogisms. *Cogntive Psychology, 10,* 64–99.

Johnson-Laird, P.N., & Tagart, J. (1969). How implication is understood. *American Journal of Psychology, 82,* 367–373.

Johnson-Laird, P.C., & Wason, P.N. (1970a). Insight into a logical relation. *Quarterly Journal of Experimental Psychology, 22,* 49–61.

Johnson-Laird, P.N., & Wason, P.C. (1970b). A theoretical analysis of insight into a reasoning task. *Cognitive Psychology, 1,* 134–148.

Kahneman, D., Slovic, P., & Tversky, A. (Eds.) (1982). *Judgment under uncertainty: Heuristics and biases.* Cambridge, UK: Cambridge University Press.

Kahneman, D., & Snell, J. (1992). Predicting changing taste: Do people know what they will like? *Journal of Behavioral Decision Making, 5,* 187–200.

Kahneman, D., & Tversky, A. (1972). Subjective probability: A judgment of representativeness. *Cognitive Psychology, 3*, 430–454. Reprinted in part in D. Kahneman, P. Slovic, & A. Tversky (Eds.) (1982), *Judgment under uncertainty: Heuristics and biases.* Cambridge, UK: Cambridge University Press.

Kahneman, D., & Tversky, A. (1973). On the psychology of prediction. *Psychological Review, 80*, 237–251. Reprinted in part in D. Kahneman, P. Slovic, & A. Tversky (Eds.) (1982), *Judgment under uncertainty: Heuristics and biases.* Cambridge, UK: Cambridge University Press.

Kahneman, D., & Tversky, A. (1979). Prospect theory: An analysis of decision under risk. *Econometrica, 47*, 263–291.

Kahneman, D., & Tversky, A. (1996). On the reality of cognitive illusions. *Psychological Review, 103*, 582–591.

Kareev, Y., Halberstadt, N., & Shafir, D. (1993). Improving performance and increasing the use of non-positive testing in a rule-discovery task. *Quarterly Journal of Experimental Psychology, 46A*, 729–742.

Keane, M.T. (1987). On retrieving analogues when solving problems. *Quarterly Journal of Experimental Psychology, 39A*, 29–41.

Keane, M.T., Ledgeway, T., & Duff, S. (1994). Constraints on analogical mapping: A comparison of three models. *Cognitive Science, 18*, 387–438.

Keeney, R.L., & Raiffa, H. (1976). *Decisions with multiple objectives.* New York: Wiley.

Kirby, K.N. (1994). Probabilities and utilities of fictional outcomes in Wason's four-card selection task. *Cognition, 51*, 1–28.

Klayman, J., & Ha, Y.-W. (1987). Confirmation, disconfirmation, and information in hypothesis testing. *Psychological Review, 94*, 211–228.

Koehler, J.J. (1996). The base rate fallacy reconsidered: Descriptive, normative, and methodological challenges. *Behavioral and Brain Sciences, 19*, 1–53.

Laming, D. (1996). On the analysis of irrational data selection: A critique of Oaksford and Chater (1994). *Psychological Review, 103*, 364–373.

Lea, R.B., O'Brien, D.P., Noveck, I.A., Fisch, S.M., & Braine, M.D.S. (1990). Predicting propositional logic inferences in text comprehension. *Journal of Memory and Language, 29*, 361–387.

Legrenzi, P., Girotto, V., & Johnson-Laird, P.N. (1993). Focusing in reasoning and decision making. *Cognition, 49*, 37–66. Also in P.N. Johnson-Laird & E. Shafir (Eds.) (1994), *Reasoning and decision making.* Oxford, UK: Blackwell.

Lichtenstein, S., Fischhoff, B., & Phillips, L.D. (1982). Calibration of probabilities: The state of the art to 1980. In D. Kahneman, P. Slovic, & A. Tversky (Eds.), *Judgment under uncertainty: Heuristics and biases.* Cambridge, UK: Cambridge University Press.

Lichtenstein, S., Slovic, P., Fischhoff, B., Layman, M., & Combs, B. (1978). Judged frequency of lethal events. *Journal of Experimental Psychology: Human Learning and Memory, 4*, 551–578.

Light, P., Girotto, V., & Legrenzi, P. (1990). Children's reasoning on conditional promises and permissions. *Cognitive Development, 5*, 369–383.

Loomes, G., & Sugden, R. (1982). Regret theory: An alternative theory of rational choice under uncertainty. *Economic Journal, 92*, 805–824.

Lovie, A.D. (1992). *Context and commitment: A psychology of science.* Hemel Hempstead, UK: Harvester Wheatsheaf.

Manktelow, K.I., & Evans, J.StB.T. (1979). Facilitation of reasoning by realism: effect or non-effect? *British Journal of Psychology, 70*, 477–488.

Manktelow, K.I., & Over, D.E. (1990a). Deontic thought and the selection task. In K.J. Gilhooly, M.T.G. Keane, R.H. Logie, & G. Erdos (Eds.), *Lines of thinking: Reflections on the psychology of thought* (Vol. 1). Chichester, UK: Wiley.

Manktelow, K.I., & Over, D.E. (1990b). *Inference and understanding*. London: Routledge.

Manktelow, K.I., & Over, D.E. (1991). Social roles and utilities in reasoning with deontic conditionals. *Cognition, 39,* 85–105.

Manktelow, K.I., & Over, D.E. (1995). Deontic reasoning. In S.E. Newstead & J.St.B.T. Evans (Eds.), *Perspectives on thinking and reasoning. Essays in honour of Peter Wason*. Hove, UK: Lawrence Erlbaum Associates Ltd.

Manktelow, K.I., Sutherland, E.J., & Over, D.E. (1995). Probabilistic factors in deontic reasoning. *Thinking and Reasoning, 1,* 201–220.

Margolis, H. (1987). *Patterns, thinking, and cognition: A theory of judgment*. Chicago, IL: University of Chicago Press.

Markovits, H. (1984). Awareness of the "possible" as a mediator of formal thinking in conitional reasoning problems. *British Journal of Psychology, 75,* 367–376.

Markovits, H., & Savary, F. (1992). Pragmatic schemas and the selection task: To reason or not to reason. *Quarterly Journal of Experimental Psychology, 45A,* 133–148.

Marr, D. (1982). *Vision*. San Francisco, CA: Freeman.

Mynatt, C.R., Doherty, M.E., & Dragan, W. (1993). Information relevance, working memory, and the consideration of alternatives. *Quarterly Journal of Experimental Psychology, 46A,* 759–778.

Mynatt, C.R., Doherty, M.E., & Tweney, R.D. (1977). Confirmation bias in a simulated research environment: An experimental study of scientific inference. *Quarterly Journal of Experimental Psychology, 29,* 85–95.

Mynatt, C.R., Doherty, M.E., & Tweney, R.D. (1978). Consequences of confirmation and disconfirmation in a simulated research environment. *Quarterly Journal of Experimental Psychology, 30,* 395–406.

Neumann, J. von, & Morgenstern, O. (1944). *Theory of games and economic behaviour*. Princeton, NJ: Princeton University Press.

Newell, A. (1973). You can't play 20 questions with nature and win. In W.G. Chase (Ed.), *Visual information processing*. New York: Academic Press.

Newstead, S.E. (1989). Interpretational errors in syllogistic reasoning. *Journal of Memory and Language, 28,* 78–91.

Newstead, S.E. (1995). Gricean implicatures and syllogistic reasoning. *Journal of Memory and Language, 34,* 644–664.

Newstead, S.E., & Evans, J.St.B.T. (1993). Mental models as an explanation of belief bias in in syllogistic reasoning. *Cognition, 46,* 93–97.

Newstead, S.E., Girotto, V., & Legrenzi, P. (1995). The THOG problem and its implications for human reasoning. In S.E. Newstead & J.St.B.T. Evans (Eds.), *Perspectives on thinking and reasoning. Essays in honour of Peter Wason*. Hove, UK: Lawrence Erlbaum Associates Ltd.

Newstead, S.E., Griggs, R.A., & Chrostowski, J.J. (1984). Reasoning with realistic disjunctives. *Quarterly Journal of Experimental Psychology, 36A,* 611–627.

Newstead, S.E., Pollard, P., Evans, J.StB.T., & Allen, J.L. (1992). The source of belief bias in syllogistic reasoning. *Cognition, 45,* 257–284.

Nisbett, R.E., Krantz, D.H., Jepson, D., & Kunda, Z. (1983). The use of statistical heuristics in everyday inductive reasoning. *Psychological Review, 90,* 339–363.

Nisbett, R.E., & Ross, L. (1980). *Human inference: Strategies and shortcomings of social judgment*. Englewood Cliffs, NJ: Prentice-Hall.

Noveck, I.A., & O'Brien, D.P. (1996). To what extent do pragmatic reasoning schemas affect performance on Wason's selection task? *Quarterly Journal of Experimental Psychology, 49A*, 463–489.

Oakhill, J.V., Johnson-Laird, P.N., & Garnham, A. (1989). Believability and syllogistic reasoning. *Cognition, 31*, 117–140.

Oaksford, M.R., & Chater, N. (1993). Reasoning theories and bounded rationality. In K.I. Manktelow & D.E. Over (Eds.), *Rationality*. London: Routledge.

Oaksford, M.R., & Chater, N. (1994a). A rational analysis of the selection task as optimal data selection. *Psychological Review, 101*, 608–631.

Oaksford, M.R., & Chater, N. (1994b). Another look at eliminative and enumerative behaviour in a conceptual task. *European Journal of Cognitive Psychology, 6*, 149–169.

Oaksford, M.R., & Chater, N. (1995a). Two and three stage models of deontic reasoning. *Thinking and Reasoning, 1*, 350–357.

Oaksford, M.R., & Chater, N. (1995b). Information gain explains relevance which explains the selection task. *Cognition, 57*, 97–108.

Oaksford, M.R., & Chater, N. (1995c). Theories of reasoning and the computational explanation of everyday inference. *Thinking and Reasoning, 1*, 121–152.

Oaksford, M.R., & Chater, N. (1996). Rational explanation of the selection task. *Psychological Review, 103*, 381–391.

Oaksford, M.R., Chater, N., Grainger, B., & Larkin, J. (1997). Optimal data selection in the reduced array selection task (RAST). *Journal of Experimental Psychology: Learning, Memory, and Cognition, 23*, 441–458.

Oaksford, M.R., & Stenning, K. (1992). Reasoning with conditionals containing negated constituents. *Journal of Experimental Psychology: Learning, Memory, and Cognition, 18*, 835–854.

O'Brien, D.P. (1993). Mental logic and irrationality: We can put a man on the moon, so why can't we solve those logical reasoning problems? In K.I. Manktelow & D.E. Over (Eds.), *Rationality: Psychological and philosophical perspectives*. London: Routledge.

O'Brien, D.P. (1995). Finding logic in human reasoning requires looking in the right places. In S.E. Newstead & J.St.B.T. Evans (Eds.), *Perspectives on thinking and reasoning. Essays in honour of Peter Wason*. Hove, UK: Lawrence Erlbaum Associates Ltd.

O'Brien, D.P., Braine, M.D.S., & Yang, Y. (1994). Propositional reasoning by mental models? Simple to refute in principle and in practice. *Psychological Review, 101*, 711–724.

Ormerod, T.C., Manktelow, K.I., & Jones, G.V. (1993). Reasoning with three types of conditional: Biases and mental models. *Quarterly Journal of Experimental Psychology, 46A*, 653–677.

Osherson, D.N., Smith, E.E., Wilkie, O., Lopez, A., & Shafir, E. (1990). Category-based induction. *Psychological Review, 97*, 185–200.

Over, D.E., & Manktelow, K.I. (1993). Rationality, utility, and deontic reasoning. In K.I. Manktelow & D.E. Over (Eds.), *Rationality: Psychological and philosophical perspectives*. London: Routledge.

Parfit, D. (1984). *Reasons and persons*. Oxford, UK: Oxford University Press.

Payne, J.W., Bettman, J.R., & Johnson, E.J. (1992). Behavioral decision research: A constructive processing perspective. *Annual Review of Psychology, 43*, 87–131.

Payne, J.W., Bettman, J.R., & Johnson, E.J. (1993). *The adaptive decision maker.* Cambridge, UK: Cambridge University Press.

Pelham, B.W., Sumarta, T.T., & Myaskovsky, L. (1994). The easy path from many to much: The numerosity heuristic. *Cognitive Psychology, 26,* 103–133.

Peterson, C.R., & Beach, L.R. (1967). Man as an intuitive statistician. *Psychological Bulletin, 68,* 29–46.

Platt, J. (1973). Social traps. *American Psychologist, 28,* 641–651.

Poletiek, F.H. (1996). Paradoxes of falsification. *Quarterly Journal of Experimental Psychology, 49A,* 447–462.

Politzer, G., & Nguyen-Xuan, A. (1992). Reasoning about conditional promises and warnings: Darwinian algorithms, mental models, relevance judgements or pragmatic schemas? *Quarterly Journal of Experimental Psychology, 44A,* 401–412.

Politzer, G., & Noveck, I.A. (1991). Are conjunction rule violations the result of conversational rule violations? *Journal of Psycholinguistic Research, 20,* 83–103.

Popper, K.R. (1962). *Conjectures and refutations.* London: Hutchinson.

Pulford, B.D., & Colman, A.M. (1997). Overconfidence: Feedback and item difficulty effects. *Personality and Individual Differences, 23,* 125–133.

Ray, J.L., Reynolds, R.A., & Carranza, E. (1989). Understanding choice utterances. *Quarterly Journal of Experimental Psychology, 41A,* 829–848.

Reeves,L.M., & Weisberg, R.W. (1994). The role of content and abstract information in analogical transfer. *Psychological Bulletin, 115,* 381–400.

Revlis, R. (1975). Syllogistic reasoning: logical decisions from a complex data base. In R.J. Falmagne (Ed.), *Reasoning: Representation and process.* New York: Wiley.

Rips, L.J. (1975). Inductive judgments about natural categories. *Journal of Verbal Learning and Verbal Behavior, 14,* 665–681.

Rips, L.J. (1994). *The psychology of proof.* London: MIT Press.

Ritov, I., & Baron, J. (1990). Reluctance to vaccinate: Omission bias and ambiguity. *Journal of Behavioral Decision Making, 3,* 263–277.

Roberge, J.J. (1971). Some effects of negation on adults' conditional reasoning abilities. *Psychological Reports, 29,* 839–844.

Roberge, J.J. (1974). Effects of negation on adults' comprehension of fallacious conditional and disjunctive arguments. *Journal of General Psychology, 91,* 287–293.

Roberge, J.J. (1976a). Effects of negation on adults' disjunctive reasoning abilities. *Journal of General Psychology, 94,* 23–28.

Roberge, J.J. (1976b). Reasoning with exclusive disjunction arguments. *Quarterly Journal of Experimental Psychology, 28,* 419–427.

Roberge, J.J. (1978). Linguistic and psychometric factors in propositional reasoning. *Quarterly Journal of Experimental Psychology, 30,* 705–716.

Roberts, M. (1998). Inspection times and the selection task: Are they relevant? *Quarterly Journal of Experimental Psychology, 51A,* 781–810.

Rosch, E. (1978). Principles of categorization. In E. Rosch & B. Lloyd (Eds.), *Cognition and categorization.* Hillsdale, NJ: Lawrence Erlbaum Associates Inc.

Rosch, E., Mervis, C., Gray, W., Johnson, D., & Boyes-Braem, P. (1976). Basic objects in natural categories. *Cognitive Psychology, 7,* 573–605.

Ross, B.H. (1987). This is like that: The use of earlier problems and the separation of similarity effects. *Journal of Experimental Psychology: Learning, Memory, and Cognition, 13,* 629–639.

Ross, M., & Sicoly, F. (1979). Egocentric biases in availability and attribution. *Journal of Personality and Social Psychology, 37*, 322–336.

Rumelhart, D.E. (1980). Schemata: The building blocks of cognition. In R.J. Spiro, B.C. Bruce, & W.F. Brewer (Eds.), *Theoretical issues in reading comprehension*. Hillsdale, NJ: Lawrence Erlbaum Associates Inc.

Savage, L.J. (1954). *The foundations of statistics*. New York: Wiley.

Shafir, E.B. (1993a). Intuitions about rationality and cognition. In K.I. Manktelow & D.E. Over (Eds.), *Rationality: Psychological and philosophical perspectives*. London: Routledge.

Shafir, E.B. (1993b). Choosing versus rejecting: Why some options are both better and worse than others. *Memory and Cognition, 21*, 546–556.

Shafir, E.B., & Tversky, A. (1992). Thinking through uncertainty: Nonconsequential reasoning and choice. *Cognitive Psychology, 24*, 449–474.

Simon, H.A. (1957). *Models of man: Social and rational*. New York: Wiley.

Simon, H.A. (1978). Rationality as a process and product of thought. *American Economic Review, 68*, 1–16.

Simon, H.A. (1983). *Reason in human affairs*. Stanford, CA: Stanford University Press.

Sloman, S. (1993). Feature-based induction. *Cognitive Psychology, 25*, 231–280.

Sloman, S. (1994). When explanations compete: The role of explanatory coherence on judgments of likelihood. *Cognition, 52*, 1–21.

Sloman, S. (1997). Explanatory coherence and the induction of properties. *Thinking and Reasoning, 3*, 81–110.

Slovic, P., Fischhoff, B., & Lichtenstein, S. (1980). Facts versus fears: Understanding perceived risk.

Reprinted in D. Kahneman, P. Slovic, & A. Tversky (Eds.) (1982), *Judgment under uncertainty: Heuristics and biases*. Cambridge, UK: Cambridge University Press.

Smith, E.E., & Medin, D.L. (1981). *Categories and concepts*. Cambridge, MA: Harvard University Press.

Smith, E.E., Shafir, E., & Osherson, D. (1993/94). Similarity, plausibility, and judgments of probability. *Cognition, 49*, 67–96. In P.N. Johnson-Laird & E. Shafir (Eds.), *Reasoning and decision making*. Oxford, UK: Blackwell.

Spellman, B.A., & Holyoak, K.J. (1996). Pragmatics in analogical mapping. *Cognitive Psychology, 31*, 307–346.

Sperber, D., Cara, F., & Girotto, V. (1995). Relevance theory explains the selection task. *Cognition, 57*, 31–95.

Sperber, D., & Wilson, D. (1986). *Relevance: Communication and cognition* (2nd ed. 1996). Oxford, UK: Blackwell.

Springston, F.J., & Clark, H.H. (1973). *And* and *or*, or the comprehension of pseudoimperatives. *Journal of Verbal Learning and Verbal Behavior, 12*, 258–272.

Staudenmayer, H. (1975). Understanding conditional reasoning with meaningful propositions. In R.J. Falmagne (Ed.), *Reasoning: Representation and process*. New York: Wiley.

Stenning, K., & Oaksford, M.R. (1993). Rational reasoning and human implementations of logic. In K.I. Manktelow & D.E. Over (Eds.), *Rationality: Psychological and philosophical perspectives*. London: Routledge.

Stevenson, R.J., & Over, D.E. (1995). Deduction from uncertain premises. *Quarterly Journal of Experimental Psychology, 48A*, 613–643.

Stich, S.P. (1985). Could man be an irrational animal? *Synthese, 64*, 115–135.

Stich, S.P. (1990). *The fragmentation of reason*. Cambridge, MA: MIT Press.

Sutherland, S. (1992). *Irrationality: The enemy within*. Harmondsworth, UK: Penguin.

Thagard, P., & Nisbett, R.E. (1982). Variability and confirmation. *Philosophical Studies, 42,* 379–394.

Thaler, R. (1980). Toward a positive theory of consumer choice. *Journal of Economic Behavior and Organization, 1,* 39–60.

Thaler, R.H., & Shefrin, H.M. (1981). An economic theory of self-control. *Journal of Political Economy, 89,* 392–406.

Thompson, V.A. (1995). Conditional reasoning: The necessary and sufficient conditions. *Canadian Journal of Psychology, 49,* 1–58.

Traugott, E.C., ter Meulen, A., Reilly, J.S., & Ferguson, C.A. (1986). *On conditionals.* Cambridge, UK: Cambridge University Press.

Tukey, D.D. (1986). A philosophical end empirical analysis of subjects' modes of inquiry in Wason's 2–4–6 task. *Quarterly Journal of Experimental Psychology, 38A,* 5–33.

Tversky, A. (1969). Intransitivity of preferences. *Psychological Review, 76,* 31–48.

Tversky, A. (1972). Elimination by aspects: A theory of choice. *Psychological Review, 79,* 281–299.

Tversky, A., & Kahneman, D. (1973). Availability: A heuristic for judging frequency and probability. *Cognitive Psychology, 5,* 207–232. Reprinted in part in D. Kahneman, P. Slovic, & A. Tversky (Eds.) (1982), *Judgment under uncertainty: Heuristics and biases.* Cambridge, UK: Cambridge University Press.

Tversky, A., & Kahneman, D. (1974). Judgment under uncertainty: Heuristics and biases. *Science, 185,* 1124–1131. Reprinted in D. Kahneman, P. Slovic, & A. Tversky (Eds.) (1982), *Judgment under uncertainty: Heuristics and biases.*

Cambridge, UK: Cambridge University Press.

Tversky, A., & Kahneman, D. (1981). The framing of decisions and the psychology of choice. *Science, 211,* 453–458.

Tversky, A., & Kahneman D. (1982a). Evidential impact of base rates. In D. Kahneman, P. Slovic, & A. Tversky (Eds.) (1982), *Judgment under uncertainty: Heuristics and biases.* Cambridge, UK: Cambridge University Press.

Tversky, A., & Kahneman, D. (1982b). Judgments of and by representativeness. In D. Kahneman, P. Slovic, & A. Tversky (Eds.) (1982), *Judgment under uncertainty: Heuristics and biases.* Cambridge, UK: Cambridge University Press.

Tversky, A., & Kahneman, D. (1983). Extensional versus intuitive reasoning: The conjunction fallacy in probability judgment. *Psychological Review, 90,* 293–315.

Tversky, A., & Kahneman, D. (1986). Rational choice and the framing of decisions. *Journal of Business, 59*(4), S251–S278.

Tversky, A., & Kahneman, D. (1992). Advances in prospect theory: Cumulative representation of uncertainty. *Journal of Risk and Uncertainty, 5,* 297–323.

Tversky, A., & Shafir, E. (1992). The disjunction effect in choice under uncertainty. *Psychological Science, 3,* 305–309.

Tweney, R.D. (1985). Faraday's discovery of induction: A cognitive approach. In D. Gooding, & F.A.J.L. James (Eds.), *Faraday rediscovered: Essays on the life and work of Michael Faraday, 1791–1867.* London: Macmillan.

Tweney, R.D., & Chitwood, S.T. (1995). Scientific reasoning. In S.E. Newstead & J.St.B.T. Evans (Eds.), *Perspectives on thinking and reasoning. Essays in honour of Peter Wason.* Hove, UK: Lawrence Erlbaum Associates Ltd.

Tweney, R.D., Doherty, M.E., Worner, W.J., Pliske, D.B., Mynatt, C.R., Gross, K.A., & Arkkelin, D.L. (1980). Strategies of rule discovery in an inference task. *Quarterly Journal of Experimental Psychology, 32,* 109–123.

Vallée-Tourangeau, F., Austin, N.G., & Rankin, S. (1995). Inducing a rule in Wason's 2–4–6 task: A test of the information-quantity and goal-complementarity hypotheses. *Quarterly Journal of Experimental Psychology, 48A,* 895–914.

Wason, P.C. (1960). On the failure to eliminate hypotheses in a conceptual task. *Quarterly Journal of Experimental Psychology, 12,* 129–140.

Wason, P.C. (1966). Reasoning. In B. Foss (Ed.), *New horizons in psychology 1.* Harmondsworth, UK: Penguin.

Wason, P.C. (1968). Reasoning about a rule. *Quarterly Journal of Experimental Psychology, 20,* 273–281.

Wason, P.C. (1977). Self-contradictions. In P.N. Johnson-Laird & P.C Wason (Eds.), *Thinking: Readings in cognitive science.* Cambridge, UK: Cambridge University Press.

Wason, P.C., & Brooks, P.J. (1979). THOG: The anatomy of a problem. *Psychological Research, 41,* 79–90.

Wason, P.C., & Evans, J.StB.T. (1975). Dual processes in reasoning? *Cognition, 3,* 141–154.

Wason, P.C., & Green, D.W. (1984) Reasoning and mental representation. *Quarterly Journal of Experimental Psychology, 36A,* 597–610.

Wason, P.C., & Shapiro, D.A. (1971). Natural and contrived experience in a reasoning problem. *Quarterly Journal of Experimental Psychology, 23,* 63–71.

Wetherick, N.E. (1962). Eliminative and enumerative behaviour in a conceptual task. *Quarterly Journal of Experimental Psychology, 14,* 246–249.

Wetherick, N.E. (1993). Human rationality. In K.I. Manktelow & D.E. Over (Eds.), *Rationality: Psychological and philosophical perspectives.* London: Routledge.

Wetherick, N.E., & Gilhooly, K.J. (1990). Syllogistic reasoning: Effects of premise order. In K. Gilhooly, M. Keane, R. Logie, & G. Erdos (Eds.), *Lines of thinking: Reflections on the psychology of thought* (Vol. 1). Chichester, UK: Wiley.

Wharton, C.M., Cheng, P.W., & Wickens, T.D. (1993). Hypothesis-testing strategies: Why two goals are better than one. *Quarterly Journal of Experimental Psychology, 46A,* 750–758.

Wilkins, M.C. (1928). The effect of changed material on ability to do formal syllogistic reasoning. *Archives of Psychology,* No. 102.

Woodworth, R.S., & Sells, S.B. (1935). An atmosphere effect in syllogistic reasoning. *Journal of Experimental Psychology, 18,* 451–460.

Author Index

Author index

Subject Index

Subject index